Visions of Lincoln

Nebraska's Capital City in the Present, Past and Future

Written by James L. McKee

Photography by Joel Sartore

Krista Burlae, Editor
Larry McDonald, Art Director

Parrish McDonald, Project Coordinator

Additional Contributions by
Barbara Bartle
Wendy Birdsall
Morgan Fry
Cindy Lange-Kubick
Andrew McDonald
Polly McMullen
Marilyn Moore
Harvey Perlman
Mary Pipher
Kent Seacrest

Acknowledgments

This book began as a conversation between neighbors. When Parrish McDonald said how much she loved living in Lincoln, Joel Sartore replied that if she loved it that much, she should do a book on it. She said she would put it together, if he would do the photography. When Jim McKee agreed to write the history, that sealed the deal. Over a year of continuing conversations and invitations resulted in this marvelous project. Each one of these initial three has contributed countless hours to this book. Thanks to them for their vision and tireless efforts.

A great debt of gratitude is owed to every one of the contributing writers. Their willingness to share expertise and insight has been inspiring. A city moves forward when it has the kind of citizens who will step out and take the risk of casting a vision. Lincoln is fortunate to have these civic leaders. Krista Burlae's editorial work has been truly remarkable. When the project's scope just kept growing, Krista responded with grace and outstanding professionalism. We were blessed to have her as the editor. We are grateful to all our Partners in Progress who have made this book possible. It takes a truly visionary company to want to tell the city's story in this form. Thank you all. And a special word of gratitude to the folks at BryanLGH who were the first to catch the vision.

Todd McGreevy of AdMospheres stepped up in the early days to offer invaluable counsel on business and editorial matters, as did Shelley Weih. Ed Mueller, the publisher of *Chef* magazine, came through with a pemmican recipe we could all enjoy.

Our thanks go to the Nebraska State Historical Society, including the Library and Archives Division and especially Linda Hein, Mary-Jo Miller, Deb Arenz and Dale

Published by TankWorks, LLC

E. Lawrence McDonald
Managing Partner

Sherri Lynn
Associate Publisher

The Visions of Lincoln Project is a subsidiary of TankWorks, LLC

ISBN

978-0-9798794-0-1

Copyright 2007 by TankWorks, LLC. All rights reserved. No portion of this book may be used or reproduced in any manner whatsoever without written permission from the publisher, except in the case of brief quotations embodied in critical reviews and articles.

Permission to reprint selected excerpts from Mary Pipher's *The Middle of Everywhere: Helping Refugees Enter the American Community*, pp. 5-23, (ISBN 0151006008) has been granted by Harcourt, Inc. All rights reserved. No part of the material protected by this copyright may be reproduced or utilized in any form or by any means, electronic or mechanical, including photocopying, recording, broadcasting or by any other storage and retrieval system without the written permission from Harcourt, Inc.

Bacon for their help, insight and photographs. We are grateful to the Museum of Nebraska History for their photographs and expertise. And our gratitude to the folks at Morrill Hall for keeping their ancient residents with us. The Lincoln Chamber of Commerce and the Lincoln Partnership for Economic Development were tremendously helpful in both the contribution of staff time and the material they have prepared. Leadership Lincoln provides a tremendous introduction to this city. The first chapter has many insights from their executive director, Deane Finnegan. Thanks for your warmth and help. The state's Department of Economic Development was forthcoming in contributing supplemental photography.

Gary Reichel at Reichel Graphic Design dropped everything else to solve our website and IT problems. You can bet we will be working with him again. Speaking of information technology, Boomer's Printing Company and Patti Wenzel did a nice job of turning delicate archival photographs into bulletproof digital files. Holly Pepper did some Photoshop work that is as wonderful as she is.

Every city needs a professional planner and Lincoln is fortunate to have Crandall Arambula filling that role. The term, Architect of Cities, comes to mind. Debra Ames from that office was especially helpful in providing illustrations for Polly McMullen's essay.

The folks at Harcourt were expeditious in licensing us to use Mary Pipher's quotes. It is nice to see that big publishers can be so kind to small publishers.

To Kathy Sartore and to the staff at Joel Sartore Photography–Katie Joseph, Frances Schoonveld, Grace Young, and Dave Norris–we could not have done this without your help.

Finally, to the children whose parents spent so many hours on this project, Cole, Ellen and Spenser Sartore and Edison, Field and Trinity McDonald – a very special thanks. A great city and great kids deserve each other.

– ELM

Contents

Lincoln

Today

When you look at the heart of Lincoln, Nebraska, you see why people love to live here. Of course, with a population of more than 240,000 people, exciting things are going on every day. As the Capital City, it is the place where important discussions are held and

debates decided. With five colleges, including the flagship campus of the University of Nebraska, it is an intellectually exciting city. Lincoln's businesses in manufacturing, pharmaceuticals, health care, insurance and technology touch places around the country and around the globe. And with a wide diversity of entertainment possibilities, Lincoln is an outstanding place to relax and play.

Yet there is something more about Lincoln that draws people here. Every city has a different feel and its own unique character. A city is like a sponge. It soaks up the values of the people who founded the city. Then those values get wrung out, watering future generations. This soaking and watering go back and forth over the generations. Eventually these values grow into the enduring heart of a city. To paraphrase Churchill, first you build your city, then it builds you. The people who formed Lincoln, and those who continue to shape it, have made a city that is, as one of its monuments says, "a place most beautiful."

Again and again, people say what they value most about Lincoln is the quality of life. The dedication to family, the deep aspirations of the people, the opportunities

Andrew McDonald

that people have to pursue their passions – these are the types of reasons so many people choose to live here. The quality of life is also why so many people who have moved away decide later in life to return.

Lincoln is a place that feels like home. Just take a walk down the streets of Lincoln. People make eye contact and greet you with a smile and a "hello." Frequently, they will stop and make a comment about the weather, ask about your child or the dog at the end of your leash. Perfect strangers make you feel as if you belong here.

Torn Notebook epitomizes the creative process of celebrated sculptors Claes Oldenburg and Coosje van Bruggen.

Photograph by P. Drickey, Nebraska DED

Lincolnites are good at "telling their story." Spend time with someone who has been around the community a while and they will tell you how the quality of life shaped their lives and made them who they are today. Old-timers are likely to tell you about going to the long-gone Miller and Paine's tearoom for the cinnamon rolls, or after high school football game gatherings at King's Drive-Inn. There is a collective community nostalgia that is passed down. While newcomers might not have experienced those events or activities first hand, the stories are ingrained in the community as part of the enduring values of something special. When you hear those stories, it is an invitation to become part of a living community. They want "their story" to become part of "your story."

Neighborhoods in Lincoln flourish. It is common to find residents, old and young, gathered together on a summer's evening, enjoying a potluck dinner, streets having been blocked off so the youngest members can ride tricycles and bikes, while teens hop on skateboards or bring out the guitars as their parents and elders sit in lawn chairs and visit. People expect to know those around them and to care. The friendliness even shapes the formal parts of the city. The Lincoln Police Department is a community-based department. Officers responsible for your part of town will, more often than not, join you at your block party or event. Neighborhood Watch and other national safety programs flourish in Lincoln. In Lincoln, it's natural because neighbors watch out for neighbors.

New families in town are "adopted" by long time residents and are invited to spend a leisurely evening downtown at "Jazz in June" or take a walk along one of Lincoln's beautiful tree-lined streets. Newcomers are asked to join book groups or to consider becoming involved in one of the many not-for-profit groups serving the community. Most people moving to Lincoln learn quickly that there are hundreds of opportunities of which to become involved.

The friendly spirit of Lincoln is experienced in many ways, but one example may say it best. While in other cities, major sports events are often filled with harsh insults and over-the-top competitiveness, Lincoln is different. Home football games are like big family reunions. Visitors are treated like guests. And whether the opposing team wins or loses, as they leave the stadium, the home team people in red stand and applaud. Every team that comes says it loves playing at Nebraska. It happens in the heart of this city, the capital of the state that shares these values.

Talent Plus

A commitment to Talent A commitment to Lincoln

Talent Plus has called Lincoln home since 1989. When Talent Plus built its corporate headquarters in 2004, Lincoln continued to make sense. "The number one reason we stayed is the people; the human capital in Lincoln is extraordinary," says Talent Plus Chairman Doug Rath.

Talent Plus has over 200 world-class, growth-oriented clients and nearly 150 associates. The Science of Talent® dates back to the 1960s when we began studying selection and talent; listening to what top performers think, believe and feel; and building structured interviews to help companies identify, select and develop the best, building Talent-Based Organizations℠.

When talent's cast in the right position and developed long term – people, companies and communities thrive. Talent Plus and its associates are thriving in Lincoln.

Talent+ ®

One Talent Plus Way . Lincoln, NE . 68506
402.489.2000 . talentplus.com

Partner In Progress

Wendy Birdsall

July 1870 was an important month for Lincoln. The town had just settled into its role as the Capital City of the thirty-seventh state. Lincoln was in the midst of a population boom, and the Burlington and Missouri Railroad clanged to a stop at 5th and "R" streets for the first time on July 26.

The gleaming steel rails meant Lincoln finally was in the selling position to entice other businesses and industries to invest in the future of the city. With that objective in mind, several Lincoln community leaders gathered in the 10th street school house on a hot July 28.

Their purpose was to form a Board of Trade, and although they didn't realize it then, they were laying the groundwork for a community development task force that would eventually come to be called the Lincoln Chamber of Commerce.

The war in Europe occupied much of the space in the Nebraska State Journal the following morning, but there was an item that some of the more substantial citizens

of the fledgling community were looking ahead. The Journal noted that a group of businessmen met on Wednesday evening for the purpose of organizing the business interests of the community.

Those at the meeting organized the Board of Trade and C. H. Gere, Chairman of the Board of Town Trustees and Editor of the Journal, was elected chairman. G. A. Randall was named secretary with A. J. Cropsey and A. C. Tichenor as vice chairmen. Rounding out the first "Executive Committee" were Paren England, A. M. Ghost, and S. B. Galey.

The first order of business was to draw up a constitution and obtain signatures and subscriptions. England, Ghost, and Galey were instructed to report back on July 30. They missed the deadline, but on August 1st, they reported subscriptions totaling $245.50.

A Place Where Commerce has Deep Roots

and Tall Aspirations

With many of the city's businessmen backing the Board of Trade, Lincoln did indeed have a chance to grow. The first Executive Committee was obviously optimistic about their possibilities because the preamble to the Board's constitution stated:

"We, the undersigned citizens of Lincoln, believing that Lincoln is possessed of advantages which, if made known to the public would result in soon making it a large and prosperous city, do for the purpose of judiciously advertising said town and presenting its many advantages before the public, hereby organize ourselves into an association and agree to be governed by the following constitution."

The rules of the association allowed any person to become a member by signing the constitution and paying the sum of five dollars into the treasury. After that, a member paid $2.50 on or before the first day of January, April, July and October. Each additional $2.50 over the quarterly sum entitled the member to one additional vote.

A copy of one of the original membership certificates of stock hangs in the Chamber offices today.

The dues weren't too expensive when you stop to consider that in 1870, you paid $3.00 for a chicken and forty cents for coffee.

Prior to 1870, Lincoln had been viewed as something of an outpost of civilization with the main routes following the Missouri River to the city's east. Lincoln's only waterway was what at that time was described as "The Beautiful Clear Waters of Salt Creek."

It is only natural that, under those circumstances, members of the Board of Trade placed great importance upon the establishment of additional roads into town.

One of their earliest actions was the following amendment to their constitution:

"Resolved, that the Lincoln Board of Trade is in favor of voting for $150,000 in county bonds to the Midland Pacific Railway Company, the said bonds to be issued upon the completion of the road from Nebraska City to Lincoln; PROVIDED, it be completed by the first day of February, 1871."

The amendment was passed and signed by some of the leading figures in the city, county, and state politics and business. The issuance of the county bonds, not only helped bring the Midland Pacific into Lincoln, but played a small part in bringing in other new roads as well.

The Board of Trade was a mobile force in Lincoln and Southeast Nebraska. It had, however, been hastily put together and by 1874 it became obvious that a more tightly-knit organization was needed – particularly in view of the phenomenal growth rate of the city.

In March of 1874, the Lincoln Board of Trade was abolished and a new organization called the The Board of Trade at Lincoln was incorporated in its place. Capital stock amounting to $1,000 was set and a provision was made so increases in capitalization could be made. The corporation also gave itself a definite life span from March 15th, 1874 to January 1, 1900.

Admittance rules were also tightened. Under the old constitution, anyone could join by signing the constitution and paying his dues. New rules stated "any male citizen, of good moral character and over 21 years of age" could purchase stock and become a voting member of the corporation. The ladies were excluded. A few years later, women were allowed to participate in some matters. Today the woman's role in the Chamber has expanded to include the organization's first woman president, Wendy Birdsall.

The new Board of Trade, because of, or in spite of its painstakingly detailed constitution, remained a driving force in the economic life of the city. Some of the town's greatest strides were made over the next few years.

The board's major concern was bringing new business into the city. One of the earliest attempts in this field was an unsuccessful bid to move a plow manufacturer from Nebraska City to Lincoln. Why the attempt failed is unknown. The firm wanted to relocate to the capital city; the Board of Trade offered to buy a building site but nothing ever came of it. However, as a result of the early endeavor, the Board asked the city council to remit taxes for ten years to any new industry that wanted to locate in Lincoln.

Although books of meeting minutes don't mention it, other sources indicate that another re-organization took place around 1880 with the organization reverting to its original name, the Lincoln Board of Trade.

After this re-organization it is apparent that the Board took a more aggressive approach in industry, civic affairs, and problems of business in general. In 1880 the Board was active in establishing packing plants in west Lincoln. The next year, the Board worked for construction of a city waterworks, and members hassled over whether the utility should be publicly or privately owned. The membership finally voted in favor of public ownership. The Board then worked

to pass a $75,000 bond issue that made the waterworks a reality.

In 1882, Lincoln continued to experience tremendous growth and now transitioned from a village to a city. As a result, Lincoln began to number its streets. The Board of Trade urged the City Council to adopt the "Philadelphia System." Under this system, O Street would be the dividing line for north and south Lincoln. First Street would be the starting point for numbering east and west. Today, that system remains in place thanks to the work of the Lincoln Board of Trade.

In December of 1891, the Board took an interest in an issue that affected the entire state. In only its second year of existence, sugar beet farming remained a hit and miss proposition since Nebraska farmers knew little or nothing about the crop. The Board realized the importance of sugar beets and gathered all of the state's beet farmers in Lincoln for a grower's convention. Later, this convention would lead to the formation of the Beet Growers Association of Nebraska.

The following year, the Board sent a representative to New York to talk to a group who was interested in locating a sugar beet plant in Nebraska. Today, of course, the beet industry is a multi-billion dollar business and at least some of that credit goes to the Lincoln Board of Trade.

Records cease to exist for the Board of Trade after August, 1892. Whether the organization disbanded or failed to keep meeting records isn't clear, but the organization faded from the public view.

In losing the trail of one organization, we pick up that of two others. The Union Club was a men's social organization founded around 1878 and the Lincoln Commercial Club was formed fifteen years later in 1894. The two groups voted to consolidate in 1897, forming the Union Commercial Club.

This new organization first moved into Walsh Hall at 12th and N, before eventually outgrowing that facility and settling into the Y.M.C.A. building at just one block east at 13th and "N."

R. H. Townley was named office manager at a salary of $25 a month. That was later raised to $50 when Townley was called to duty in the Spanish-American war and E. R. Sizer took the job.

J. C. Seacrest succeeded Sizer as club secretary in 1899. Soon, he realized the value of hosting conventions in Lincoln and organized a drive to induce state associations to hold their conventions in the Capital City. He also started a Lincoln advertising campaign in various publications around the country.

Between 1901 and 1903, the club reduced its emphasis on social activities and began placing more emphasis on commercial development. This change of philosophy is noted in the group's decision to change its name to the Lincoln Commercial Club.

With this renewed interest in commercial development, the club hired its first full-time, paid executive. Walter S. Whitten took the position.

By 1913, Club membership had jumped to 1,625 and the group needed a larger office space. The group bought a parcel of land on the corner of 11th and P Streets and opened its own office at a cost of $175,000.

Just one decade later, the Lincoln Commercial Club underwent a change that set the foundation for today's success. The Commercial Club officially changed its name to the Lincoln Chamber of Commerce.

The 1920s brought busy times for the City of Lincoln. In 1924 the Chamber led the drive to raise $150,000 to pay for the city's share of construction costs for a new football stadium on the University of Nebraska – Lincoln campus. That stadium is still known today as Memorial Stadium.

A veteran's hospital became a reality in 1928. Twenty-six members of the city's Chamber of Commerce pledged the $17,000 necessary to close the gap between the cost of the land and a federal appropriation.

The Depression hit Lincoln in the 1930s. When relief offices had to be moved from the Capitol, the Chamber of Commerce successfully defeated Omaha's bid and kept the $500,000 payroll in the city. The Chamber underwrote $6,775 worth of State Fair tickets and $6,000 in funding went to insure the city could offset the cost of hosting the A.A.U. Track and Field Meet.

During World War II, the city found itself shaping many of its activities toward national defense. The first step was forming an industrial team composed of business leaders and Chamber of Commerce members to go after wartime industries. The team's biggest catch was the Goodyear Tire and Rubber Company. Goodyear officially began business in Lincoln in December of 1943 with 700 workers employed at the plant.

During the 1950s, what was a booming industrial sector took a tumble. The number of people employed in industry jobs fell from a high of 10,000 in 1953 to 7,750 in 1960.

It was at this time that business leaders decided to put their money together and become more aggressive at attracting manufacturing businesses to Lincoln. Industrial developers set about a ten-step process designed to grow Lincoln's manufacturing industry: basic economic data had to be compiled, industrial property had to be developed, a list of industrial prospects had to be made, the community had to be sold on the advantages of these new industries, an advertising and marketing program had to be devised and prospective companies had to be contacted so business leaders could answer questions about the city, specialists had to be hired in the fields of transportation, finance, labor, and utilities, and an industrial park had to be created.

The Lincoln Chamber of Commerce chose a site across from the State Penitentiary near 14th and Highway 2 as the location. Today businesses such as Square D and Weaver's still remain as active tenants in the park.

In the 1970s and 1980s Lincoln continued to grow, but the progress was nothing like what was about to happen to the city in the 1990s.

The 1990s ushered in a ten-year growth spurt like nothing the city had ever seen before. Areas such as North 27th Street and Cornhusker Highway underwent tremendous redevelopment. The housing market exploded in south Lincoln. Areas like Cripple Creek, Williamsburg and The Ridge became synonymous with prosperity.

Today, the city remains as vibrant as ever. New businesses like Verizon are choosing Lincoln as the location for new facilities while current businesses like Kawasaki, Molex, and Bryan Memorial Hospital continue to expand their existing operations. Industry remains strong. New steps are also being taken to ensure that our future continues its promising outlook. A public-private program called The Lincoln Partnership for Economic Development was created to act as a recruiter and conduit for new business opportunities in Lincoln. A business expansion and retention program has been enacted to maintain existing businesses and continues to work to streamline the business process in the city.

It's been a long journey from that hot July day in 1870 to where we are today. Programmed for progress, the business community continues on in search of the next project in which it can assert its influence and demonstrate that Lincoln truly is a community of opportunity.

Lincoln Electric System

Once you've experienced Lincoln's unique ambience, growing cultural diversity and energized business environment, we think you'll agree it's one of the Midwest's best kept secrets. Another well kept secret is the fact the community owns the local electric utility. The nonprofit Lincoln Electric System (LES) is recognized for providing superior, reliable energy services at rates that are among the lowest in the nation.

Low Rates Are Appealing

For 20 consecutive years, a survey of electric rates in 106 U.S. cities has shown LES is one of the most efficient energy providers in America. The most recent survey ranked LES rates 9th lowest, overall.

Lincoln's low rates are attributable to a balanced mix of efficient and reliable power resources that use coal, water, oil, gas and wind to keep production costs low. Low operating costs and access to wholesale markets to buy and sell replacement power also contribute to Lincoln's low rates.

LES keeps a close eye on expenses to fulfill its commitment to provide low-cost electricity to customers. Another factor is low-cost financing. LES' bonds and commercial paper are rated 'AA', enabling the utility to borrow money at low interest costs.

LES' low electric energy rates make Lincoln an appealing business site, and are a major factor in the decision of businesses and manufacturing firms to make Lincoln their home.

Service That's Reliable

Customers receive extremely reliable service from LES. Millions of dollars are spent annually to install, upgrade and replace equipment and facilities, keeping LES' infrastructure reliable. The latest reports show LES' delivery of electricity is 99.99 percent reliable, with the average amount of time that customers were without electricity at just 18.3 minutes. The national average outage time is 88 minutes.

Services Save Money

Businesses and residents have saved thousands of dollars in annual energy costs by utilizing LES' energy-saving services. LES offers a customized, online analysis to businesses and homeowners and a quick, no-hassle "walk-through" to help businesses save money and increase profits by implementing no-nonsense, cost-effective ideas that save on energy bills. The energy experts at LES can help businesses analyze electricity use patterns to determine when and how to use electricity to minimize costs, as well as how to manage and schedule daily and seasonal electric loads. In addition, rate plans can be matched to a company's electricity use profile to provide effective cost management.

From energy-saving services for residents to the largest manufacturers, LES helps customers find ways to reduce their electricity use and their monthly bills.

The city-owned Lincoln Electric System's performance, reliability, service and value help Nebraska's "Star City" shine.

Focused On Customers' Needs

Electricity is essential to our way of life. LES' customers know that at home and at work, at any time of the year and in any type of weather, they can count on LES to keep this vital commodity flowing. When they flip a switch or push a button, customers have the energy they need to power their lights and their production lines. LES' performance, reliability, service and value help Nebraska's "Star City" shine.

Partner In Progress

Commercial Development

At a recent informational event, five CEOs of Lincoln's largest businesses were asked the question, "What is Lincoln's biggest asset for businesses?" To a person, their response was, "The people." As each took time to expand, it was Lincoln resident's work ethic that was noted again and again. People are reliable and hard working, taking time to get the job done in a professional manner.

Businesses are also greatly attracted by Lincoln's reasonable labor costs, low cost of living and well-educated work force. Major commitments to education have been made across the board, from preschools to postgraduate programs. The people of this city place a high value on quality education. A well-educated city contributes to Lincoln's intelligent and motivated labor force. Lincoln businesses understand that a populace prepared educationally along with a solid work ethic is key to success.

In its overall development, Lincoln has been a "planned" community since its founding. Streets are laid out in an easy-to-follow grid, numbered streets running north and south and lettered streets running east and west. Growth and development are guided by Lincoln's Comprehensive Plan which is adjusted routinely. Citizens play an important role in updating the plan, volunteering their time to assist the city government in gaining a good vision for the future.

Community of Opportunity

Andrew McDonald

> **"I'VE NEVER HAD A PROJECT GO THROUGH A CITY AS QUICKLY AS THIS PROJECT IN LINCOLN AND I'VE WORKED IN THIRTY STATES AND EUROPE."**

Lincoln is an attractive place to locate a business due to a variety of state and local incentives. This includes Nebraska Advantage, a package of economic incentives. These incentives cover property purchases, investment tax credits, sales tax refunds for capital purchases and tax exemptions for qualifying facilities. Research and development activities are encouraged with various tax advantages. And there are state and local tax exemptions for qualifying manufacturing equipment and services.

In the past, like many other cities, Lincoln tended toward simply responding to companies that showed an interest in locating here. In recent years, the focus on economic development has shifted from response-to-inquires to a new strategy of development preparedness. Companies looking for new sites want a quick turnaround on their questions and interest. The Lincoln Partnership for Economic Development (LPED) is a community-based public and private collaboration. It recognizes that the public and private sectors work best when they work together. They work to attract industries, nurture a positive economic environment for existing businesses, and cultivate local entrepreneurial development. They also coordinate marketing strategy and events along with various sectors of the city to help attract business. They recognize the types of companies with a propensity to locate in or around Lincoln. The LPED also has identified a software company to develop an integrated website aimed at helping people quickly acquire information about properties in the Lincoln area. They have a comprehensive data base of development sites. There is an infrastructure work group to help identify sites, including information on the resources that are available. They identify how existing utilities can be enhanced or expanded. There is also a good flow of information with commercial brokers so new and existing listings can be quickly identified and examined. Where land is available, there are possibilities for tax increment financing that can help attract potential new businesses.

With these changes, Lincoln is ready for a rapid response. Armed with advance information, interested businesses are able to readily recognize which possibilities are the most feasible. This coordinated effort has made a significant difference. Recently, when Verizon chose Lincoln as a key site for its expansion, one company official said, "I've never had a project go through a city as quickly as this project in Lincoln and I've worked in thirty states and Europe."

Some of the nation's most sophisticated technology allows development professionals to explore Lincoln's commercial real estate using a variety of criteria.

Technology Park

The University of Nebraska Technology Park is a high-tech business incubator designed to bring together creative minds and new technologies. It embodies the spirit in the greater Lincoln community that is willing to boldly move into the future with creative new ideas. Technology Park offers support, services and amenities for both new and established technology companies. Since it began in 1997, Technology Park has expanded to house twenty-three high-tech companies employing

approximately 820 people. The number of jobs will double to 1,600 over the next two years with the addition of its newest business partner. And there is plenty of room for further expansion.

The mission of this high-tech consortium is "To promote synergy among the park companies, and facilitate technology transfer and collaboration with the private sector via the basic and applied research of technology-based products and services. The results are intended to foster economic development and new jobs for the State of Nebraska." Located for easy access, Technology Park is adjacent to Interstate 80, near Lincoln Municipal Airport, and only five minutes from both downtown and the University of Nebraska campus.

The most recent addition, Verizon Wireless, is opening a new 33-million-dollar customer service center within Technology Park. The 112,800 square-foot facilities will house state-of-the-art equipment and bring another 800 jobs to the Technology Park. Verizon consistently ranks as one of the top 100 companies to work for in the United States. Their choice of

Lincoln for this facility fits with the established goals and vision of Technology Park. Verizon chose Lincoln for many reasons, but especially for the quality of the people in the workforce. That this nationwide corporation chose Lincoln speaks well about Lincoln's future, and about the possibilities that Technology Park offers for future high-tech businesses.

Business Facilities magazine ranks Nebraska as one of only two states to place in the top ten of its major categories for biotechnology research. One of the companies at the University of Nebraska Technology Park that contributes to that strength is Nature Technology Corporation (NTC). NTC is a bioengineering technology company and is part of the geonomics revolution that is rapidly changing the world of applied biological study. NTC is working to develop, among other things, safe DNA-based vaccines for prevention of pandemic flu, such as avian flu, and other infectious diseases. They provided the DNA-

manufacturing process used by the National Institutes of Health as they seek to develop their own vaccines.

The current list of other Technology Park businesses and some of their services is impressive. These outstanding, creative companies include: Alpaca Registry, Inc. (Animal registry); ALTS (educational testing/ assessment software tools); Cabelas (Worlds Foremost Bank, MIS/IT support group, customer service center); Cranze Technology Group (financial transaction software); Donovan Networks (network security products and consulting); Eide & Associates (animal health products development and contract research); GeneSeek (animal genotyping & gene discovery); Highway Bridge Services (engineering services and software support products); Ingenient Technology (DSP hardware and embedded software development); Invest Nebraska (statewide equity capital network); Little Big Endian (contract software development); Mars Veterinary Services (animal genotyping, animal health products); Merial (animal genotyping and animal health products); Nebraska Center for Excellence in Electronics (full service EMC, environmental and safety testing laboratory, contract engineering services); Southeast Community College (electronics and engineering software training services); Specialized Network Systems (computer network design and support services); Technology As Promised (on-line corporate training products, continuous and process improvement training and certifications) and Z3 Technology (embedded software/hardware products development.)

Digital Vision

Lincoln has an eye on the future. That this diverse collection of high-tech companies can grow in just a few years shows the payoff for creative thinking, hard work and collaboration. There is a creative energy here on the prairie. According to the Partnership for Economic Development, the National Policy Research Council has termed Lincoln an "entrepreneurial hot spot." *Expansion Management* magazine ranked Lincoln in the top ten Best Places in the U.S. to locate a company. *Forbes* ranked Lincoln as the 4th best city in terms of overall business climate and one of the best small cities for business and careers.

Cost of Living and Readily Available Housing

Owning your own home is part of the American dream. In some areas of the country, economic realities make this an impossible dream. It is different in Lincoln. The cost of living in Lincoln is significantly lower than other places in the country. In one estimate by the Director of Planning, a $100,000 lifestyle in Lincoln would cost over $7,000 more in a nearby large city. And Forbes.com ranks Lincoln among the top sixty cities for stretching your dollar

The median price of owning a home in Lincoln is significantly less than the average when comparing it either to the country as a whole, or to many other Midwestern cities. In 2006, the average sale price of a new home in Lincoln was a $246,000, while the average price for an existing home is an even more modest $153,000. The stability of the market has made housing a good investment. In Lincoln about 60 percent of households own their own home.

There are houses of all types, styles and sizes. Lincoln is divided into a series of neighborhoods, and each area has its own style and story. There is a house for just about every desire and pocketbook. Some neighborhoods were first developed in the 1870s. Many historic mansions create beautiful vistas in the established neighborhoods.

Child magazine ranked Lincoln as the twentieth best city in the country for raising a family. Safe neighborhoods, good schools, and a commitment to family are part of this. So are parks and activities for children. The strengths of neighborhood communities along with a strong economy contribute to Lincoln's low crime rates.

For a long time, Lincoln has been growing at a reasonable rate. The emphasis on both "reasonable" and "growing," as Lincoln's population has continued to grow by an average of 1.5 to 1.8 percent for more than fifteen years. Every year the edges of the city keep expanding. Still, this rate of increase means is that the city is able to keep up with the necessary infrastructure that continues to make the good life good. That means while new schools are built in growing areas, the older neighborhoods and their schools are kept in a high state of repair. While other cities have sacrificed quality for quantity, Lincoln has a balanced approach to growth. While businesses and housing keep expanding, Lincoln is also growing the infrastructure of schools, roads, sidewalks, utilities, parks and public swimming pools

Festivals and Nightlife

Festivals and activities highlight the times and seasons of life in Lincoln. Summertime is filled with great events. The Jazz in June concert series is held in the Sheldon Sculpture Garden and surrounding University of Nebraska campus. These free concerts often draw up to 7,000 people. They come for the great music, the beautiful setting and to meet friends in the

balmy, early summer evenings. Also, in June, the International Thespian Festival is held at the University of Nebraska. In Antelope Park, the Lincoln Municipal Band has been putting on free concerts since 1911. Each week the music is based on a different theme. As someone remarked, music in the park band shell makes you feel like you're living in a Norman Rockwell painting.

The Celebrate Lincoln Ethnic Festival turns the streets and sidewalks of downtown into an "out of this world" experience. Multiple ethnic cultures are represented in food, music, dancing and a "world market" array of goods. This is a celebration that everyone can enjoy.

Americruise makes regular stops in Lincoln in late June or early July. Fifteen hundred participants bring their antique and classic cars as well as restored hot rods. The diverse display is moving in more ways than one. Besides riding around town, the cars are shown over the course of two days at the Nebraska State Fairgrounds. One of the special attractions to Lincoln for car lovers is Speedway Motors. The Smith Collection Museum at Speedway Motors houses the world's largest collection of antique racing engines as well as a great variety of antique and one-of-a-kind automobiles

The Nebraska State Fair comes to Lincoln in late August each year. People from far and wide come for the festivities. The carnival rides always include a new thrill. High school bands from across the state perform. And 4-H clubs bring a wide array of animals for livestock judging competition. Nationally-known musicians put on concerts that are highlights of the fair. It is a time when people across Nebraska come together. The Capital City Ribfest is also in August. Barbecue chefs from around the country come vying to win the title of best ribs. Music is always included as dessert.

The Star City Holiday Parade in November is the largest event of its kind in a five-state area. Floats, marching bands, vintage vehicles, and live animals, all wind through the streets of Lincoln. Participants are granted entrance based on their ability to entertain children of all ages. It kicks off Lincoln's winter wonderland season.

Pershing Auditorium with its arena and exhibition hall has year-round events with up to 7,500 attendees. Included are national concert tours, trade shows, ice skating, basketball, wrestling and even rodeos. Within walking distance of the Capitol building and downtown restaurants, it has been a center of celebration in Lincoln for many years.

A newcomer on the scene is the Nebraska Bluegrass Festival at the Lancaster Event Center. This is one of the genuinely American styles of music. It's relaxed. It's all about the music – listening to those on stage, taking a workshop or jamming with some folks you met. New events keep on coming to this diverse, growing city.

The Arts and Cultural Amenities

Artists and those who care about the arts have made the whole city of Lincoln a place for creative experiences. The Lied Center for the Performing Arts is at center stage. Its annual array of Broadway plays, opera, diverse music, dance and children's events engage thousands of people every year. The Lied also hosts the E.N. Thompson Forum on World Issues. These free public lectures are designed to bring diverse perspectives on international public policy issues to Nebraska in order to promote discussion and debate. Speakers have included such world-renowned figures as Mikhail Gorbachav, poet Maya Angelou, Archbishop Desmond Tutu, Bill Gates and UNL alumnus Warren Buffet.

Nebraska Wesleyan's McDonald and Enid Miller Theaters provide high quality productions. A wide range of theatrical events is offered, with plays and music by authors from Aristophanes to Elton John, and from Shakespeare to Broadway shows. The quality of the plays and intimacy of the theaters make this a special experience.

The Sheldon Memorial Art Gallery boasts one of the nation's most important collections of 20th century American art. With more than 12,000 objects in its permanent collection, there are works by such artists as Edward Hopper, Jackson Pollock, Mary Cassatt, Andy Warhol and Georgia O'Keeffe. A trip to the Sheldon is always a rewarding experience. Surrounding the gallery on the outside is the Sheldon Sculpture

Lincoln's Symphony Orchestra performs under the baton of Music Director Edward Polochick to an audience of more than 30,000 at the second annual "Uncle Sam Jam," a free community concert on July 4, 2007.

Garden. It has grown from its original two and one half acres to now include works spreading into downtown and East Campus. Represented are outstanding sculptures from the early 20th century to the present. Strolling through the sculptures is an interactive and insightful journey.

Lincoln's Symphony Orchestra began in 1927. In its first program it was said that this was

" . . . an institution of which all Lincoln may be unprejudicedly proud." Over the years, the members of the Orchestra have continued the tradition of bringing the finest in live performance music to Lincoln. The list of guest musicians who have performed with the Orchestra includes such notable figures as Itzak Perlman, Aaron Copland, Henri Mancini and Ray Charles.

The Mary Riepma Ross Theater offers a variety of artistic films, including independent, foreign, documentary and experimental films. Douglas Theatre's locations around the city, including their new landmark multiplex in downtown, make sure that a wide diversity of

popular films keeps movie buffs' tickets punched.

The vision of the Lincoln Arts Council is to inspire creative community through the arts. Recently they reached this goal in two widespread exhibitions. To highlight Lincoln's nationally recognized trail system, various artists created seventy one different sculptures of bicycles. These playful and beautiful full-size creations were individually displayed throughout the city, sharing visions of excitement and joy.

Next came the Stories of Home project. Led by renowned artist, Pepon Osorio, a dozen professional artists listened to the stories of a dozen diverse families. Then they created sculptures celebrating that which brings us together – family – and that which sets us apart – diversity. These artistic creations were displayed throughout the community, in homes, community centers, churches, and businesses. Through this great diversity of images, people found a shared yearning to find a place that feels like home. A documentary was made about the event, so that other cities can follow this pattern. It is telling that a grand vision such as this was conceived in Lincoln.

Educational Opportunities

Education is one of the greatest strengths of life in Lincoln. As a key to success, from family life to economic life, schools receive broad support in the city. Lincoln Public Schools (LPS) are ranked second in quality in an eight-state Midwestern area, according to the Lincoln Chamber of Commerce. A low classroom ratio of teachers to students is a goal that keeps the schools strong. LPS consistently have achieved the fourth highest percentage of graduating high school seniors in the nation. In addition, there are also nearly 30 private and religious schools serving a wide variety of students. In Lincoln, 90 percent of adults have at least a high school diploma.

This commitment to education is part of the belief that education and hard work can make dreams come true. Estimates are that there are approximately 40,000 full-time and part-time college students in Lincoln. Thirty-three percent of adults in Lincoln have at least a Bachelor's degree. And 40 percent of employees in temporary positions are currently earning college credit. The array of schools is impressive for a city this size.

The University of Nebraska, chartered in 1869, is a land-grant university that has established an internationally recognized reputation for excellence. It is a research leader in a wide variety of grant-funded projects, as well as one of the nation's leading teaching institutions. The University of Nebraska is rated by *U.S. News & World Report* as one of the

top fifty public universities. The Carnegie Foundation recognizes it as a doctoral/research extensive university. The University of Nebraska-Lincoln, with more than 22,000 students, offers over 150 undergraduate majors and 275 programs of study, as well as seventy-three masters degree and thirty-nine doctoral degree programs.

Nebraska Wesleyan University is ranked by *U.S. News & World Report* as the number one liberal arts college in Nebraska. With 1,500 students in forty-eight majors and a faculty-student ratio of one to thirteen, Nebraska Wesleyan emphasizes quality education through outstanding teachers and small class size. Wesleyan has an active relationship with the United Methodist Church and welcomes people of all faiths.

Union College is rated by *U.S. News & World Report* as one of the top colleges, ranking twenty-eighth in the category of Baccalaureate Colleges in the Midwest. With fifty majors and a faculty to student ratio of one to thirteen, students are taught by professors in a campus atmosphere of strong faith. One-fifth of Union's out-of-state students choose to stay in Nebraska after graduation, contributing to the state's "brain gain." Union College is in association with the Seventh-Day Adventist Church.

Doane College is located on three campuses, including Lincoln. The Lincoln campus is especially prepared to serve nontraditional undergraduate and graduate students who need to juggle career and family. Doane has a faculty whose qualifications and professional experience are impressive.

Hamilton College offers Bachelor's and Associate's degree programs. Centered on career-oriented academic programs, Hamilton

enrolls between 600 and 700 students. Hamilton students contribute to the strength of many Lincoln businesses.

BryanLGH College of Health Sciences offers Bachelor of Science and Associate of Science degrees as well as other outstanding

Family & Implant Dentistry

Cosmetic dentistry can give you a smile that is both beautiful and healthy. Using the latest materials and dental techniques in combination with artistry, Dr. Roger Plooster, our in-house ceramist and dental team can give you the smile you have always wanted Today's dentistry can add value to an individual's life through the improved health, happiness and self confidence that results from a healthy mouth and a beautiful smile. Most make overs can be completed in two painless appointments.

Everyone at Family Implant & Dentistry values patient relationships and in many cases, three generations of families have benefited from Dr. Plooster's 25 years of experience.

Roger Plooster and Family and Implant Dentistry are proud to be dental providers to the Lincoln community.

For more information telephone 402/486-0825 or visit fidentistry.com

educational services. It provides professional education marked by standards of academic excellence and clinical competence.

Southeast Community College offers Associate's degrees and undergraduate academic transfer programs as well as career,

technical, adult basic education and continuing education programs. Multiple locations make Southeast Community College a college of choice to more than 7,000 full-time and part-time students.

Health Care

The nation wide system of 911-calling for emergencies was first developed and used in Lincoln, Nebraska. This may be a great image for Lincoln – a city ready for a great range of urgent health

Family Implant DENTISTRY

chest pain center are ranked among the top tier in the nation in response time to heart attacks. Saint Elizabeth provides services to more orthopedic patients than any Lincoln hospital and offers the state's premier radiation therapy center. In a personal touch, every time a baby is born, the Brahm's

I n 1959, Arnott Folsom, along with key community leaders, recognized the importance of creating an environment where children could connect with nature. Their dedication to the project led to the opening of the Lincoln Children's Zoo. Since 1965, the Zoo has enriched the lives of people in Lincoln and surrounding communities by helping its visitors connect with wildlife through unique hands-on encounters and engaging experiences.

The Lincoln Children's Zoo is a treasure for the Lincoln community as it is one of only five zoos in the nation dedicated to educating children. Its design is tailored specifically for children, providing viewing areas at a child's height, animals that are within reach, signs that are read easily–all surrounded by botanical gardens. The numerous hands-on learning exhibits, such as Firsthand Farm and Critter Encounter, encourage children to touch animals and ask questions of the staff. This one-on-one interaction makes lasting memories and inspires children of all ages not only to care about nature, but also to take action to protect our environment.

care needs. Life is precious, and Lincoln's assets for health care are significant.

The Community Health Endowment (CHE) has a goal of Lincoln becoming the healthiest community in the nation. In 1998, Lincoln sold its public hospital, Lincoln General Hospital, and created CHE with the funds. It was a visionary move. Every year this multimillion dollar public health endowment generates hundreds of thousands of dollars. These funds financially support specific projects aimed at improving the health of the city's residents. Innovation and community collaboration make CHE a pillar upon which Lincoln is building a healthy future.

BryanLGH Medical Center offers health care on two different campuses. BryanLGH is ranked as one of the top 100 hospitals in the nation. It is rated among the nation's top neuroscience programs and is designated as a Neuroscience Center of Excellence. For more than thirty years it has been a leader in fighting against heart disease, and its Heart Institute is nationally recognized in the areas of heart and vascular disease. It

has earned a five-star ranking for overall orthopedic excellence five years in a row from HealthGrades, an independent rating service. It is a five-time recipient of the Solucient™ 100 Top Hospital Award for excellence in cardiovascular care. Among BryanLGH Medical Center's special areas of focus are childbirth, cancer treatment, mental health, sleep disorders, diabetes and substance abuse.

S aint Elizabeth Regional Medical Center has been recognized as one of the nation's "100 Top Hospitals" by Solucient™ in the overall category. They were also awarded Magnet status, the highest award in nursing. It is a full-service hospital that cares about patients physically, emotionally, and spiritually. The burn unit is internationally recognized for outstanding research and treatment of serious burns and wounds that are resistant to healing. Their well-recognized Children's Services includes the state's highest level NICU. The emergency room and certified

Lullaby is played over the hospital intercom to share the celebration throughout the hospital.

Madonna Rehabilitation Hospital has been ranked as one of the top ten rehabilitation hospitals in the country. Its focus is on helping children and adults with physical disabilities through research, rehabilitation and support. State-of-the-art technology helps guide diagnosis. A primary aim is to help people to redevelop practical skills. One rehabilitation area contains such practical equipment as the front half of a car, an actual tractor cab, and movie theater seating, in order to help people to learn to move again in real life situations. This Catholic organization is living out its core value of being "dedicated to the healing ministry of Christ."

The Nebraska Heart Institute Heart Hospital opened its doors in 2003, and has rapidly

Lincoln Children's Zoo

Enriching lives everyday.

Lincoln Children's
ZOO

Learn firsthand.

Lincoln Children's Zoo
1222 South 27th Street
Lincoln, NE 68502
(402) 475-6741
www.lincolnzoo.org

Not only has the Zoo been nationally recognized for the outstanding care and conservation efforts for the West African dwarf crocodiles, tree kangaroos, red panda, and Amur leopard, but also for its remarkable educational programs noted numerous times by the Institute of Museum and Library Services. Some of those community focused programs include:

• Children at the Zoo–Providing free admission and scholarships for at-risk children to visit and participate in Zoo events.

• Our Zoo to YOU–Placing the Zoo's education animals in 85 classrooms providing children with an extended exposure to caring for wildlife. In the summer, animals visit people living in assisted living centers and retirement communities.

• Sensory Safari–Providing a hands-on opportunity for those who are visually impaired to experience animals.

The Zoo's mission to "enrich lives through firsthand interaction with living things" is accomplished everyday when a child connects with the wonders of the natural world through playful interaction. It is here that the youngest learners discover new animals as they explore their way through the natural landscape of the Zoo.

See you at the Zoo!

The Lincoln Children's Zoo is sponsored by  WR LLC.
Real Estate & Investments

Partner In Progress

achieved widespread acclaim. As an exclusive Heart Hospital, it offers a full-range of cardiology services, including cardiac, vascular and thoracic care services. The cardiologists and surgeons at NHH focus on an interactive relationship with the patient, family and referring physician. The sixty-three bed facility offers state-of-the-art technology and a personal atmosphere.

The commitment to health is also seen in also in leading local businesses. Lincoln Industries developed one of the first wellness programs in the nation. Their vision has been that wellness encompasses the body, mind and spirit. They encourage a balance of work, home and personal goals. In helping people to learn to make healthier lifestyle choices, they have increased productivity, lowered absenteeism, lowered turnover, lowered health care costs, and supported their employees to make a happier company.

Commerce and Shopping

Lincoln's shopping has changed in the last decade. As the population grew, national stores began to put Lincoln on their map. Now you can choose between Lincoln and bigger cities like Chicago, St. Louis, or Kansas City, if you want to: go to lunch at Granite City,

choose between that new shirt at the Limited or the other at Banana Republic, pick up your glasses at Lenscrafters, get your hair cut at Master Cuts, pick up some bon bons at the Rocky Mountain Chocolate Factory, indulge in new footwear at Tradehome Shoes, snack on a fresh pretzel at Auntie Anne's, get a gift-wrapped shirt at Aeropostale, ogle the power tools at Sears, pick out a new novel at Barnes & Noble, get some new chinos at Eddie Bauer, remember your vitamins at GNC, and decide whether to go to dinner at the Olive Garden or Macaroni Grill. You can do any of this and more in either in one of those bigger cities or Lincoln. The stores are the same, but there is just a lot less traffic and hassle to get there in Lincoln. Westfield Gateway has 111 stores and SouthPointe Pavilions has 57 shops and upscale restaurants.

Particularly enjoyable are the unique shops and restaurants that you discover as you explore the city. Unlike a whole lot of medium size cities, Lincoln actually has a downtown. Exploring downtown is an adventure. Traveling through all the artist shops in The Burkholder Project is a creative event in itself. Then wander around Ten Thousand Villages with its handmade objects from around the world. Nearby, be amazed by the Michael Forsberg Gallery and its Nebraska nature scenes. Wander in the Mission Arts building. Or go up to Sartor Hamann Jewelers and dream about what you would like to give next Christmas. Then stroll over to Dietze Music and let your musical imagination

wander. And make sure you have lunch at the Blue Orchid in historic Federal Place, or one of the many other outstanding restaurants you can find only in Lincoln. There is a lot going on in downtown.

Lincoln has a Blue Ribbon Roster of Utilities

For twenty consecutive years, Lincoln Electric System's (LES) rates have ranked among the lowest in the United States. In a study of 106 cities, the average LES electric bill ranked ninth lowest overall. People never think about electricity much until it goes out. Losing power is a frequent fact of life in other cities, including rolling brownouts that happen every summer when all the air conditioners overload their electric systems. It is different in Lincoln, where the reliability of the electric system is ranked at 99.996 percent. Winter, summer, spring and fall, the power stays on.

Lincoln is served by multiple power plants, including two owned by LES, the Salt Valley Generating Station and the Walter Scott Jr. Energy Center Unit 4, that *POWER* magazine ranked as among the best in the world. The strength of LES' system is attributed to the variety of energy resources, low operating and repair costs, the way the system was built, and the way it is managed. When you have a child in a winter storm who needs to keep warm, or a business that needs to keep on schedule, reliability is critical.

Runza

If you wonder where the water is in Nebraska, is it under your feet – way down under the ground. Nebraska sits on top of the Ogallala aquifer, which stretches over eight states, from South Dakota to Texas, and from Wyoming and Colorado to Nebraska. This is one of the world's largest, and perhaps the largest, water source of its kind. Of those states, Nebraska has both the largest amount of water and the most favorable recharge rate. It is an important natural resource. Nebraska and other states are concerned that it is used in ways that are wise and environmentally sound.

The city of Lincoln is supplied by a series of wells located along the Platte River. According to the City of Lincoln Public Works and Utilities Department, Lincoln uses about 14 billion gallons of water a year. According to the Lincoln Partnership for Economic Development (LPED), Lincoln's average daily water demand is 38 million gallons a day while its average water capacity is 114 million gallons a day. The city and state pay close attention to this valuable resource, both in terms of conservation practices and environmental stewardship.

Wireline telephone service provided by Windstream includes 240 route miles of cable fiber and 11,600 fiber strand miles in the city, acccording to LPED. Windstream offers Broadband and DISH Network, with digital high definition technology TV.

Time-Warner Cable is the second largest cable operator in the U.S.

Locally, Time-Warner Cable offers digital phone service, digital cable, high definition television (HDTV), and high speed online access. Serving 110,000 Nebraska customers, Time-Warner has a goal of serving its customers with the most up-to-date advancements in technology, programming and service. Road Runner, AOL High Speed Broadband and EarthLink High Speed Internet connections are available through Time-Warner. Other local and national internet service providers include Netzero, and Juno.

Sports

Year round nationally ranked college sports teams play in Lincoln—baseball, football, gymnastics, softball, track and volleyball. The enthusiastic support of the community for each of these teams makes Lincoln a place that attracts athletes from all over the country and the globe. In a mutual exchange of support, reasonable ticket prices and availability make it possible for people to attend often and to bring the whole family.

+ CATHOLIC HEALTH
INITIATIVES

**Saint Elizabeth
Regional Medical Center**

Taking healthcare to a higher level.

Saint Elizabeth has again been named one of the nation's "100 Top Hospitals.®" While we're turning heads nationally, we're changing lives right here in Lincoln.

SaintElizabethOnline.com

ANCC MAGNET RECOGNITION

SOLUCIENT
TOP HOSPITALS
1993 2003 2004 2006

As one enters downtown on the Interstate, UNL's Memorial Stadium football complex towers impressively on the horizon. The Huskers have amassed an historic list of awards and accomplishments, including five national football championships, three Heisman Trophy award winners, ninety-two first team All-American awards, and ninety Academic All-American awards. What is far more impressive is entering the stadium on game day, and experiencing what it is like to come into "a sea of red." The fans are as passionate about football as the players. The traditions are deep and the festivities are nonstop, including the hotdog-firing bazooka. When the crowd sings, "There Is No Place Like Nebraska," you have to agree.

While football may be what first comes to mind, the University of Nebraska fields twenty-one men's and women's teams in fifteen NCAA Division 1 sports. Nebraska Women's Volleyball has earned three NCAA titles, including 1995, 2000 and 2006. The Nebraska Men's Track and Field Team

has been represented in every Olympics since 1956. And in the overall record, they have amassed a total of 228 Outdoor Conference champions. The Women's Gymnastic team has twenty-eight All-American gymnasts, including three female gymnasts crowned NCAA champions.

The Lincoln Saltdogs are an American Association independent minor league baseball team. They offer an exciting season of professional baseball in a wonderful setting. Recently-constructed Haymarket Park has seating for more than 4,500 and additional space for an additional 4,000 on the grassy berm. A family-friendly playground for kids overlooks the field. In addition, the stadium contains sixteen luxury suites. The American Association of Independent Professional Baseball Clubs voted Haymarket its top honor as "Best Playing Field" for the superior overall aspects of the park.

The Lincoln Stars are a Tier One junior ice hockey team playing in the West Division of the United States Hockey League. The Stars

made the playoffs nine out of their first ten seasons. Playing in the 4,610 seat Ice Box on the Nebraska State Fairgrounds, the team has some of the best fan support in the league.

Lincoln is the host to the USA Indoor Speed and Figure Skating National Championships. These

Since 1907 TierOne Bank has built a solid reputation as a leading financial institution throughout the Midwest. Rooted in the rich spirit and tradition of strong Midwestern values, the Bank has grown to become one of the most innovative and successful financial institutions in the history of Nebraska.

TierOne Bank's foundation of financial strength, broad resources and community bank philosophy, blended with highly trained employees focused on customer responsiveness, provides a successful combination that customers have trusted and relied upon for generations.

Throughout its history, TierOne Bank has proven itself an innovator and financial pioneer. It was one of the first savings associations to apply for a federal charter; the first Lincoln savings and loan to offer insurance on savings; the first mortgage lender in Nebraska to make veterans' loans; one of the first mortgage lenders to receive Federal Housing Administration accreditation; the first Nebraska savings and loan to install

events are displays of speed, skill, endurance, athleticism and grace. Thirty-five hundred athletes from across the country come to Lincoln to show their skill in the various events of this twenty-two-day festival. The National Museum of Roller Skating, located in Lincoln, is home to the world's largest collection of roller skates as well as photos, films, videotapes and trophies.

In November, the Nebraska high school state football championships are played at Memorial Stadium. In March, the Nebraska high school boys' and girls' basketball tournaments are held in the Bob Devaney Center. In these events, school spirit, intensity, inspiration, and teamwork come together in great moments that are remembered for a lifetime.

TierOne Bank

Full-service consumer, commercial and agricultural banking products and services

data processing operations; the first financial institution in the nation to develop and implement money cards and electronic funds transfer; a pioneer of in-store banking through the use of remote terminals in grocery stores; and one of the first financials in the nation to introduce telephone bill paying.

Though the bank has experienced significant growth over the years, its values of integrity, reliability and innovation and its commitment to providing customers with superior service remain constant and strong. TierOne Bank employees are dedicated to the bank's brand promise of *"Taking the extra step"*

for customers and for the community.

Today, because of this commitment, TierOne Bank is favorably positioned among an elite group of super community banks with a network of 69 banking offices in Nebraska, Iowa and Kansas and ten loan production offices in Arizona, Colorado, Florida, Minnesota, Nevada and North Carolina.

Exemplary customer service...a diversity of competitive financial services... innovative and convenient banking offices...an uncompromising commitment to our communities. These are just some of the many reasons TierOne Bank is—and will continue to be—one of Nebraska's premier financial institutions.

 Member FDIC   tieronebank.com

Partner In Progress

Recreational Opportunities

Lincoln has more than 100 individual parks in the city, each park having its own unique amenities. Antelope Park's band shell hosts a wide diversity of events from spring through autumn months. Among the most popular is the Lincoln Municipal Band free summer concerts. This event often draws more than 1,000 music lovers to take in the music and the park's ambiance. Nearby is a playground designed to be accessible for children of all different abilities. Impressive in its size and scope, it is a place for every child to play.

Holmes Lake Park has a winding trail surrounding this beautiful lake. There as you walk the trail, you can watch the wild ducks paddle, or see anglers fishing for large mouth bass, bullhead, carp, and blue gill. In the spring, the dam is a favorite site for kids flying kites. Holmes Lake Park is bordered by a fenced-in dog park where canine companions can run free.

Oak Lake Park, Tierra Park and Woods Park are all spacious, attractive places to relax. Large parts of the city are bordered by Wilderness Park and two stretches of tall grass prairie on different sides of the city. The ability to be back in nature is never very far away. In Pioneer Park, on the outskirts of Lincoln, you can see the buffalo roam, hear the elk trumpet and watch the prairie grass wave. Anytime you are looking for some peace and quiet, it's there waiting in Lincoln's parks.

Lincoln is a cyclist's paradise. There are nearly 100 miles of bike paths within the city, including trail bridges that keep you from having to cross heavy traffic. From dawn to dusk you see people of all ages biking, running, roller skating, strolling hand-in-hand or walking their dogs.

Lincoln offers fifteen different scenic public and private golf courses. All offer unique and beautiful experiences. The Country Club of Lincoln is a 18-hole regulation length course just minutes from downtown and is an historic place both in terms of its membership and location. Golfers play near what used to be a landing strip where Charles Lindbergh learned to fly, and the stream where famous naturalist Loren Eiseley played as a child.

Golf Digest ranked Wilderness Ridge and Firethorn (north and south) in the top 10 golf courses in the state. Newly-developed Wilderness Ridge contains a 18-hole championship course and a nine-hole executive course. These include twenty-two lakes, and a mile and half of streams. Each water feature is scenically bordered by portions of the 300 train loads of granite shipped in from Minnesota. This course has a unique feel to it, including four waterfalls, the largest one being a forty foot waterfall on the fourteenth hole.

Firethorn's outstanding facilities have made it a widely respected location for many great golfing events. It is home to both the University of Nebraska's Men's and Women's golf teams. It has been the host to the Nebraska State Amateur Championship. On a national level, it has been the host for qualifying rounds for the U.S. Open, the U.S. Seniors Open and the U.S. Women's Open.

And Firethorn has been the site for the U.S. Women's Amateur Championship and the Women's Trans-National Championship.

Highlands Golf Course opened in 1993 and is another new and challenging course. HiMark Golf Course, carved from an old apple orchard, has earned its name and often receives popular accolades from those who golf there. Jim Ager Memorial Junior Golf Course has the unique focus of encouraging the development of younger golfers. In this nine-hole course, youth receive preferential treatment.

Tennis is popular, and Lincoln offers twenty-four sites in city parks and schools. The University of Nebraska, Nebraska Wesleyan University, Union College and Southeast Community College all have courts for public use. The Woods Park Tennis Center offers leagues, tournaments and events.

Its fifteen high quality courts are open to the public, including six covered courts for play year round. The Nebraska Tennis center offers six indoor climate-controlled courts and nine outdoor courts, as well as a full-service clubhouse and stadium.

There are dozens of public and private swimming pools. When school is out in the summer, friends see each other as the swim teams rotate through the various pools for swim meets. Star City Shores is a zero-depth pool with giant slides and other water features.

The YMCA offers a host of team events throughout the year. Baseball, softball, t-ball, basketball, flag football, in-line hockey and volleyball all have eager participants. The soccer leagues are popular with boys and girls, and the leagues fill the parks in-season. Whatever the sport, kids have plenty to do throughout the year.

In winter, the sledding hill at Pioneers Park offers a ramp that adds height and helps manage the sledding traffic flow. It is lighted, so sledding after dark gives extra time for kids to play. Holmes Lake Dam is considered a shorter sledding run, but the added vertical drop and the wide range make it an inviting place for a fast running sled.

Alzheimer's Disease Steals Memories

We care about the loss of past, present & future memories.
We can help you.

Alzheimer's Association of the Great Plains
Contact us at 402.420.2540 or visit our website
www.alz.org/greatplains

Underwritten by Buckley & Sitzman CPA's

Climate

Lincoln has a true four-season climate. April and May begin the growing season. Flowering trees that line many of the city streets and open at different intervals, make this season a beautiful experience. It's the season the parks and the trail system wake up, as everybody comes outside to soak up warm spring days.

If you like sunshine, Lincoln is your kind of place. The sun shines here 234 days a year. Most often, the rain comes in the night time, meaning that day time is free for lots of outdoor activities. Three fourths of the precipitation comes in April through September, according to a climatology report by the Chamber of Commerce. Those who have lived in other areas of the country where the humidity is high will find Lincoln's moderate to low humidity levels a refreshing change. There are plenty of perfect days to spend at the pool, on the golf course, at the lake or just relaxing in the backyard.

Autumn usually sees shirt-sleeve weather through September and even into October. The beautiful changing color of the tree leaves lasts into November. Lincoln is on the migration routes of many wild birds. On fall days, you can stand in Pioneer Park and see ducks, geese and other birds flying overhead in flocks that seem to stretch for miles. And the migrating Husker football fans who flock here from across the state, enjoy the temperate autumn days too.

Snowfall throughout the winter season averages about twenty-seven inches, through much of the snow does not last long. Children in Lincoln – and some adults – take delight in the few days a year when there is enough significant accumulation to merit a "snow day." For those who believe that children deserve the wonderland that snow provides, most years there are enough sledding, snow forts and snowballs to keep everyone satisfied.

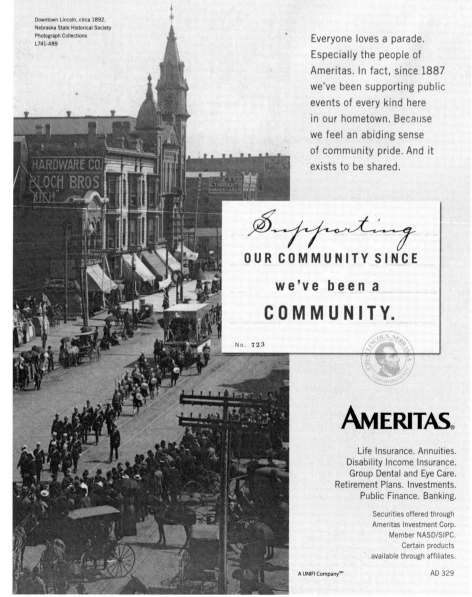

Downtown Lincoln, circa 1892.
Nebraska State Historical Society
Photograph Collections
L741-489

Everyone loves a parade. Especially the people of Ameritas. In fact, since 1887 we've been supporting public events of every kind here in our hometown. Because we feel an abiding sense of community pride. And it exists to be shared.

Supporting

OUR COMMUNITY SINCE

we've been a

COMMUNITY.

No. 723

AMERITAS®

Life Insurance. Annuities.
Disability Income Insurance.
Group Dental and Eye Care.
Retirement Plans. Investments.
Public Finance. Banking.

Securities offered through
Ameritas Investment Corp.
Member NASD/SIPC.
Certain products
available through affiliates.

A UNIFI Company℠   AD 329

Lincoln sits on top of the Ogallala aquifer, one of the world's largest water sources of its kind.

Digital Vision

Why I choose to live in Lincoln.

A life-long Nebraskan, Joel Sartore brings a sense of humor and a mid-western work ethic to all of his National Geographic Magazine assignments. Over twenty years of experience (more than 15 with the National Geographic Society) have allowed him to cover everything from the remote Amazon rain forest to beer-drinking, mountain-racing firefighters in the United Kingdom.

Besides the work he has done for National Geographic, Joel has completed assignments for Time, Life, Newsweek, Sports Illustrated and numerous book projects. Joel and his work have been the subject of several national broadcasts including National Geographic's Explorer, the NBC Nightly News, NPR's Weekend Edition and CBS Sunday Morning, as well as an hour-long PBS documentary.

Joel's work can be viewed at www.joelsartore.com, along with information on how to purchase individual prints.
He currently resides in Lincoln with his family and submits, "These photographs are a testimony to why I choose to live in Lincoln."

Photography by Joel Sartore

Commentary by Morgan L. Fry

The people in this town love to work...

The unemployment rate in Lincoln is amongst the lowest in the nation, which is especially remarkable, given the level of "under-employment."

...and work hard, with a real pride in craftsmanship.

"Under-employment," is a term used to describe a worker who chooses to work at an available job, even though they qualify for better jobs elsewhere. In Lincoln, more than 40 percent of temporary employees seeking permanent jobs are also currently earning college credit.

'Round here the weather can change in a heartbeat, but we're ready for it.

Lincoln's location in the upper Midwest experiences fantastic seasonal averages with a comfortable 75 degrees in the summer and 212 "clear days" annually. The water that does fall ends up mainly in the Ogallala aquifer, one of the world's largest underground water sources.

How do you not get caught-up in the pageantry of Big Red Football?

The University of Nebraska football team gets all the attention, but the University's Technology Development Center is a big champion in its own right. The tech park is home to a score of companies and organizations that employ hundreds in cutting edge technologies.

Lincoln is a place of faith.

For over 100 years, engaged couples have been meeting with the pastors at Westminster Presbyterian Church to plan their weddings. Celebrating life together in a faith community is part of who we are here. Lincoln has over 170 churches in a vibrant religious community.

Partner In Progress

Why I Choose to Live in Lincoln

Lincoln is a liberal town in a conservative state, which always keeps the politics interesting.

Voter apathy is somewhat difficult to find in Lincoln. The city's people are extremely interested in their government and openly participate in every aspect.

Lincoln has some great parks and they're accessible no matter where you live.

The whole Lincoln community came together to restore the Sunken Gardens. The Rotary Clubs of Lincoln joined together to help establish the golden dome as a community landmark. Rotary Club #14 was the first service club in Lincoln, and remains the 14th oldest Rotary Club in this international organization whose goal is "Service Above Self."

Partner In Progress

Lincoln's great. But sometimes it's nice to get out of the city and see the real beauty of Nebraska.

Lincoln is surrounded by outdoor escapes for everyone. There are dozens of golf courses, parks and lakes, minutes from town. Fishing, boating and hiking are everyday adventures.

Malls and strip-malls, whether they're in New York or California, are pretty much the same.

Lincoln still has a <u>Downtown</u>.

Downtown Lincoln is home to a variety of arts and culture, dining, entertainment and shopping. There has been a continuous and uplifting stream of major public and private redevelopment projects.

Lincoln Children's Museum:

- invites children to create, discover and learn through the *power of play*
- Is open to children and families since 1989
- Welcomes 130,000 guests each year (that's 260,000 feet of all sizes!)
- is one of the top twenty children's museums in the United States – as rated by Parents Magazine
- Has more than 4,400 member families
- Serves nearly 1,000 low-income families each year by offering free admission to the Museum through the Have a Heart program
- Partners with over 250 organizations to bring unique and quality programs to area children each year
- is the only place where your child can be a prairie dog, a firefighter, an artist, a pilot and an actress or actor – all before nap time

Kids love this place. It's kinda' like a three floor jungle gym. The best part is they never get in trouble for touching the exhibits. They're encouraged to.

Lincoln
Children's
MUSEUM

(402) 477-0128
1420 P Street Lincoln, NE 68508
www.LincolnChildrensMuseum.org

The Lincoln
Children's
Museum is
sponsored by

Partner In Progress

There's a spark
of wonderment
in the kids of
Lincoln. The
schools here make
sure of that.

Lincoln Public Schools (LPS) are some of the
strongest in the nation, with test scores higher
than the national average. Seventeen percent
of LPS students scored above 28 percent
on the ACT's, compared to the 11 percent
statewide, and 10 percent nationally.

The University of
Nebraska State
Museum exhibits
some of the most
phenomenal
relics of the
past. We hope to
keep a present
day species from
becoming a relic.

The Salt Creek Tiger Beetle, unique to the
Lincoln area, is on Nebraska's endangered
species list. Activists are working to further
protect it.

The people of
Nebraska are
proud of their
roots. It's an honor
to live in Lincoln.

Why I Choose to Live in Lincoln

Older
neighborhoods
offer the sense
of community I
prefer.

Others want new
construction on
the outskirts.

Regardless,
housing in Lincoln
is affordable.

Everywhere you look in Lincoln there's a little piece of history or art that anyone can get caught up in.

Even if you live to be 100, you'll never see the same sunset in Nebraska twice.

How this city got to be the way it is.

The great-grandson of Lancaster County pioneers, Jim McKee is a life long resident of Lincoln, Nebraska. Currently, he has authored nearly 1,000 articles and books on Lincoln and Nebraska history including:

Lincoln: A Photographic History 1976
The Lincoln Trivia Game 1980
Lincoln: The Prairie Capital 1984.
Havelock: A Photo History and Walking Tour 1993
Remember When. A collection of articles on Lincoln history 1997.

His weekly history column appears in the Lincoln Journal-Star Sunday newspaper, 1960s and 1993 to present. Additionally, Jim is an adjunct professor at Southeast Community College, lecturing on subjects such as history, copyright law and publishing. A popular public speaker, Jim gives about fifty talks a year to church, civic, professional and historical groups including a number through the Nebraska Humanities Council.

The unattributed quotes at the beginning of each chapter are from the author's lifelong collection of amusing quotes about Lincoln.

All images in this section, except as noted, are from the collection of the author.

Text by
James L.
McKee

The N.
Ameri
and The Salt Legend

tive
cans

Salt Creek:
"There is a cheerless look about it. It winds its way through the prairie with a withering influence, blighting every green shrub."

This supposedly contemporary oil painting, which languished in a local antique shop for years, shows Luke Lavender's cabin. The 1864 cabin, often erroneously termed Lincoln's first house, was located just south of O Street, north of the Bennett Martin Public Library, on 14th Street.

Two features of the painting, often overlooked, are the tree behind the cabin and the well at the front. The story told is that the tree, a maple switch, was transported from a site near the present penitentiary. This would have been the first "planted" tree in the city of Lincoln, once virtually treeless and today a literal forest.

The well actually stood at the north door of the cabin. When the footings and pilings for the present Chapin Building were set, workmen actually uncovered the hand dug well's casings near the southeast corner of the intersection.

In any Great Plains history it is common to forget that the first settlers usually referred to were preceded by the American Indian. In Lancaster County a number of village sites have been uncovered which date from 1,000 to 1,500 AD or some 350 to 900 years

before John D. and son, John W. Prey, settled near the present village of Sprague, southwest of Lincoln in the summer of 1856. The largest probable village, whose location is known as the Schrader Site, sits on about fifteen acres on the west bank of Salt Creek between Saltillo Road and Roca, Nebraska. The site was excavated and studied several decades ago then reburied so it could be farmed while preserving it for future archeologists.

One of the earliest recorded histories of Indians in Lancaster County was written by John T. Irving Jr. and published in 1835. The two volume work represents a diary kept by Irving while accompanying a federal government investigatory party which was charged with securing Pawnee lands. This induced the Pawnee to then move north of the Platte River thus reducing the fierce strife then existing between the Pawnee and Delaware. Salt Creek was, at that time, a boundary between the Pawnee, who primarily lived to the west, the Otoe to the east and the less amicable Sioux to the northwest. Easily the most dramatic discovery they made was the dry lake bed "of pure salt of dazzling whiteness, which is

highly prized by the Indians" who had reportedly been visiting and harvesting salt there since 1550.

The Indians had a legend explaining the area salt deposits which are now generally purported to be the mineral remnants of a salt lake. Irving related the story which centered around a "chief warrior…a terror to old and young" both in other area tribes as well as to his own people. The warrior's sole love was the beautiful daughter of a neighboring village's chief. His goal of marrying the woman was unchallenged because of both fear and respect. After their marriage he became a new man, "he was a tiger tamed." Sadly his wife died and the warrior turned inward, taking no notice of events or people around him. After a month's absence from his village he returned "laden with the scalps of men, women and children."

After only one day he again left, returning a week later and told of his most recent travels. After walking many miles he laid down in the grass to sleep as the moon rose. Shortly afterward he was awakened by a woman's cries. In the distance he saw an old decrepit hag threatening a young woman with a tomahawk. The warrior approached as the two women fought and when he quickly buried his own tomahawk in the old woman's head, the young woman turned revealing his wife's face. Before he could react the earth opened and swallowed both women leaving only a rock of salt.

Irving noted that even in the 1830s the local tribes all felt the basin was under the control of the old hag. Before they could harvest salt they felt it necessary to subdue the hag by beating the ground with tomahawks or clubs.

With John D. Prey and his two sons in 1856, perhaps the county's first settlers, others began to slowly arrive in what is today Lancaster County and with them encounters with the local Indians naturally commenced.

The first recorded Indian encounter resulting in bloodshed occurred in 1857 after John Davis settled near Salt Creek in what today would be the northern section of Wilderness Park. Bachelor Davis made no secret of his desire to kill an Indian. When two Pawnee calmly wandered onto his claim, Davis promptly shot and killed one of them. The other settlers, fearful of retaliation, packed up and went to Weeping Water until the outcome was settled. Mr. Davis was soon charged with murder and fled, never to be heard of again. The reprisal likewise passed without initiation and the settlers returned to their homes. The same year, just as corn planting was about to start, John Prey shot at an Indian but missed him and grazed Mr. Loder's head.

The following year a group of Pawnee camped adjacent to William Donovan's cabin near the salt flats. Donovan, who had been sharing what supplies he had with the Indians, found he was down to the last of his flour and bacon. Several of the Pawnee walked into Donovan's cabin demanding food but were told there was none to share. They immediately grew angry and threatened Donovan. One Indian, She-cool-al-col-la-ca, who happened to be sleeping on the floor by Donovan's stove, immediately came to his defense, explaining that Donovan was a government agent who could call the U. S. Army down on them at will. Although it was a complete bluff, the party moved on. Later in 1858 Mrs. Donovan was alone while her husband and sons were away and broke a chair over an intruder. When Mr. Donovan returned, the Indians again retreated. A few months later the Donovan family moved to the Stevens Creek area returning to Yankee Hill in 1861.

The following year the Cheyenne and Arapahoe arrived at the salt flats. Waiting until John Prey was away from his cabin, a small band of Indians descended on Mrs. Prey, their twelve year old daughter, Rebecca, and two sons aged eight and fifteen. After Rebecca tried to hide in a field the Indians seized her and took her away. Mrs. Donovan and her sons immediately sought help from their neighbors who chased down the Indians and secured the girl's release without further incident.

In the spring of 1859 the cabin of James Bogus and Mr. Beals was raided by a group of Pawnee in the men's absence. When they returned and discovered the robbery they formed a posse of about ten men and met at Sophir's cabin near Crabb's Mill, today's 1st and Van Dorn Streets. The following morning the Indians, who were camped near the present penitentiary, were approached by Joel Mason who attempted to retrieve the stolen property. Mason was chased back to Sophir's and as soon as he was inside, the shooting started, killing three Pawnee and wounding five.

About the same time a man living near Olathe (Roca) reported the theft of a steer from his herd presumably by area Pawnee. A neighbor, Jeremiah B. Garrett, gathered some men and pursued the Pawnee to their camp. There they discovered the Indians skinning the steer. Garrett killed one Indian but in the process was shot between the ribs with an arrow. Garrett pulled the arrow out but assumed he was done for, even reciting his supposed last words of "Boys, I sold my life dearly." The Indians abandoned the camp and Garrett recovered completely.

In September of 1862 John S. Gregory, a would-be salt boiler, wrote "where West Lincoln now stands was a camp of about 100 Pawnee wigwams. I rode over, and that night slept upon my blanket by the side of one of them." This was on the floor of the salt basin which was "smooth and level…covered with an incrustation of salt about a quarter of an inch deep, white as the driven snow."

During the winter of 1862 to 1863 Gregory decided to rid the area of wolves. Using a common practice, he rolled balls of fat around strychnine and scattered the poison in the snow. The wolves were attracted by the smell, devoured it and were quickly dispatched. Gregory then skinned the animals

selling the pelts and piled up the frozen –stiff carcasses like firewood to prevent domestic animals from eating them. By spring his cache amounted to several cords. Gregory then observed several Pawnee women examining the animals and rode over to warn them of the poison with which they had been killed just as some began carrying a few off. The accompanying chief thought Gregory wanted his carcasses back and they were begrudgingly restacked. Another Indian, who spoke some English, arrived and the threat was explained with Gregory saying he only wanted to protect the Indians. When this was translated to the women it merely brought peals of laughter and they again gathered the wolves to be taken back and cooked for meat. The chief then explained that they were well aware of this method of killing wolves and had been eating the meat for some time without ill effects.

In 1862 a small group of local citizens became alarmed by a rumor that there was about to be an Indian uprising. They fled to the south taking cover in a small pocket cave north of the area where the penitentiary would later be built. If there had indeed been an uprising, their shelter would have been extremely ill advised as the site was in fact what others knew as the Pawnee Council Cave where important meetings and trials were convened, the spot they felt was the highest point of land in their territory. No uprising occurred. The rumor was just that, a rumor.

Another false alarm spread through the area around the salt flats in 1864 when word arrived that a Sioux raiding party was approaching from the south in Gage County along the east bank of the Blue River. Virtually all of the settlers evacuated leaving eight men behind as observers. After

several days of waiting Captain W. T. Donovan, John Gregory, E. W. Warnes, Richard Wallingford, James Morgan, John Loder, Aaron Wood and one other unnamed man ventured to the west to see if any signs of the advancing party could be discerned. One lone warrior was spotted behind them. When they

---

The Plains Indians of North America were nomadic in nature and traveled across a wide portion of the central United States, including Lincoln. In those pre-I-80 days, they required a high-energy, food-on-the-go solution. Pemmican, a sort of meat lover's veggie burger was the answer.

Of course, the recipes for pemmican varied a great deal, according to tastes and available ingredients. What is common is the requirement that the finished product have long shelf-life without refrigeration. The key component to preservation was separating those elements prone to spoilage, drying them, then recombining them with the oily elements as a binder.

So give this recipe, with Americanized alternatives, a try. Stalk and kill one buffalo, bison, elk or deer, any size. Carve several pounds of lean meat off the shoulder or rump.

At the same time, carve out several pounds of fatty material from the loins. Set remainder of buffalo, bison, whatever, aside.

If game is not plentiful, or the folks at Pioneer's Park are taking a dim view of you

stopped and turned, they suddenly found their retreat blocked by several hundred Indians. Just as they decided to fight their way out, one warrior approached. As he drew closer he threw his rifle to the ground and explained he was a Pawnee, a friend and that they too were looking for the Sioux, a common enemy which did not materialize.

As Union troops were called to the Civil War much of Nebraska was plagued with Indian skirmishes but virtually all encounters with unfriendly or even those perceived as unfriendly, ended. Settlers were often confronted with Indians, particularly Pawnee but they were primarily looking for food and even if rebuffed did not provide any real threat.

Pemmican, Fast Food for the Plains Indian

stalking the park wildlife, just snag some bison, venison or sirloin carried in Lincoln's finer grocery stores.

Using a sharp flint knife, cut lean meat into flat, bacon-like strips and lay on flat rock to dry in sun. Instruct children to shoo flies away. Although children may be recalcitrant, be aware they may nevertheless steal part to play with, and they may eat the remainder when you are not looking.

During winter, the strips of meat can be hung in front of an open fire. The point is to get the meat as dry as possible.

Spread out whatever fruits, nuts or grains are available to also dry. Then place fatty parts of aforementioned beast in a pot of water over fire, effectively bringing all the fat to the surface, when cooled.

When the ingredients are thoroughly dried, it's time for you to let out a little steam yourself. With a medium-sized club, beat the heck out of the dried meat. Then go for the nuts and grain. Then go for the dried fruit. Then go back to the meat, until it is fairly shredded. Or until it's time for you to go to bed.

In the morning, gather the ingredients that your spouse salvaged from the mess you left the night before. Mix dried meat, fat from top of pot and a bit of honey. Form into golf ball-sized balls, then roll around in dried fruits. Then roll around in dried nuts and grains.

Tightly pack meatballs into small doe-skin bag. In a pinch, Baggies® will do just fine. Store in cool, dry place.

Or you could just shuck all the messy preparation, along with the obligatory lecture from the spouse on housekeeping. Go to the nearest convenience store, grab a hunk of beef jerky and glue it to a granola bar with some peanut butter. The ingredients and nutritive value will be about the same.

Banksy

– Edward J. Mueller

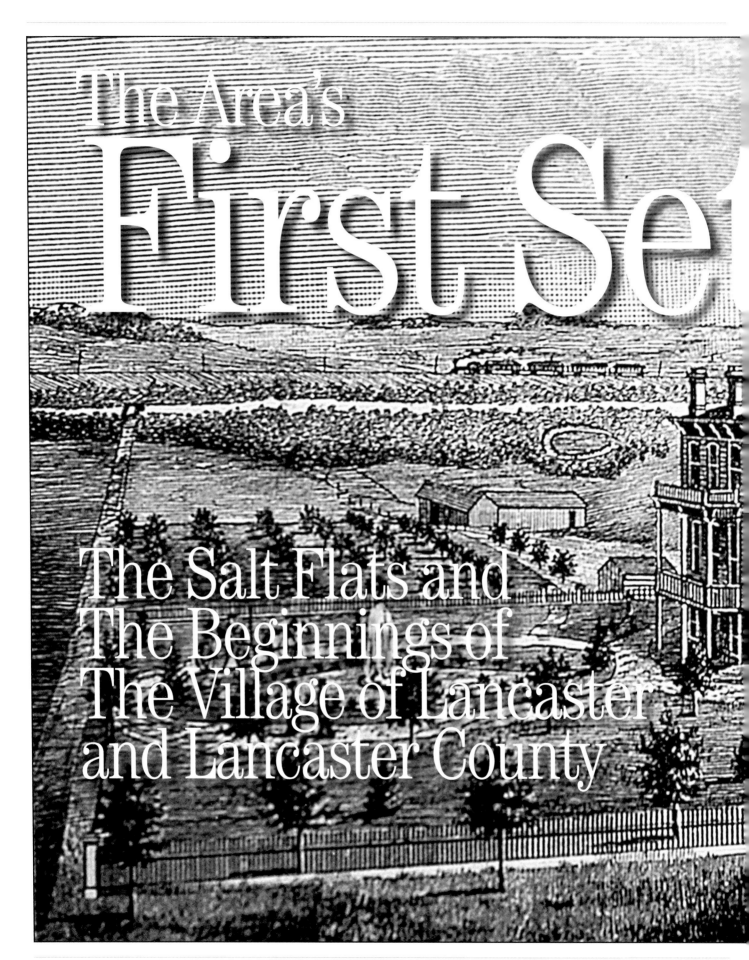

The Area's
First Se

The Salt Flats and
The Beginnings of
The Village of Lancaster
and Lancaster County

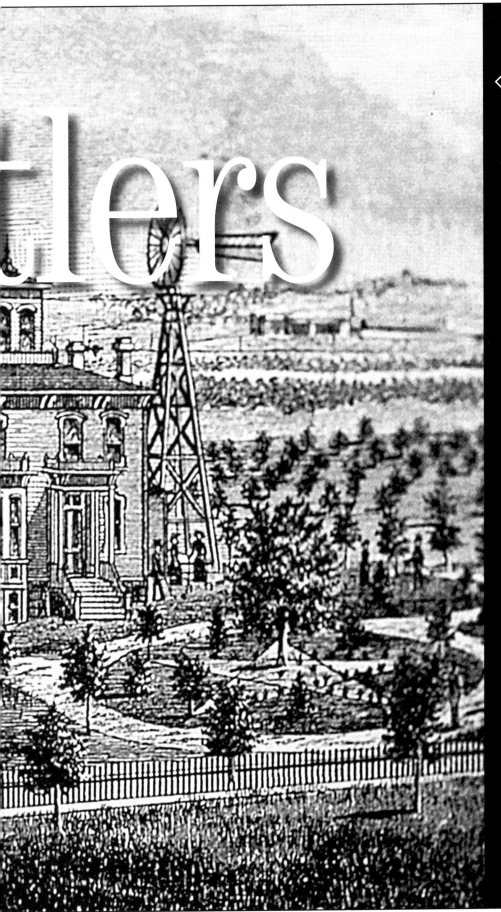

ers

"the weary traveler
will be lulled to
sleep upon his
down couch by
the incessant
barkings of
the numerous
denizens of the
adjacent prairie
dog town"

In the spring of 1856 John D. and his son John W. Prey headed from Milwaukee for Iowa where they intended to settle but there they chanced to meet Zebediah Buffington, also shopping for a site to homestead. Finding the area pretty well already

settled he explained he was heading further west. The Preys agreed with his assessment and bought a wagon and two oxen and headed west for the Elkhorn River valley. Even before they arrived there however they heard tales of the Salt River (Creek) area where timber was supposedly in better supply and again changed their destination.

On June 15 the Preys camped on the Salt, probably in the area now known as Wilderness Park, and met a small party of land speculators who had just filed claims on land to the southeast near today's Hickman. The speculators' plan was simply to take possession of the land and then sell it as soon as buyers could be found. The Preys continued south filing on land for themselves and Thomas, the other of John D. Prey's sons, near the Buffington claim and ultimate village of Sprague.

While John D. returned to Milwaukee for his family, his father stayed and helped Buffington build a cabin but even before the cabin was completed, Buffington left for greener pastures and was never heard from again. John W., his wife and children returned in July and set out to build a bridge over the

Salt and erect a tent while they began construction of a proper cabin.

In the spring, after a particularly harsh winter with one storm producing over two feet of snow and an accumulated depth said to average three to four feet, the Preys discovered a number of other settlers had arrived. In 1857 the Preys hosted a group of federal surveyors who were mapping Nebraska Territory (NT) allowing land descriptions and making settlement considerably easier.

Although the Preys settled in what was originally called Clay County, it was dissolved in 1864, giving the south half to Lancaster County and the north to Gage County in a political ploy to make Lancaster a larger and more prestigious area for John Cadman's political ambitions. Thus, even though they were not technically even in Lancaster County, John D. and Margaret Prey are usually considered its first permanent settlers though this is sometimes disputed by John Dee who resided near the present city of Waverly.

During the earliest days about the only visitors to the general area of the salt basin were Native Americans, those traveling through and a few men who came from Plattsmouth, Nebraska City and later Beatrice to gather the salt either by boiling the brine when firewood was obtainable or by

Overleaf
John Cadman's home, where the Capital Commission stayed in 1867 while examining Yankee Hill as a potential state capital location, would be on today's West Calvert Street. In the 1881 steel engraving the Burlington & Missouri River Railroad is visible just east of Salt Creek and the State Penitentiary is on the hill on the right. When the Capital Commission met there, only the lower, stone basement would have been in existence. This view shows the house, looking east, at the height of its splendor.

simply scraping it from the basin. As salt was a scarce and expensive commodity, with salt and flour selling at the same price per pound, people came from other trails to the south as far as 100 miles, traveling at three to four miles an hour to gather salt before heading back to the westward trails. Others came from Iowa, Kansas and Missouri on periodic visits.

The basin flooded with brine twice a day at about 3:30 AM and again at 3:30 PM to a depth of a few inches. This most probably occurred as subsurface hydrostatic pressure, perhaps like those creating Old Faithful Geyser, forced the solution up through the dry, cracked lake bed. Because this salt lake then mysteriously receded back into the ground less than an hour later, a thin film of salt was produced by the sun and breezes. So long as the weather remained dry the twice daily flooding and draining caused salt to accumulate, sometimes three-quarters of an inch thick. Thus salt could simply be scraped from the basin floor but when it rained the salt layer melted and disappeared back between the cracks. One man reported seeing some men who had traveled nearly a hundred miles arrive just in time to see a brief rain wash away the salt in a moment.

The unpredictable nature of the dry salt layer allowed the formation of a salt gathering business with salt selling locally for $0.50 to $1 per hundred pounds. One of the first of these entrepreneurs was Capt. W. T. Donovan who came from Plattsmouth with the Crescent Salt Co. in 1856. With the completion of the federal land survey Donovan and his family had settled on the west bank of Salt Creek at about

what would be 3rd and T Streets today. Those who arrived with little money seeking salt would eagerly trade "meat, flour, chickens, butter, fruit, potatoes" or as one man from Winterset, Iowa exchanged 5,000 pounds of his flour for 5,000 pounds of salt.

Because what little timber which existed in the area was soon exhausted, the local salt merchants also traded for wood which had to be imported from ever increasing distances. The wood was then used to boil the brine in large flat steel pans or sorghum sugar pans. On some occasions the "salt boilers" would take wood in exchange for allowing the travelers to use their pans. With hundreds coming and going, business became brisk.

In order to substitute a method of extraction for wood-required boiling, a system of shallow ponds were formed by railroad tie-like timbers joined with pitch. The brine was captured in the ponds and transferred to tall, circular, wooden vats with hinged lids. In the summer months, with warm winds and the sun beating down, the cylinders also took advantage of the chimney effect allowing the retrieval of several tons of salt in each vat. As the daylight shortened and temperatures dropped in the fall, the salt gatherers would retire for the winter spending their time hunting and constructing buildings.

At the end of June, 1861 W. W. Cox met Donovan in Nebraska City with Cox joining Donovan on a visit to the salt basins near the confluence of Salt and Oak Creeks. Following the faint path worn by "salt pilgrims" they entered the valley on July 2 and saw a drove of antelope where the old post office, also the old city hall, would later appear at 9th and O Streets. Fighting head-tall grass and sunflowers they crossed Salt Creek and saw "the basin was as smooth as glass and

resembled a slab of highly polished, clouded marble…geese, brant and pelicans had undisputed sway." A dozen families lived to the north east and south, to the west was a wilderness."

Late in the summer of 1859 a meeting was called "under the Great Elm" on the east bank of Salt Creek near Capt. Donovan's earlier home and what today would be in the Burlington rail yards northwest of the depot. The men chose Festus Reed as chairman, then elected Donovan, A. J. Wallingford and Joseph Forest as County Commissioners to Lancaster County, whose name was suggested by Donovan after his earlier home in Lancaster, PA. The commissioners were charged with investigating a site for the county seat and, though no written record survives, this was apparently all the business which was discussed.

On January 2, 1863 Donovan filed for the first official homestead in Lancaster County, a quarter section just east of today's Regional Center. It was at Donovan's house that the first county election was held that October 9. Twenty-nine votes were cast, officially electing the three originally designated commissioners and fixing the county seat at the village of Lancaster.

John S. Gregory arrived at the basin in 1862, established a salt works and the following spring built a small frame house near what is now Charleston Street and the subsequent village of West Lincoln to replace his dugout. On May 28, 1863 Gregory opened the first post office in the county which he named Gregory's Basin intending his name would forever be associated with the area. As an official postmaster, Gregory received an annual salary of $3, but also collected an additional $12 as he had to retrieve the mail at Yankee Hill where the Oregon Trail Cut-Off and all government wagons stopped. Gregory was also elected to the Territorial Legislature in October of 1863 and admitted to the bar in 1866 becoming the first attorney in the county.

On July 4, 1863 Mr. Cox, who was picking goose berries, was surprised by a group of men. John M. Young, Rev. Peter Schamp and Jacob Dawson (Capt. Donovan's son-in-law), Luke Lavender, E. W. Warnes and Dr. J. McKesson (Young's cousin), all of whom lived in Nebraska City and were on a visit to the area seeking a site for a potential Methodist colony and female seminary. The party then joined Cox for dinner and that Sunday Elder Young preached what is believed to be the first sermon delivered in Lancaster County. The group returned to Nebraska City and on July 10, Young acquired eighty acres in the southeast quarter of Section 23 from Julian Metcalf for $140. In a portion of this land Young situated the village of Lancaster, named for the county, giving parcels to the county for a hoped-for courthouse, a school site and about half to the Methodist Protestant Female Seminary, sometimes simply called the Lancaster Seminary. Some of these lots were then sold to raise funds to erect the seminary building. The footprint of the village would today cover the area roughly bounded by 5th, 14th, O and U Streets. Dr. McKesson's property lay north of Lancaster and his cabin was located about where Avery Hall sits on the current University of Nebraska campus.

On September 15, 1864 Jacob Dawson was appointed the village of Lancaster's first postmaster. Like many Nebraska and Great Plains post offices, its location was in Dawson's home, a double-walled log cabin on the south side of O Street at about 7th. On November 8, 1864, the day Abraham Lincoln was reelected President, in the midst of a blizzard and after some problems in finding enough men to form a jury, Lancaster's first court was held, also in Dawson's home. The court's notes indicated it was the only "finished" residence in the village meaning it was also the "first." The case revolved around a man named Pemberton who suffered an argument with one of Jim Bird's daughters. When the girls began spreading the word about Pemberton through the county, Mr. Pemberton, unamused, charged into the Bird house. Words were

The Cadman house, here looking to the southeast has begun to deteriorate: the cupola is gone along with the north porch, the hill has eroded and only the chimneys and bracketing under the eves gives evidence that the house was once much grander. By the late 1950s even the top two floors had been removed and a north-facing brick entry had been added. The lower basement level, perhaps the most historically significant portion of the house, is extant.

exchanged, shots were fired and Mr. Bird was hit in the head with the butt of Pemberton's revolver. T. Marquette represented Pemberton who was found not guilty but Marquette told his client to leave Mr. Bird alone in the future or he would personally prosecute him. Pemberton promptly left the county.

In 1867 Dawson built a new, totally symmetrical brown stone house southwest of the corner of today's 10th and O Streets where he then kept the post office for a brief time. While he was finishing the new house, Stephen B. Pound arrived and purchased the 7th and O cabin where he lived while preparing to take the local bar exam. Pound used the front room as a grocery store, probably the first in Lancaster. One of his later compatriots said that "Pound, as a merchant, was noted for his close application to his law studies."

During the winter of 1864 to 1865 the seminary building was completed. This, the first real building in Lancaster, was described as a two-story, sandstone, thirty by fifty foot building in the block bounded in Lancaster by 6th, 7th, High and College Streets, today's Journal-Star block. Although the seminary function never got off the ground due to a lack of students, Reverend Schamp used a portion of the structure as a Methodist church until a small frame building was completed on the northeast corner of the same block. Interestingly, on Sunday August 18, 1866 Reverend Reuben Gaylord, who founded Omaha's First Congregational Church in 1856, Reverend E. C. Taylor and William Coleman both of Greenwood as well as S. P. Sibley of Nebraska City, presided over a meeting at the seminary building. The meeting was comprised of community members who represented three Methodist, one Presbyterian and three Congregationalist families. The following Sunday Gaylord and Taylor performed a service, again at the seminary, after which the First Congregational Church of Lancaster County was officially organized. The Methodists were also using the seminary for services but because of a technicality the Methodist Protestant Church could only officially organize a Sunday School until their numbers increased to a specific level. Thus the first organized church in Lancaster was the Congregational Church, formed in the Methodist's building and in the village of Lancaster which was in itself, in a manner of speaking, owned by the Methodists.

Mrs. Merrill, wife of H.W. Merrill, who planned to teach at the seminary, received permission to conduct a graded, tuition school in an uncompleted, dirt-floored, carpet-covered, unglazed window room, providing her family could also live in the building. This became the first school in the community. Classes varied in size from five to thirty students depending on the weather and whether or not the children were needed to help their parents at any given time. Early in 1867 the building was gutted by fire and acquired by John Cadman, formerly from Yankee Hill, who added onto the building shell, extending it to the new streetscape of Lincoln, converting it into the Cadman House and subsequent Atwood House Hotel.

Perhaps the earliest actual photograph of the Lincoln area shows the salt flats with one of the large wooden evaporation vats which used hot winds and the sun to remove the water from brine. With the lack of firewood to boil the salt water, this proved the most successful, yet ultimately uneconomical means of large scale salt harvesting.

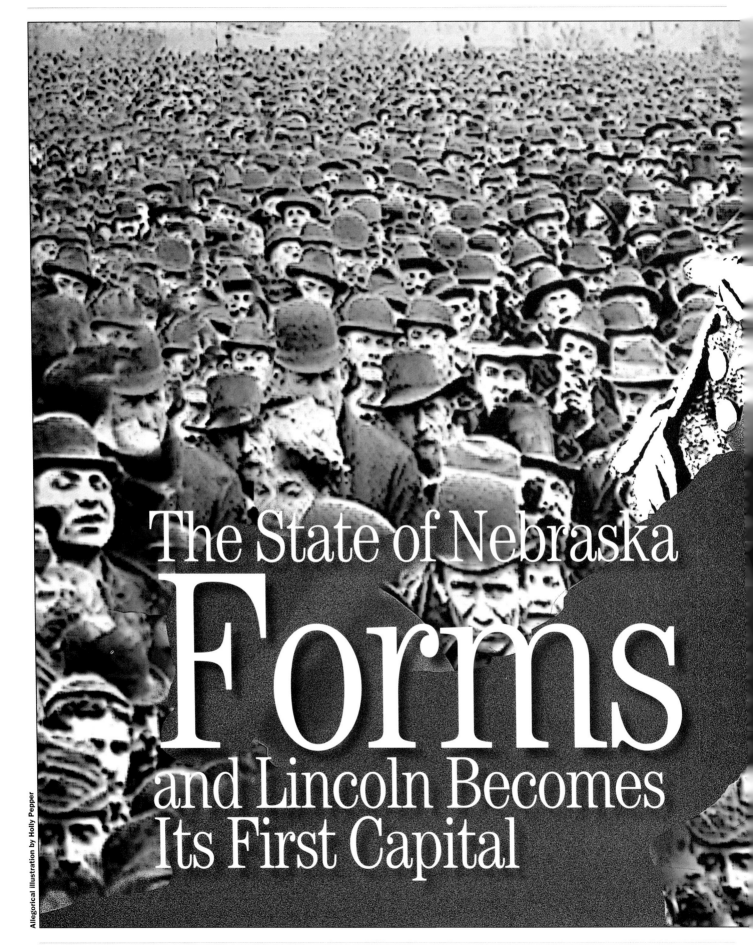

The State of Nebraska

Forms

and Lincoln Becomes Its First Capital

Allegorical Illustration by Holly Pepper

CHAPTER 3

"There would have been some decency in making Plattsmouth, Nebraska City, or Columbus the state capital, if Omaha could not be retained, but to locate it in a wild country, remote from any present or probable lines of travel, has not only the merit that either the commissioners are insane or have concluded to bring the whole 'South Platte' movement into contempt."

The "Act to Organize the Territories of Nebraska and Kansas" was signed by President Franklin Pierce on May 30, 1854. This, the original Nebraska, was many times larger than the current state and encompassed most of the Dakotas, the land to the

Rocky Mountains on the west and north to the British Possessions (Canada) at the 40th Parallel, a total of over 350,000 square miles. After several rejections Pierce appointed Francis Burt of South Carolina as Nebraska Territory's first governor on August 2, 1854. Burt arrived at Bellevue, NT on October 7 and was sworn in October 16. Sadly, two days later on October 18, having never left his bed, Governor Burt died and was succeeded by Thomas B. Cuming. Cuming, who had many alliances in Iowa announced the Territorial Legislature would convene at Omaha City, the favored capital from the point of view of Council Bluffs where Cuming also lived. By using his authority, Cuming contrived to divide the territory into counties and legislative districts so that the weight of power fell to the area north of the Platte River and Omaha even though the South Platte faction represented almost twice the population of the north. On December 30, 1854 J. Sterling Morton delivered a proclamation resolving Cuming was "neither…honest nor honorable and an unprincipled knave" and asked that President Pierce remove him from the governorship. Nonetheless, Cuming remained the governor and Omaha the capital.

By 1865 Nebraska, with the formation of new adjacent territories, assumed a shape and size approximating its current area. Talk of becoming a state was widely discussed. Proponents pointing out that as a state Nebraska would be able to elect actual voting senators affecting the rapidly growing area and perhaps influencing the transcontinental railroad. Opponents argued that as a territory nearly all local governmental expenditures were paid for by the federal government—Nebraska could not afford to become a state.

In 1866 the Democrats nominated J. Sterling Morton, a polished eloquent speaker for governor and endorsed remaining a territory. The Republicans chose David Butler, a politician able to speak to the common man and who, with the Republican Party urged statehood. A heated campaign followed. Morton "out-spoke himself—for vehemence, argument, wit and sarcasm, outstripped everything I have ever heard in Nebraska." Butler "waved the bloody shirt" of the Civil War emphasizing Morton's pro-slavery leanings.

The result was, albeit close, a near Republican landslide. Statehood and the proposed constitution carried 3,938 to 3,838 while Governor David Butler was elected 4,093 to Morton's 3,984. Votes were challenged and fraud claimed but the election results held. After lengthy debate and a February 8 veto by President Andrew Johnson, Congress passed the bill overriding his veto thirty to nine in the Senate and one hundred twenty to forty-four in the House. On March 1, 1867 President Johnson signed the proclamation making Nebraska the thirty-seventh state.

Governor Butler called for a meeting of the state legislature to be convened April 4, 1867 at Omaha to deliberate on forty-five items pertaining to statehood. Number 19 on this list was the "location of state public buildings" or capital removal which had been a topic of discussion since the inception of the territory in 1854.

The question of capital removal revolved on where in Nebraska one lived. Those to the south of the Platte River were so disgruntled at being ignored and overridden despite their numerical and economic superiority over Omaha and the Democrat-controlled, North Platte contingency that at one point they threatened to secede from Nebraska and join Kansas—bluster which was not acted on. With the election going to the Republicans in 1867 the argument was about to change directions. The South Platters, with majorities in both houses and in the governor's seat, were about to have their day.

The new state legislature convened in Omaha, at the territorial capital, on May 16, 1867. On June 4 Senate Bill 44 was introduced and provided for the location of the capital and erection of public buildings at the site. The specific location of the capital was left to a three-man

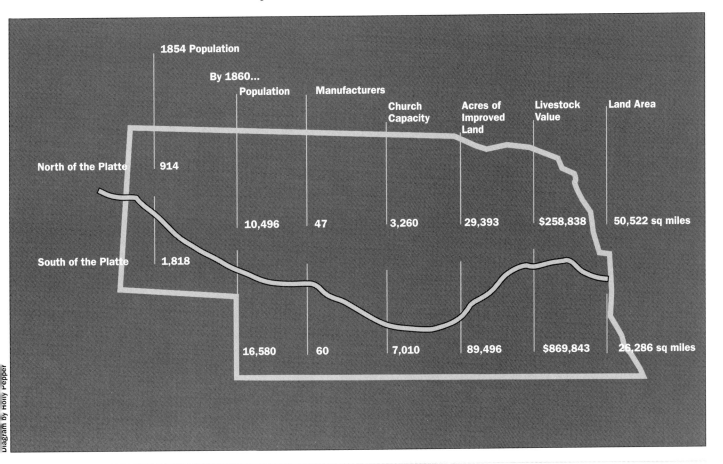

	1854 Population	By 1860... Population	Manufacturers	Church Capacity	Acres of Improved Land	Livestock Value	Land Area
North of the Platte	914	10,496	47	3,260	29,393	$258,838	50,522 sq miles
South of the Platte	1,818	16,580	60	7,010	89,496	$869,843	26,286 sq miles

Diagram by Holly Pepper

Johnson's 1854 map of the Nebraska Territory shows one of the earliest depictions of the area covered by the Kansas-Nebraska Act. The territory loosely covered an area from the 40th parallel to the British Possessions (Canada) from the summit of the Rocky Mountains on the west to the Missouri River on the east. The 351,558 square mile area covered all of present Nebraska, most of the Dakotas, Wyoming and Montana as well as tiny bits of other subsequent states. Thus the book Handbook to the Gold Fields of Nebraska and Kansas published in 1859 is really talking about present day Colorado. Within a short time other territories began forming and Nebraska's shape and size seemed to vary by the month.

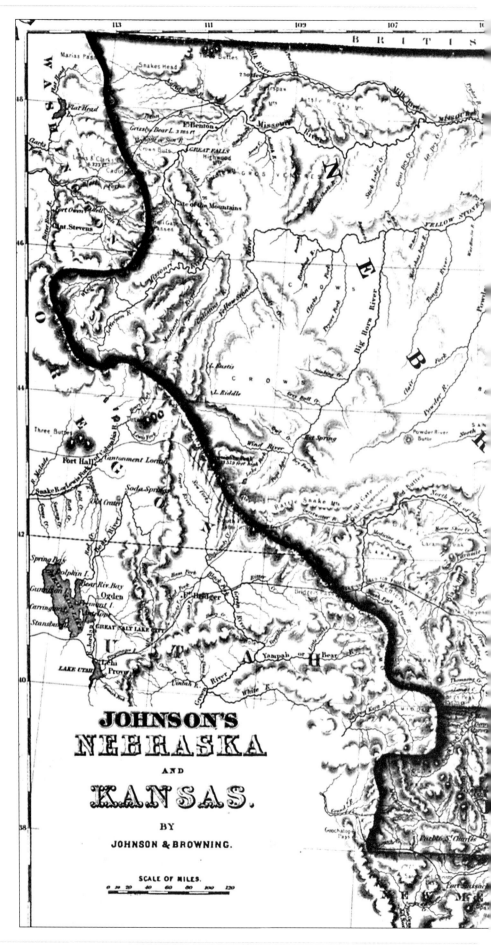

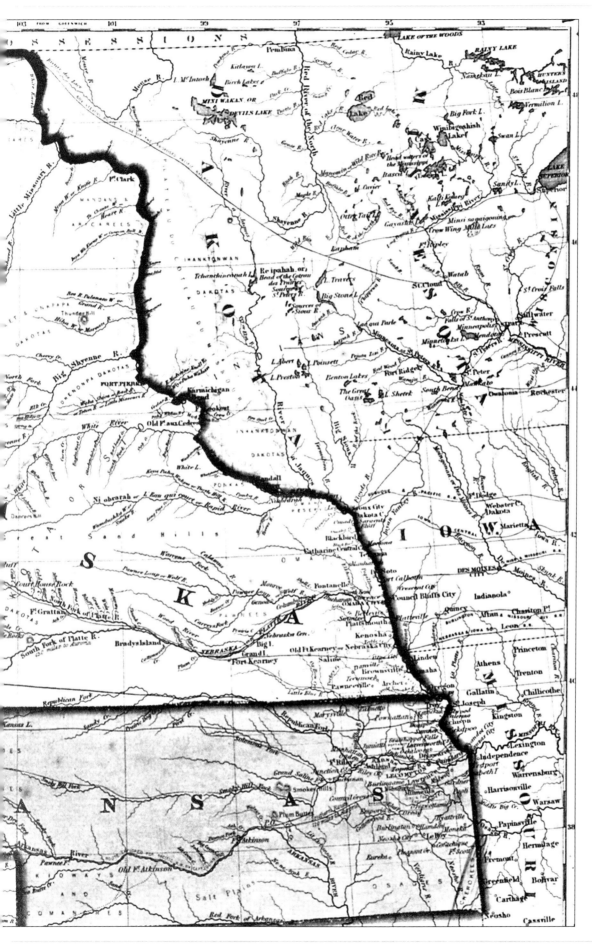

commission consisting of Governor David Butler, Secretary of State Thomas P. Kennard and State Auditor John Gillespie. The site was to be chosen by July but amended to September 1, 1867 and to be chosen from sites in the counties of Butler, Lancaster, Saunders and Seward and to be at least a full section of 640 acres. The counties were specified after examining a map of the state which showed much of the land west of a north to south line along the west edge of Lancaster County consisted of the Great American Desert where no man would ever live and nothing would ever grow. By limiting points west of this loosely defined line, it was felt the question of moving the capital close to the center of population and adjacent to the largely uninhabitable desert would not have to be reinvestigated. If no large numbers of settlers ever moved into the western desert, even though vast in land area, the population center would not materially shift. At the same time this would move the capital from the "eastern seacoast" of the state and put it closer to the demographic center. Amazingly this prediction has held nearly constant with the 2000 census still showing Lancaster County central in terms of population. The bill also specified that the name of the new site would be the unimaginative but highly memorable "Capital City."

One of the principal proponents of moving the capital from Omaha was Senator Mills S. Reeves of Nebraska City in Otoe County. Otoe County was, according to the census, where the handful of Nebraska slaves were held while Reeves himself was an outspoken and highly vocal opponent of Abraham Lincoln. One of the most eager pro-Omaha senators, ever in opposition to removal, was Democrat Senator J. N. H. Patrick of Douglas County. Knowing the vote would be close and still hoping to thwart the removalists, Patrick moved an amendment, striking Capital City as an "inexpressibly clumsy and ugly" name, substituting Lincoln which he knew Reeves would oppose and even vote against defeating the entire bill in order to avoid having the President's name attached to it. Instead of voting against the amendment and to the surprise and probable consternation of Patrick, Reeves seconded the amendment "and the motion was carried without division." On June 10, 1867 the Senate Bill passed eight to five with Reeves voting Yes and Patrick voting No. On the 13th the bill passed the House twenty-five to fourteen and was signed by Governor Butler on June 14, 1867. The Nebraska City News said the Otoe County contingent voted "to put the buildings south of the Platte River and westward from the Missouri River, not because they loved Omaha less, but Nebraska City more." The Omaha Republican responded that the "perpetrators of this outrage were 'legislative cormorants.'"

In mid July of 1867 the three commissioners, Butler, Kennard and Gillespie, set out for Nebraska City by steamboat. On Thursday, July 18, 1867 the group was joined by Augustus F. Harvey, hired as surveyor to help choose a potential site, and two reporters from the Omaha Herald. After staying the night at the Cincinnati Hotel, the party hired a wagon and driver and they headed west on the Steam Wagon Road.

The evening of July 19 was spent with a farmer near Nursery Hill and Syracuse and on the 20th they arrived at Yankee Hill, just south of Saline City. Yankee Hill, the home of state legislator John Cadman, was the favorite choice of the Nebraska City faction. It was located on the important trade and freight route of the Oregon Trail Cut-Off, had a small existing community in place, was above the flood plain of Salt Creek and thus was probably an odds-on favorite going into the inspection trip. The bulk of the party stayed with Cadman whose house was a stone-walled, dug out with a sod roof and was the site of Lancaster County's first school. Cadman himself was an enthusiastic supporter of Yankee Hill but was also known as a bit of a political rogue having engineered the dissolving of old Clay County, giving the north half to Lancaster and the south half to Gage County in 1864, partially to ensure his representing a larger and more important district in the territorial legislature and partially to garner the county seat for Yankee Hill. After promising the county capital to several sites, providing they would vote for Clay County's demise and division, the communities joined against Cadman and gave the nod to Lancaster. Cadman was therefore, understandably, doubly aggressive in pursuing Yankee Hill's bid for the state capital.

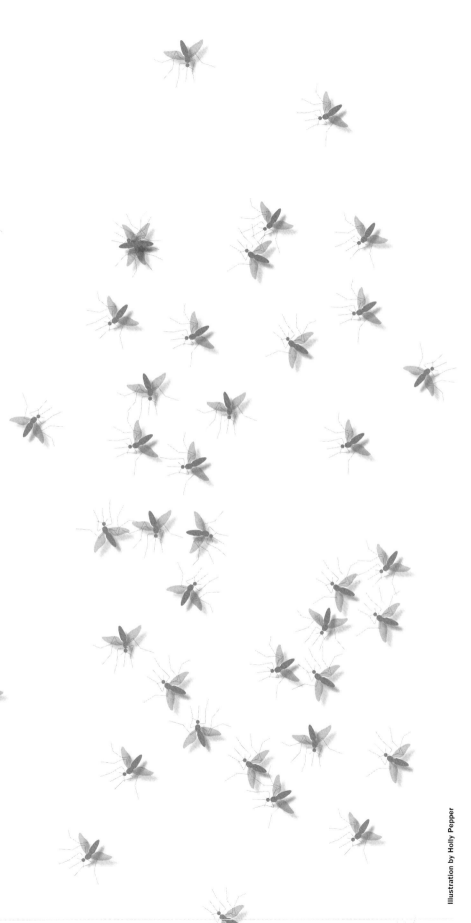

On the afternoon of the 23rd the commission journeyed "down the valley of Salt Creek" into Lancaster. Lancaster, with only about thirty residents, did not take too long to examine as its only building was the stone seminary and its two positive attributes in the salt flats and available land were well known to the committee. It was reasonably felt the salt deposits would form an industry which would economically support the capital and the Methodist Seminary Association's willingness to give the state most of the city, which meant the land requirement would not be a problem.

The 24th was spent at Ashland in the extreme southeast corner of Saunders County. Here they found abundant timber, water, an excellent outcropping of building stone and a suitable location for a capitol building which, interestingly, later became the site of the Saunders County Courthouse. The night was spent in an unfinished two-story brick building with Governor Butler, considered the senior member, sleeping downstairs and the balance of the party on the second floor. Governor Butler slept peacefully, screened away while the unprotected second floor fell prey to thousands of marauding mosquitoes.

The following day the party headed northwest into Butler County, examining the land along the old California Trail. The evening was spent with J. D. Brown "sleeping in the shade on the ground wrapped up in [their] blankets" but no sites of "commanding advantages" were noted. Leaving on the 26th, they traveled along the Blue River, stopping near Camden and Milford for the night. On the 28th they returned to Cadman's at Yankee

Illustration by Holly Pepper

Hill where Mr. Kennard noted "very nice arrangements [had been] entered into for the purpose of entertaining the Commission." Mr. Cadman had indeed decided to pull out all the stops in convincing the group that Yankee Hill was the correct spot for the capital and was assured they, so far at least, had top billing. No detail was spared as "a beautiful bower of branches of trees thrown over poles" was erected with tables groaning with treats from fried chicken to ice cream. Mr. Kennard also admitted to being lobbied by "a very beautiful young lady" on Yankee Hill's many advantages.

After another night at Cadman's, the commission returned to Lancaster on July 29 where they adjourned to W. T. Donovan's house at about 8th and Q, going directly to the second story bedroom. Here they poured over maps and notes. On the first ballot there was a single vote for Ashland but when the paper slips dropped into Governor Butler's hat were counted on the second ballot, the decision was unanimous. J. C. F. McKesson, nephew of Dr. John M. McKesson of the Methodist Seminary Association, was visiting his uncle and had been swimming and fishing with some friends at Willow Bend on Salt Creek where it meandered across O Street. As they approached Donovan's house they saw a small group of folks cheering and waving their hats. The commission had just announced their decision to choose, not Yankee Hill but Lancaster as the state's first capital city and whose name would be changed to Lincoln.

What went on in that upper room to change what many thought was a foregone decision from Yankee Hill to Lancaster? Many points were discussed in detail and it is fair to say Ashland lost due to the then insurmountable problem presented by the mosquitoes. Another point which was discussed was John Cadman's reputation as a political schemer which led to the mention of the ice cream served at his party—probably the first instance recorded in the county. Ice cream would have been a major feat, principally because the necessary ice would have had to have been harvested and stored the previous winter. As the ice cream was so extravagant, the commission agreed it constituted bribery and Yankee Hill was dismissed from further deliberations.

The commission's initial work was done. The three returned to Omaha while Mr. Harvey stayed to begin surveying the townsite and preparing the plat. On August 14, 1867 the commission presented their report to the Senate and House of Representatives.

The first settlers in Lancaster County discovered the same phenomenon that the first settlers who strayed beyond the Missouri river encountered, the paucity of trees. Most of the early settlers were familiar with the heavily treed areas of the east and surprised to discover that in 1854 less than 3 percent of Nebraska Territory was timbered, falling almost exclusively along streams and rivers. In fact the first federal surveyors found the north half of then Lancaster County had, by their count, twelve trees! The territorial legislature was so acutely aware of the lack that in 1861 they exempted $50 in property taxes for every acre of trees that were planted and although this was rescinded due to an acute need for tax revenues, it was reinstated in 1869 when every $100 of land tax in the state was exempted for the planting of an acre of trees planted. This was expanded in 1872 to include tax exemption for trees planted in cities and

J. Sterling Morton, could have been a governor, instead he changed a state.

supplemented by stringent laws against those destroying trees on others' property.

This scarcity did not miss Julius Sterling Morton who arrived from Michigan in 1854 and settled at Nebraska City. In 1869 Morton was a principal in forming the Nebraska State Horticultural Society which he addressed two years later saying "an orchard is a joy forever...if I had the power I would compel every man in the state...to plant and cultivate fruit trees." In January of 1872 Governor Furnas, himself an arborists from Brownville and president of the State Board of Agriculture, along with support from Morton and others called for what Morton called Arbor Day to encourage the planting of trees. The date was set for April 10, 1872 and called for a prize of a $25 farm library to be given to the person planting the most trees. The books were won by Lancaster County farmer J. D. Smith who planted over 35,000 trees and it was claimed that over a million trees were planted statewide. An essay prize was won by Rev. C. S. Harrison of York who basically expanded on the concept of "rain follows the plow" noting that rain, from Egypt to various dry spots in the U. S., also follows the planting of trees. Kansas and

Tennessee followed Nebraska's lead and established state holidays for Arbor Day in 1875. In 1883 the date for Arbor Day was moved to April 22, honoring Morton's birthday, in 1885 the legislature created the legal state holiday and in 1895 Nebraska's official nickname was announced as "the tree planters' state" which survived until "the Cornhusker State" took over.

Although various U. S. Presidents have, from time to time, proclaimed a national Arbor Day and all fifty states have state holidays in the name of Arbor Day, there is still not an official holiday. Each state therefore sets its own date for Arbor Day, primarily

around the best tree planting season running from January in Florida to November for Hawaii but most still occur in April with Nebraska officially set on the last Friday in April. The state of Nebraska is, of course, much smaller in area that the vast Nebraska Territory but even with the largest man-made forest in the world in the Nebraska National Forest, the state is still only about 3 percent timbered.

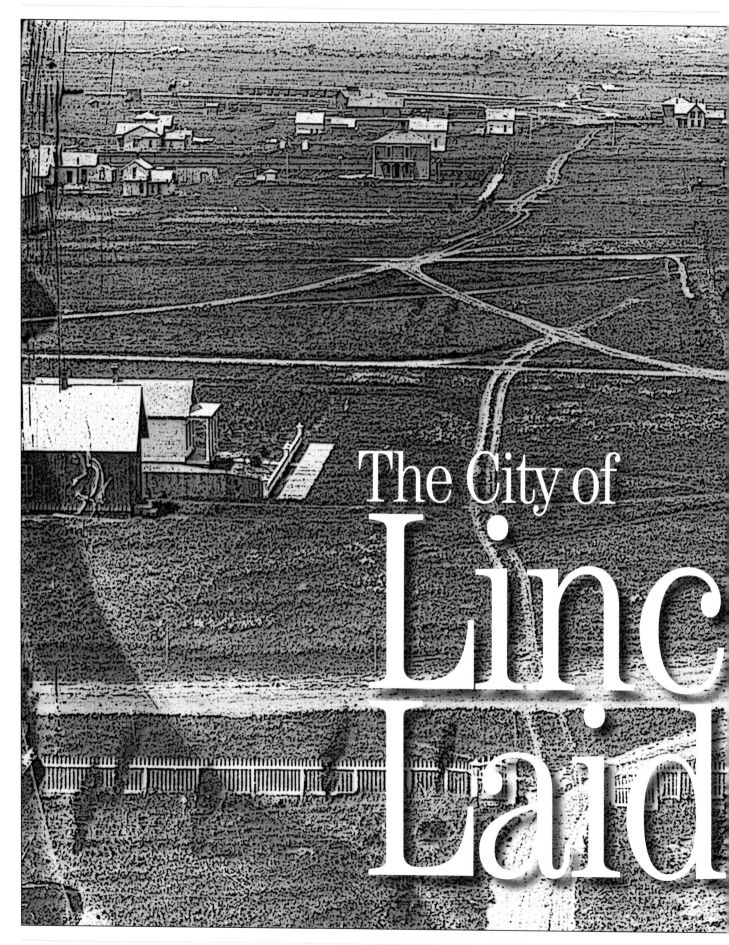

The City of
Linc
Laid

oln Is
Out

"Lincoln is too
far south to be
reached by the
Burlington &
Missouri River
Railroad and
it must remain
isolated from
every other
portion of the
state."

On August 14, 1867 Augustus F. Harvey, Anselmo B. Smith and "a corps of assistants" arrived to begin the official survey and plat of the new city of Lincoln. Virtually all of the 940 acres they would survey was unbroken prairie.

"A buffalo might have occasionally been seen," while "herds of antelope gamboled, coyotes were numerous" and settlers reported a profusion of other wildlife including deer, elk, prairie wolves, pelicans, geese, ducks, quail, prairie chickens and wild turkey. The dim track that cut through the site running east and west made its way through tall sunflowers, buffalo grass and other grasses so tall that a man on horseback would only be visible from his shoulders up. As the land sloped to the north and west to the salt flats, there were perhaps half a dozen houses, barely shacks and the stone seminary. Although

one resident said "on none of these lands was there a single tree," there was a plum thicket on the present Journal-Star block and a lone elm on Salt Creek under which the first county meeting was held. Several dry ravines crossed the area with one of the most prominent running east and west, draining from a spring at 14th and P Streets to a basin at 12th and O then running directly west between and parallel to N and O Streets, emptying into Salt Creek. Two prominences were the old City Hall block and the ultimate capitol grounds which, because of the lack of landmarks, appeared even higher. These two points were of interest to Harvey who intended to place the capitol on the highest point of buildable land looking down on the city.

Overleaf
Taken from the tower of the first state capitol, this 1870s view looks directly west down J Street. John Alford, the Governor's private secretary's house is behind the picket fence on the left. Judge Stephen Pound's home is at center, appearing to almost be built in the edge of J Street. It is the last, most westerly house on the right, north side of J Street. The large white-roofed building is the 1870 Episcopal Church of the Holy Trinity's $4,000 building and just behind it is the spired $5,000 First Presbyterian Church.

About 1870 this view, taken from the first capital's dome, looks to the northwest over the city of Lincoln. Visible on the right horizon is the just-completed University of Nebraska, virtually north of the city at 11th and R Streets. The two white buildings are the Swedish Lutheran Church at left and the First Congregational Church at 13th and L Streets at center.

This is the west front of the first state capitol in its most common and best of only a half dozen photographs. Just at the capitol's south is the corner of the extant Kennard house and to its right, the John Gillespie house. The stagecoach-appearing vehicle is actually a herdic coach, more of an inner city taxi/ omnibus which often transported passengers between the railroad depot, hotels and the capitol.

The drawing of the plat was made additionally imperative because the sale of lots in the hopefully popular and successful capital city would provide funding for building the city and state institutions as well as provide income before and as tax dollars began to flow to the then nonexistent treasury.

All streets were to be 100 feet in width with the exception of 3rd, 7th, 9th, 11th, 15th, D, J, O and S which were 120 feet wide with alleys set at 16 feet wide. Five sizes of lots were mapped from 23 feet, 8 inches by 134 feet to 50 by 142 feet. East and west street names were simply the letters from A to Z, ignoring I to avoid confusion with 1st Street and north and south streets numbers from 1st on the west to 17th on the east. It was generally felt that a sister city, East Lincoln would develop to the east and because of Salt Creek's flood plain, Lincoln would never grow in that direction beyond 1st Street. A half mile south of A Street a street was set, perhaps marking as far as they could conceive in that direction—today's South Street. The land between A and South Streets was not platted to lots at that time.

Blocks were set aside for the use of a city hall, high school, county courthouse, state historical society, five common schools and three, four-square block parcels, each about ten to twelve acres, for a city park, the capitol building and the state university. In addition the commissioners planned to offer any church denomination which applied a grant of three lots for construction of a building so long as it was started within two years and "costing some reasonable amount." Additional lots were to be offered to the I.O.O.F., the Masons and the

Good Templars, though these were never claimed. Strangely the plat of the village of Lancaster was neither abandoned nor dissolved, merely drawn over supplanting wider streets and larger blocks which meant that some existing buildings would sit off the new streetscape with the only street in common between the two cities being the old Locust and the new O Street. The survey of Lincoln did not even take a month to complete and was virtually finished and the plat files were finished on September 6, 1867.

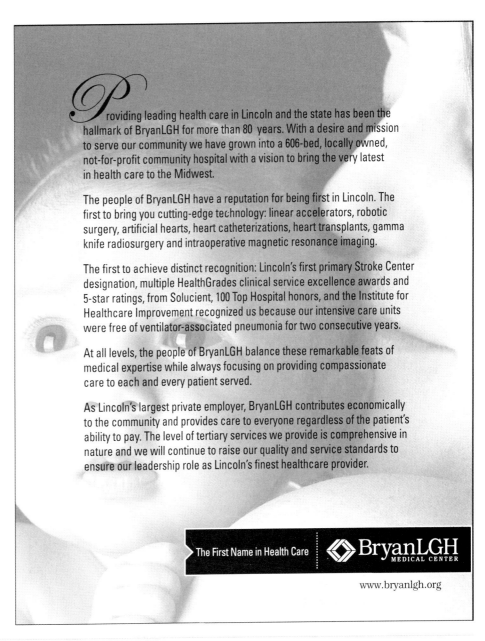

*P*roviding leading health care in Lincoln and the state has been the hallmark of BryanLGH for more than 80 years. With a desire and mission to serve our community we have grown into a 606-bed, locally owned, not-for-profit community hospital with a vision to bring the very latest in health care to the Midwest.

The people of BryanLGH have a reputation for being first in Lincoln. The first to bring you cutting-edge technology: linear accelerators, robotic surgery, artificial hearts, heart catheterizations, heart transplants, gamma knife radiosurgery and intraoperative magnetic resonance imaging.

The first to achieve distinct recognition: Lincoln's first primary Stroke Center designation, multiple HealthGrades clinical service excellence awards and 5-star ratings, from Solucient, 100 Top Hospital honors, and the Institute for Healthcare Improvement recognized us because our intensive care units were free of ventilator-associated pneumonia for two consecutive years.

At all levels, the people of BryanLGH balance these remarkable feats of medical expertise while always focusing on providing compassionate care to each and every patient served.

As Lincoln's largest private employer, BryanLGH contributes economically to the community and provides care to everyone regardless of the patient's ability to pay. The level of tertiary services we provide is comprehensive in nature and we will continue to raise our quality and service standards to ensure our leadership role as Lincoln's finest healthcare provider.

The First Name in Health Care | ◈ BryanLGH
MEDICAL CENTER

www.bryanlgh.org

With the plat, the commission purchased advertisements in several Nebraska and nearby newspapers on August 17, 1867 announcing the state lot sale to be held commencing on September 17 in Lincoln, continuing in Nebraska City on the 27th and at Omaha on the 30th. If, after these sales, sufficient monies had not been collected to pay all auction expenses and build the first capitol, sales would then continue at Plattsmouth and Brownville. Before the sale, as directed by the Capital Bill, the commission established minimum values for each lot, below which bids would not be accepted. T. P. Kennard later admitted they had been a bit arbitrary and "appraised the lots higher than people seemed to think was a right valuation," a point in fact which nearly caused the sale to flounder.

George B. Skinner from St. Joseph was hired as auctioneer with a brass band on hand to raise spirits and hopefully bids. Perhaps 100 would-be buyers congregated at Elder Young's house at about 17th and O Streets early on the morning of Tuesday the 17th. The day was described as gloomy with a drizzling rain and because the crowd was smaller than anticipated, the commissioners too were aware that many on hand were already

Looking to the southwest from the roof of the Centennial Opera House at 12th and O Streets is this late 1870s photo showing 12th Street built as a bridge south of O Street to accommodate the arroyo which ran west, down the alley between N and O Streets after crossing the O Street intersection on a diagonal. The board fence screening the clothes line would have been along O Street. The white structure in the background at center is the U. S. Land Office. To the west, across 11th Street is Lancaster County Sheriff Granville Ensign's livery stable.

predicting failure. Lot number one was announced, asking a starting bid of $40 to open the sale. After a long, resounding silence Governor Butler, who had previously agreed along with the other commissioners not to bid, opened with a bid of the asked-for $40. Rev. J. G. Miller raised the bid by $0.25 and the lot was sold. Some reports later said that the first lot was sold for a quarter but in fact it was this amount over the appraisal/minimum bid. The sale ended the day at about 10 percent of the hoped-for total.

John Cadman, early proponent of and resident of Yankee Hill, had, after losing the capital site, moved to Lincoln. Here he acquired the old Methodist Seminary building, added on to it and converted it to a hotel he called the Cadman House. It was here that the damp and disheartened commission retired after the first day's sale. The commission met there with Rev. Miller, State Treasurer James Sweet of Nebraska City and Rev. Henry T. Davis. This group decided that if the commissioners did not show their faith in the sale by bidding it would be hobbled and perhaps fail. In addition a fund of $15,000 was established which empowered Mr. Sweet to open every lot at its appraised value to help prime the pump of auction enthusiasm.

At 9:00 the following morning the sale resumed. The sun shone, spirits picked up and by day's end about $18,000 in lots had been sold. When the Lincoln leg of the sale ended, nearly $34,000 had been sold with less than half purchased by the Nebraska City syndicate and after the Omaha and Nebraska City sales concluded, the total had reached about $53,000, more than enough to clear all expenses and begin letting construction bids for the Lincoln capitol.

The next step dictated by the legislature was that the commission turn over the auction proceeds to the State Treasurer, August Kountze of Omaha "as a state building fund, and be kept by him separate from other funds." The commission had however been warned that Kountze, who was outspokenly opposed to capital removal, would accept the monies but never pay them out for capitol construction in the city of Lincoln. The commission therefore did not deposit the sale proceeds resulting in serious questions after Kountze proved that only $148 of the sale monies were given to him "and no more before or since." This and other questionable parts of the sale, including commission purchases and purchases which were not collected in cash at the time of the sale as stipulated, soon faded.

The First Ca

Is Built

CHAPTER

5

"The capitol should
be donated to
Lincoln—the
lower part for a
livery stable, the
upper as a block-
house—the upper
windows would be
good port-holes."

The commission immediately sent advertisements to local newspapers asking architects to submit plans for "a building to accommodate the six executive offices and the two houses of the legislature. The cost not to exceed $40,000." There were no architects

in Lincoln while those in Omaha and Nebraska City ignored the request. Finally an ad in the Chicago Tribune brought a response from John Morris of Chicago on October 10, 1867. Being the only design proffered, it was accepted. A similar call to local contractors to build Mr. Morris' building brought no response while the second ad in the Tribune was answered by Joseph Ward, also of Chicago.

Mr. Ward then set about finding suitable stone as close to the site as possible in order to save transportation costs. After eschewing a stone outcropping in Antelope Creek adjacent to the current Childrens' Zoo and at the quarry on Cardwell Branch as being too soft, the blue limestone about seventeen miles south of Beatrice on Mr. Mills' property was not only determined to be of a good quality which would easily be cut and would harden on exposure but would be given to the state. Thus the only expense would be in quarrying it, transporting it to Lincoln, and facing it.

Because it was hoped to have the building completed before the next general assembly the architect instructed Mr. Ward to proceed at once to dig foundations and a well even though he had yet to receive a

contract. It was reported in a local paper that Linderman's sawmill on Salt Creek and Young's steam mill west of Market Square were busy with additional lumber arriving from Nebraska City to build not only the capitol but the already growing city of nearly 300 people. There being no local stone masons, Mr. Ward hired thirteen men from Chicago. From Nebraska City the men were forced to walk two days before reaching Lincoln. After staying at the Pioneer Hotel on North 10th Street, a sod boarding house was built for them on the capitol grounds. Two weeks later stone began arriving and the men went to work earning $4 a day.

By year's end excavations were nearly done with some basement walls built up to four feet eight inches. Finally, on January 11, 1868, Mr. Ward got a contract, increased now to $49,000. Stone quality continued to plague the project which ultimately employed limestone, blue magnesia limestone, brown stone and sandstone used as a substitute for interior brick. Weather too proved a problem, causing a request for contract extension to January, 1869, which was granted. In spring lot sales resumed with brisk results. By June of 1868 the

Overleaf
One of the photos taken by the Burlington & Missouri River Railroad from the top of the capitol in 1870, this view looks southeast. Thomas Perkins Kennard, Nebraska's Secretary of State, built the house at the center of the photo. The house, without its south wing, still stands owned by the Nebraska State Historical Society. It is termed Lincoln's oldest house. To the right Nebraska's first State Auditor John Gillespie's home was razed by fire in the 20th century. The small cottage to the left, today the site of a parking lot built over the remains of the partially constructed State Historical Society building, belonged to Peter Cooper, an ice merchant.

first story was up and the Omaha Republican reported the foundation is of scabbled blue limestone, the first story of beautiful magnesian limestone and the inner walls of brown sandstone. August saw most of the second floor completed and by September parts of the roof were on while interior work continued apace. On December 3 Governor Butler announced the central part of the capitol was ready for occupancy.

north outside ends of the building were left more or less unfinished where additions could easily be added.

The total cost of the $40,000 state capitol ultimately came to $75,817.59. "The legislature approved the change of plans with 'great unanimity.'" Albert Watkins later observed that "the elegant brown stone was not only positively ugly but soon turned out to be fatally lacking in strength and durability."

The finished building was one hundred twenty feet long by eighty-five feet wide with a height of one hundred twenty feet to the top of the cupola which sat on a twenty-five foot square tower. The first story stone was rusticated with square-headed windows while the second story had arched windows. On the interior there was a vestibule open to the cupola with galleries at the sides. The first floor north wing contained executive offices and library with twelve offices in the south wing. The second floor housed a fifty-five by thirty-eight foot Senate Chamber, Representative Hall of fifty by fifty-five feet, Supreme Court and governor's office. The top floor had galleries over the senate and house of representatives domed halls and committee rooms. The south and

With the completion of the new capitol, the physical move to Lincoln was planned and since no written records are extant the story is told in several voices, after the fact with great disparity. Over thirty years after the fact Secretary of State T. P. Kennard, recounted that he and Governor Butler, "without consulting any other person," met at Butler's home in Pawnee City to write the proclamation announcing the move. The plan then was for Kennard to return home and on a specified, but not recorded, Sunday morning, go to the capitol in Omaha, "wrap the seal carefully…place it under the seat in [his] buggy…[and] drive straight to the west" to Lincoln. This more or less clandestine movement of the state seal, which signified the situs of the state government or capital, would insure that any in Omaha opposed to the move and perhaps inclined to try and prevent it would be presented with fait accompli by Monday.

Another, perhaps more contemporary and probably more accurate account was provided by "expressman" and later real estate agent J. T. Beach of Lincoln who was hired by Gillespie to head the removal. His story says that six four-horse teams left Lincoln on a December Friday in 1868, headed for Omaha. That afternoon the party stopped at the "woe-begone hamlet" of Ashland for the night and the following day crossed the Platte River at Forest in Sarpy County. On Saturday they arrived at Omaha, quartered the horses and wagons at the Checkered Barn and retired to the Douglas House Hotel. The following day was spent packing the archives including "stoves, furniture, records, blank books, boxes of paper and the state library." On Monday the wagons left at four o'clock in the morning and headed down Farnam Street where they were stopped by U. S. Marshal Yost who added two barrels marked "T. P. Kennard." Because of rain and mud they were forced to stop that evening at Bellevue. The next day they met at the Kimball brothers' ferry three miles above LaPlatte where they planned to cross the river into Cass County. The Kimballs were not only opportunists but known opponents of the removal of the capital. For exactly what purpose one can only speculate but the Kimballs intentionally broke the rope pulley system which propelled the flat-bottomed boats across the river. Tom Keller, a desperado later killed in a shoot-out in Elkhorn, came to the group's aid and repaired the pulley wheel. Unfortunately the boat hit an ice snag and failed to reach the south shore by 100 feet necessitating driving the horses and wagons into the water well before the shore. It is unclear but they may have spent the night near Oreapolis in Cass County near the south shore before heading west.

Faced with blinding snow they traveled as far as either Stove Creek at Elmwood or a farmstead near Greenwood. By Carr's account the farmer was disinclined to allow them to spend the night in his cabin so they attempted, unsuccessfully, to burrow into his haystack. Then with the gift of a pocket watch and a promise to send back a cash payment, they were allowed inside. Depending on which version you hear, the journey to and from Omaha lasted four, five, six or even ten days. This disparity may result from some wagons leaving Omaha at different times, even different days. Kennard said he got to Lincoln on Monday where he impressed the seal on the official proclamation declaring the capital at Lincoln "open for business." The proclamation was then published in several Nebraska newspapers on December 3, 4, and 5, 1868.

Several days later, when the snow had abated, Gillespie reported that while he was in the virtually empty Omaha capitol, he was approached by John R. Meredith who was astonished to find the furnishings gone and asked where everything was. Gillespie told him it had moved to Lincoln, prompting Meredith to scurry to Fort Omaha to fetch General S. A. Strickland who in turn contacted the U. S. Secretary of Interior who assured him the move was indeed legal.

In an 1888 newspaper interview Carr reported that while several men from Omaha, who had assisted in the move, had been given $5 each from Gillespie's own pocket before they returned home and that he, Carr, had never received the $60 promised him and his crew. Carr did not mention if he had kept his bargain to send cash to the farmer where they had spent the night before getting back to Lincoln.

While close examination of Kennard's story seems full of conflicting dates and information, Jim Potter, Senior Research Historian for the Nebraska State Historical Society points out that it is probable that Kennard would not have entrusted the state seal's transportation to anyone but himself. This version also likely prompted the widely circulated story that Lincoln had stolen the capital from Omaha and influenced the large oil painting in the Historical Society's collection which shows the seal in a gunny sack under a buggy seat driving away from Omaha in the dead of night.

The first legislature convened at the new Lincoln capitol January 7, 1879. This was in fact the Fifth Session of the State Legislature though it is sometimes referred to as the First since the last meetings in Omaha were in essence dealing with territorial legislature business but were sometimes called "Sessions of the State body."

Like the extant Kennard house and Gillespie's now gone house, Governor David Butler's home at 7th and Washington Streets was designed by John Keyes Winchell. After his impeachment the house served as a ranch house, home of the Lincoln Country Club, truck garden sales store, radio station, grocery store, KKK headquarters and a road house before being torn down in the winter of 1949-1950.

The Jewish Community of Lincoln

Congregation B'nai Jeshurun

Congregation B'nai Jeshurun, also known as the South Street Temple, has a proud history dating back nearly 120 years. Lincoln's first Jewish congregation, the Temple was founded in 1884, principally by German immigrants.

Because of its relatively small size and its distance from large Jewish population centers, our congregation has often been served by newly trained Rabbis. During the early years of the congregation, several young rabbis began distinguished careers in Lincoln. One of them, Rabbi Israel Mattuck went on to become the leader of the liberal Jewish movement in London. His writing appears in Gates of Repentance and he is considered one of the leaders in 20th Century Reform Judaism. Another, Rabbi Solomon Starrels, served the Reform congregation in Savannah for more than 50 years.

Our Temple has always provided leaders for both the Jewish and greater Lincoln communities. A number of older families have been involved in agriculture, clothing, wholesale and retail food products, banking, auto parts, and other retail and service businesses. One of

the Temple's founders, Henry Schleisinger, helped to found the Anti- Defamation League of B'nai B'rith in 1913 after moving to Denver. His grandchildren and great-grandchildren are still members of our congregation. The current membership contains many individuals in the fields of education, law, social services and medicine.

Today the Temple is the only Reform Synagogue between Omaha and Denver. We serve Jews throughout Nebraska, including those who live in the smaller towns outside of Lincoln.

South Street Temple

Our Temple building, our second permanent home, was built in the early 1920s. It is of the Moorish style, and is similar in appearance (albeit smaller) to its contemporary Reform Synagogues, notably Congregation Rodef Shalom in Philadelphia. It features a hand-carved walnut ark and pulpit (carved by a congregant's father), vaulted ceilings, and a beautiful stained glass Star of David rose window. It is reminiscent of some of the surviving synagogues of eastern Europe, and is listed on the National Register of Historic Places.

The Reform Movement is the largest Jewish religious movement in North America, with 1.5 million Reform Jews and more than 900 congregations that are part of the Union for Reform Judaism. Although each congregation is autonomous and very individual in its programs, worship style, and culture, all are characterized by the same core values.

Congregation Tifereth Israel

Although there were Jews in Lincoln from the time of its incorporation as a city, the majority of the founders of our congregation came to America as refugees from the persecutions that decimated the Jewish communities of Eastern Europe in the 1890's. The early Jewish settlers met for worship in private homes; but at a meeting on October 19, 1903 a congregation to be known as Tifereth Israel, Israel's Glory (referring to God) was founded. Twenty-eight members subscribed at the time to a building fund that would eventuate in a House of Worship for the congregation.

On July 24, 1898 there had been organized in Lincoln a congregation known as Congregation Talmud Torah. Records indicate that it was Mr. Louis Stine who purchased in 1910 the lot at the corner of 18th and L streets, which became the site of the first permanent synagogue. Only a few months after the lot was transferred to Mr. Stine, a merger of Congregation Tifereth Israel and Congregation Talmud Torah was effected, and plans were laid for the construction of a synagogue building. Subsequent expansion of the Jewish population of Lincoln resulted in an addition to the building, which was completed in 1936. Until the time that it was sold, the beloved red brick edifice served the Jews of Lincoln for forty-one years.

Although the merged congregations voted as early as 1913 to apply to the Jewish Theological Seminary of America for a rabbi to serve as their spiritual leader, it was not until 1925, under the presidency of Mr. Dan Hill, that formal affiliation with the United Synagogue of America (now the United Synagogue of Conservative Judaism) took place. Mr. Leo Hill, son of Mr. Dan Hill, was elected to office in 1948 and it was under his guidance and direction that the Congregation erected its new edifice at 32nd Street and Sheridan Boulevard. The lot on which it was constructed was acquired in 1952; groundbreaking ceremonies were held on April 19, 1953, the anniversary of the burning of the Warsaw Ghetto; and the cornerstone was laid on June 6, 1954.

The roots of the Conservative Movement run deep, nurtured by an understanding of the richness of Judaism that balances tradition with modernity. The strength of Conservative Judaism lies in its commitment to tradition as interpreted for today, but with a serious understanding of history, values, language, and law.

Tifereth Israel Synagogue

The University
of Nebraska, the State
Insane Asylum
and State
Penitentiary
Are Built

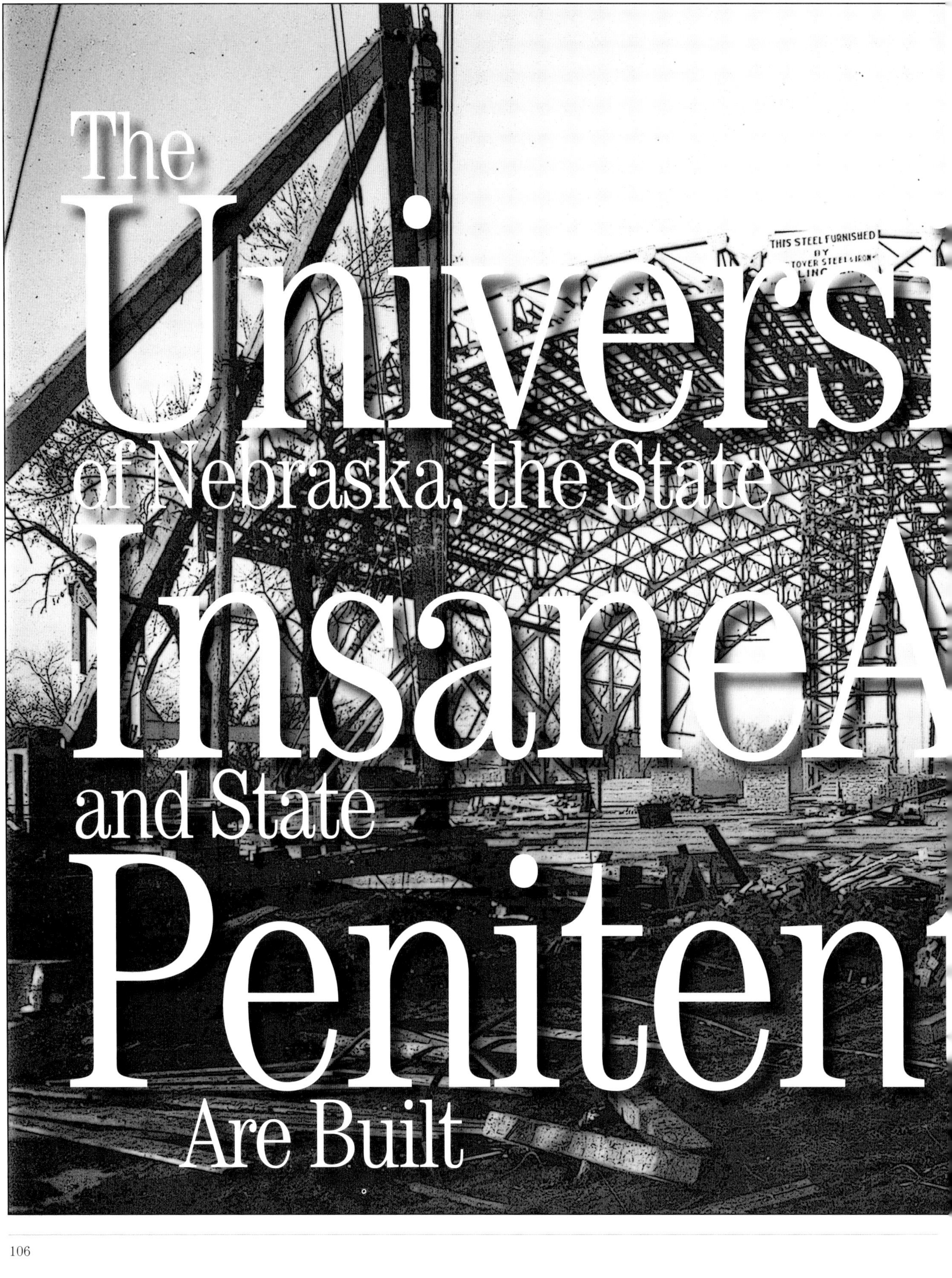

yslum

iary

"The massive
penitentiary
heaving up its
solid walls in
another point of
the horizon, and
the Insane Asylum
(mostly occupied
by members of
the legislature of
1867) bounding
the view on
another side."

"Nebraska needs a
university about
as much as a cat
needs two tails."

In many ways the Morrill Land-Grant College Act of 1862 laid the groundwork for the University of Nebraska whose charter was drawn by Lincoln's "architect" Augustus F. Harvey and was born as Senate File 86 in February 1869. The legislature

had been busy chartering universities and colleges for two years with fourteen proposed before the inception of the state university. Every city and village wanted a university and the legislature saw no problem with granting their incorporation from Nebraska University at Wyoming to Nebraska University at Fontanelle north of Omaha in Washington County. So popular was the incorporation of universities that it was said the clerk kept a supply of blank forms for the purpose. Likewise every legislator was eager to have the state university in his district. One senator suggested the University of Nebraska at Undesignated be formed while another opined it might be named the University of Nebraska on Wheels so that it might be moved annually. Harvey's charter however stopped all speculation in placing the University of Nebraska at University Place, the four-square, ten acre tract the Capital Commission had set aside at 11th and R Streets on the original plat of the city of Lincoln. The bill was signed by Governor Butler on February 15, 1869 becoming known thereafter as Charter Day. The legislature approved $100,000 for construction of the first university building and on April 10, 1869 the Capital Commission advertised for plans for a State University and Insane Asylum. The architectural plans of J. M. McBird of Logansport,

Indiana, which described a Franco-Italian building, were approved though McBird questioned whether the design, even with his modifications, could be built for the $100,000 limit established by the legislature.

Eleven days later contractor R. D. Silver, also from Logansport, arrived in Lincoln and, though he had no contract, began to set up a brick burning yard. In order to finance construction, the Capital Commission reinstituted Lincoln lot sales and reported selling 105 lots the first day for a total of $30,000. Mr. Silver meantime, continued to amass construction materials and was soon set up to "burn" 12,000 bricks a day for which he was forced to pay $10 a cord for wood which had to be hauled from twenty to thirty-five miles. Eighty-two days later, with 1,500,000 bricks done, he was ready to begin actual construction. As if by magic, Mr. Silver, who would be elected Lincoln's mayor in 1873, received a contract for $128,480 from the Capital Commission on August 18, 1869 despite the legislature's not approving any expense above the original $100,000, an overrun which would soon plague Governor Butler.

Overleaf
By 1915 the University of Nebraska's Alumni Association and others agreed that Grant Memorial Hall's gymnasium was totally inadequate for the school's basketball games. About 1920 the University began actively buying up land adjacent to and particularly north and east of the original campus. One popular idea was to build a multi-purpose structure to accommodate a Nebraska soldiers and sailors' memorial auditorium building, stadium, gymnasium and open-air Greek theatre. The gymnasium alone would seat 5,000 and serve not only as a basketball venue but also hold convocations and graduation exercises. Although initial plans for Cornhusker Hall or Nebraska Auditorium called for a dirt floor, which could be temporarily covered, the regents disagreed. Because a permanent floor, stage and swimming pool were included, the Coliseum was paid for by taxation in place of what would have initially been financed by donations. The $445,000, 9,000-seat building, shown here in initial construction, was completed in 1925 and used for commencement services June 5, 1926. Still a widely-used campus venue, basketball games were moved to the Devaney Center on its completion.

Built as a privately owned boarding hall for the use of University of Nebraska students in 1879, the ninety-four by fifty-four foot, three-story building at 14th and U Streets proved too far from the University to be accepted by the students. Even though board was only $2.50 per week and included "an ample closet and [was] furnished with a stove, a bed stead, chairs, a table, a washstand and a coal-box" the experiment failed. Purchased by "Lincoln's first millionaire" John Fitzgerald, it was given for use as the Convent of the Holy Child which also failed having, at its peak, twelve teachers and thirty-five students. After serving as a hospital the building was razed becoming the second location of Bancroft School, a joint venture of the Lincoln Public Schools and the University of Nebraska where it was used as a laboratory school. At the beginning of the 20th century that building was also razed and is now a landscaped area north of the Kauffman Center and east of Morrill Hall.

On September 23, 1869 a banquet for 1,000 people was held in conjunction with the University's cornerstone laying celebration. The dinner and band, which reportedly cost $2,000 were paid for by Lincoln donations. After sundry remarks, Attorney General Seth Robinson spoke on Popularized Education followed by a dance which lasted until 4:00 AM the following morning.

Although there was no building, the mechanics of the university began to fall into place. Construction was pushed by the commission, fearful of not qualifying for the federal land grants which amounted to 90,000 acres of land for the school. The charter called for a twelve member Board of Regents, the first nine of which would be appointed by the governor, three from each legislative district plus three ex-officio members. By 1875 this had been amended by the legislature to six members, all elected by the people to run the university's operation. Allan R. Benton of Alliance, Ohio was chosen January 1, 1870 as the first Chancellor. The first year his salary was placed at $5,000 but after that, since the work of setting up the university would be done, he was reduced to $4,000 per year and expected to also teach classes. This level of chancellor's salary stood without increase for thirty years despite the university's growth. Four professors were also hired at $2,000 per year each and one tutor who received $1,000 to round out the staff for the five colleges called for in the charter. As required by the Land Grant Act, R.O.T.C. and agriculture classes had to be offered and "tuition is free to all [only] a matriculation fee [of $5] is charged," all of which was to be set aside for the purchase of library books.

The brick walls of the university began to go up and lumber arrived in 1870. The lumber was primarily shipped from Chicago to East Nebraska City in Iowa, opposite Nebraska City, Nebraska, ferried across the river "then hauled to Lincoln in wagons over wretched roads."

Primarily at the instigation of an Omaha faction, three professional architects were hired to examine the building in June of 1871, partially because the stone which had been utilized in the construction of the foundation was identical to that employed in building the capitol which suddenly seemed to be dissolving. This report brought an offer to build a new stone building for the university by Nebraska City, followed by a similar offer from Omaha but after the foundation under the north wing and chapel was replaced at a cost of $747, the architects felt the building was safe, at least for the time being.

University Hall itself was a fairly simple "very handsome brick structure with sandstone finish, four stories high, including the mansard roof." All floors had identical plans except the two-story, forty-two by sixty foot chapel in the north wing. The building

W. H. B. Stout and J. M. Jamison were awarded the contracts to build the first state penitentiary. The stone was quarried, cut and primarily laid by prison labor and completed n 1876. The last of the old structure was removed in 1982, completely replaced by the present campus on the original site.

housed twenty classrooms, offices, the library, men's dormitory in the attic and military science room. The basement furnace was considered a joke, requiring students to supplement it with thirty, coal-fired baseboard heaters, twenty-four hours a day until the first steam plant was built to the north of the building in 1888. An ever-growing ash and cinder heap accumulated beside the building allowing neighborhood children to look into the second floor windows while climbing the mountain.

On September 6, 1871 University Hall opened for classes. The university claimed there were over 120 students admitted but on closer examination it appears 8 students and 12 "irregulars" made up the official class roster in the Literature, Science and Arts College, while 110 were taken into the preparatory or Latin School. Chancellor Benton admitted "some difficulty had been experienced in making the roof impervious to rain" and that "citizens tethered their family cows [on the four square block campus while] children picked violets and

This 1908 view of the original four-square-block University of Nebraska campus was taken from the roof of the just-completed Temple Building on the southeast corner of 14th and R Streets. The tiny cottages at left were referred to as the professors' houses though they may never have served that purpose.

buffalo beans there." Hundreds of red cedars and Osage orange borders were planted to landscape the campus but all died. While the total expenses for the first year totaled only $26,840.69 the Omaha Herald editorialized that "Butler and his forty thieves [reveal] utter inefficiency, lawlessness and total depravity."

The first commencement was held June 26, 1872 and though there were no graduates, an honorary LL.D. was awarded to Episcopal Bishop, R. H. Clarkson. The following year saw two actual graduates, J. Stuart Dales and Wm. H. Snell. The "Hesperian Student" described the class as "about eleven feet one inch in height, and weighs nearly 260 pounds."

In 1877 new fears surrounding the building surfaced as the faculty abandoned the north wing, believing it might collapse. This time the four architects who examined the building suggested razing the structure and rebuilding with an edifice costing not less than $60,000 with Lincoln financing at least $40,000 of the cost. Lincoln countered with their own experts who felt that a new foundation was all that was needed. To that end University Hall was literally jacked up and a new $6,012 foundation was constructed under the building. Lincoln financed this by using $4,000 in city funds, raising $1,810 from individual gifts and selling

The just-completed east side of Memorial Stadium is shown above in 1923 or 1924. Proceeded by the original field on the northwest corner of the ten acre campus and the east-west Nebraska Field which sat directly west of Avery Hall where the South Stadium now sits, the new field was proposed in 1919, the fiftieth anniversary of the University's founding. The original concept was to honor General Pershing and the 2,300 alumnae who had served in World War I. Fundraising stumbled until 1921 when the legislature approved $350,000 for Soldier's Memorial Stadium. The legislation however was vetoed by Governor McKelvie who felt it should not be paid for by the taxpayers. Financed by contributions, the original construction phase of $548,849 was won by the Parsons Construction Co. The first game on October 20, 1923 saw the University of Kansas and Nebraska play to a scoreless tie witnessed by a crowd of 32,000 which filled the stadium to capacity. With additions on every side, the current Memorial Stadium fills Saturday game days with nearly three times the original capacity.

the old foundation stone for $200. The state assured the city it would repay the expense but this never occurred.

In 1879 at the beginning of the university's second decade, total enrollment numbered only 284 causing the entrance exam to be shortened to one question: can you read? Still improvements were being made. In 1877 the University rented the old Tiechnor House Hotel on the southwest corner of 13th and K Streets for use as a boy's dormitory. Somewhat later the old Grand Hotel on the northwest corner of 12th and Q would become the girl's dormitory. In 1885 the second building on the campus, the $25,000 Chemistry Building, was completed which would become Pharmacy Hall in 1919 and stand until 1958 when it was razed for Sheldon Art Gallery's construction. The grounds too were being ameliorated and described as "well ornamented with a large variety of forest and evergreen trees...[while] graveled driveways and winding walks cross the grounds." University Hall's tower foundations were replaced and basement cross walls were added in 1887 and though the first building continually deteriorated, it stood and was in constant use until razed in 1949 and 1950.

In room 205, in the northeast corner of University Hall, Dr. Amos G. Warner, Professor Howard and W. Caldwell held a joint seminar in history and economics in 1889 which was noted as the first graduate school class held in a state university west of the Mississippi River. Although one Omaha newspaper referred to the University as "Lincoln High School" and others questioned why Nebraska even supported

a university "when the state is practically bankrupt" and "had accomplished nothing and academically was a travesty," the University of Nebraska was entering a period known as the Golden Years and indeed academically at the forefront of American higher education.

Although Territorial Governor Alvin Saunders managed the lack of an insane asylum by contracting to send nine patients to Iowa's facility at Mount Pleasant, little specific attention was given to the problem and mental health problems and questions were left

to the individual's families. The Capital Removal Act empowered the Capital Commission to set aside a 154.5 acre site on saline lands "two miles southwest of the old town of Lancaster" at Saline City for a state lunatic asylum. On April 10, 1869 commissioners Butler and Kennard advertised for plans for an insane asylum to cost no more than $50,000. Although he warned a suitable building could probably not be built for $50,000 or even $100,000, the plans submitted by Chicago architect John Keys Winchell were accepted and, as

Our banks have changed with the times, but our commitment to service hasn't.

The current day Union Bank & Trust Company was founded in 1917 as the Farmer's State Bank. A great deal has changed over the years—new technology, more locations—but our core values remain the same. Providing excellent service to our customers, upholding our commitment to the community and creating an atmosphere that encourages our employees to perform their best are all part of the Union Bank culture—a culture that is right at home in Lincoln.

ubt.com

Member FDIC

You Belong Here.

he was just finishing construction on the capitol, Joseph Ward began work on the foundation even though he had not received a contract, "to save time." Despite the legislative $50,000 cap, Ward got the construction bid for $128,000 on August 15, 1869 with the instruction to have the building completed by December of 1870. To finance construction, sale of odd numbered city lots was opened along with 40,000 acres of nearby state-owned land. The seventy-two by ninety foot, five-story, frame building was nearly completed when a fire broke out on November 7, 1870. The apparent cause of the blaze was a candle accidentally set near wood shavings on an attic joist. Because cisterns had been filled, a bucket brigade kept most of the fire confined to the attic with slight smoke damage to the upper floors. Minor repairs were immediately effected allowing the first patient to be admitted November 26 with the official opening on December 1, 1870. The building, which was to cost no more than $50,000, ultimately totaled $137,000.

Land for the Nebraska State Penitentiary was donated by Capt. Donovan and G. H. Hilton in 1867. The site considerably south of Lincoln was purposely given because it was not considered particularly suitable for farming and far enough from the city that should there be disturbances, they would not affect the citizenry. In July of 1870 the building illustrated above was completed while the entire penitentiary itself was built around it. The building served as a shop, stable and storage shed within the compound until razed about 1940.

After only a few weeks it was becoming apparent that the building, like the capitol, was not well planned or built. The university's contractor pointed out that inferior materials had been employed and that the outer finish or ashlar stone, which had been quarried from the nearby Cardwell's Branch outcropping, did not have a good foundation supporting it and was sinking and pulling away from the foundation. The Omaha Herald, ever ready to publicize any short-comings in Lincoln, said the asylum had been built of "indigenous hardened dirt" and that the fire had actually been arson to cover up the shoddy construction. Matters were not helped by the janitor's refusal to stay in the south wing because he thought it might collapse. In March of 1871 the legislature responded by sending an inspection committee which generally agreed with the current rumors. Their report called for corrections but at 3:00 AM on Monday April 17, 1871 the building virtually burned to the ground with at least one and possibly four deaths ensuing. The exact cause of the second fire was never clear as the administrators felt an inmate had set the fire. One Lincoln newspaper pointed to a faulty flue while the Omaha Republican suggested that ten penitentiary inmates had been purposely allowed to escape with instructions to set the fire so that the fire insurance could be collected. Another legislative investigation felt it was arson but could go no further. The insurance company said they would not pay out on the $95,000 policy if the fire was truly arson but after continued pressure from the state, they settled the claim for $71,999.95. This sum allowed the state to select William Foster, a Des Moines, Iowa architect, to design a new stone building which was completed by Robert Silver & Sons late in 1872. An interesting and potentially valuable feature of the new four-story Atchison, Kansas stone building was that there was an artesian well in the basement, as good a fire deterrent as was possible. With subsequent additions this structure stood, in constant use, until March 9, 1958 when, after being judged unsafe for over thirty years, it burned to the ground. This time the 385 patients living in the hospital were evacuated in less than twenty minutes with no injuries. Although it proved of no value, it is said the artesian well is still flowing in 2007.

Although the Territorial Legislature "located" a penitentiary at Tekamah, provided that the city donate ten acres for the purpose, no funds were ever appropriated and all state prisoners were confined in county jails. It was noted that the only the jail in the basement of the Omaha courthouse would "hold a man who has the least desire to get away." The governor was empowered to contract with any adjoining state to house prisoners but again nothing seems to have occurred. Subsequently the city of Bellevue was considered and likewise was not chosen.

With statehood, the problem was again addressed and Nebraska accepted 32,044 acres of federal land to be sold to build a penitentiary with counties reimbursed for quartering prisoners in the meantime. In 1870 the legislature created the State Prison Inspectors Board to sell the federal land and oversee construction of the prison. This board advertised the sale of the federal land plus other state-owned lands in April of 1870 and approved Stout & Jamison's bid of $307,954 to construct the building. The site of the penitentiary was a gift from Judge Hilton and Captain Donovan

A.G. Edwards & Sons, Inc.

You've built a large nest egg. It's our job to help you preserve it.

For more than 120 years, we've been fully invested in our clients. That includes providing wealth management services to help high net worth investors such as you preserve the nest eggs you've worked hard to establish.

Celebrating 30 years serving the Lincoln area

Call or visit us today.
**A.G. Edwards & Sons, Inc.
6003 Old Cheney Road, Suite 200
(402) 475-3644**

A.G. EDWARDS.
FULLY INVESTED IN OUR CLIENTS®

**Please consult "Important Information About Your Relationship With A.G. Edwards"
on agedwards.com/disclosures for a discussion of the differences between our
brokerage and advisory services.
2007 A.G. Edwards & Sons, Inc • Member SIPC • agedwards.com**

Partner In Progress

When completed, the front, north door of the Nebraska State Penitentiary was almost directly situated on Pioneers Blvd. The sidewalk, looking south to the main entrance connected to the old warden's house about a block to the north.

from Lincoln who offered land south of Lincoln which could not easily be farmed and which was felt to be so far from the city that any uprising or disturbance would be far from the population. The forty acre site was accepted and a temporary brownstone building costing $6,661 was built with the idea that when the main structure was completed around it, the temporary jail would become a workshop. The temporary jail accepted thirty-seven convicts and on the day the Insane Asylum burned, ten inmates easily broke out. Some say they were allowed or helped to escape in order to set fire to the asylum.

W. H. B. Stout also worked out a plan whereby the inmates themselves would quarry the stone and build the penitentiary at a cost to Stout & Jamison of $0.42 per inmate, per day. The stone was to be quarried from Stout's own land at Bennett some twelve miles distant on the Midland & Pacific Railroad and some at a quarry at Saltillo. The original building, including warden's house, was completed in the fall of 1876 and eighteen inmates were immediately transferred from various county jails in the state. The temporary building inside the walls was used for various purposes until the 1940s when it was razed. The current building completely replaced the original penitentiary in 1984, this time with no inmate labor.

Judging from the finery this photo shows a Sunday stroll at the second State Insane Asylum probably in the 1920s. The present grounds of the Regional Center are part of a series of area arboretums, still a great place for a Sunday walk.

The three State of Nebraska institutions were then operational in Lincoln which led historian, E. P. Brown to comment in 1930, perhaps with tongue firmly in cheek:

"The solons had justified their claims to wisdom in erecting in one legislative day both University and Asylum. The Asylum would be needed to provide teachers for the University. The University would be needed to provide inmates for the Asylum. Opponents of the whole set-up admitted that a University was needed to instruct the fools who wanted the Asylum; and that the Asylum was needed for the nitwits who thought the state needed or could ever have a University. Both sides agreed upon the necessity for a prison. It would be needed to confine the criminal other side."

"The solons had justified their claims to wisdom in erecting in one legislative day both University and Asylum. The Asylum would be needed to provide teachers for the University. The University would be needed to provide inmates for the Asylum. Opponents of the whole set-up admitted that a University was needed to instruct the fools who wanted the Asylum; and that the Asylum was needed for the nitwits who thought the state needed or could ever have a University. Both sides agreed upon the necessity for a prison. It would be needed to confine the criminal other side."

A 1905 view looks over Lincoln's second Market Square northeast to the University of Nebraska. When Lincoln sold the original Market Square at 9th and O Streets to the federal government for a post office which also served as a federal courthouse the city simply took the block which had been set aside for the state historical society for use as a new Market Square. After a questioning law suit the courts later sided with the city saying the original state gift proposed for the historical society had "lapsed by the non-user."

In the foreground is the City Scales. By the late 1880s the original market use of the center of the block had been eliminated by a city ordinance requiring a permanent hitching post be erected at the front of any place where goods were sold. This eviction allowed the city to erect a fire station which also served as a police station and city hall on the southeast corner of the block, barely visible at the right. Two University of Nebraska buildings, Brace Hall and Architecture Hall are the only structures still standing from the picture. The block itself is now the site of the Journal-Star Printing Company.

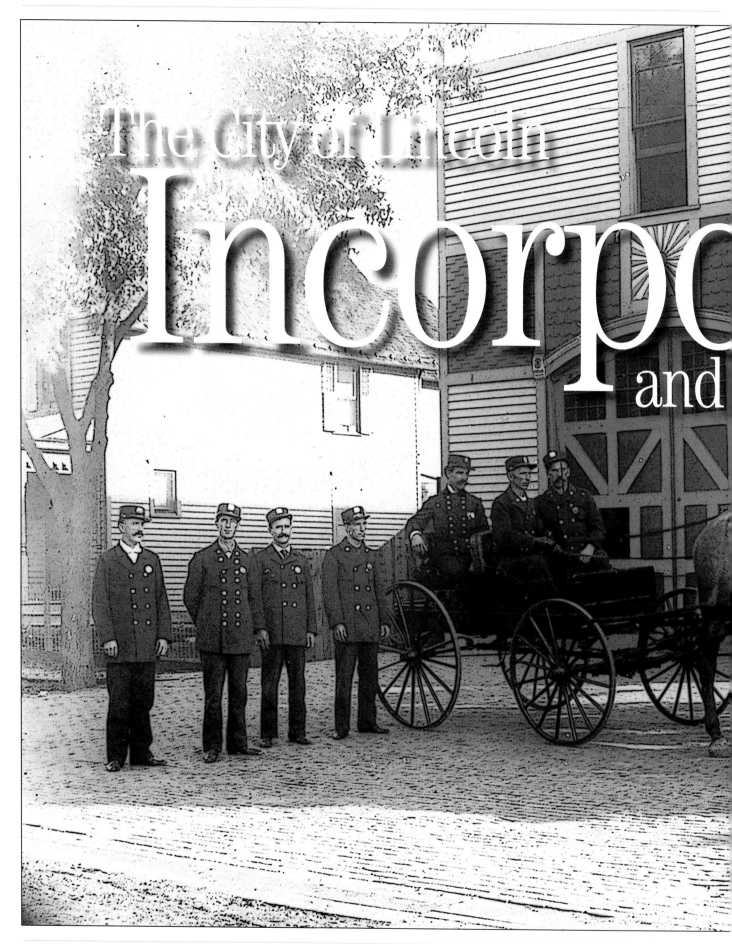

The City of Lincoln
Incorpo
and

rates
ts Underway

"There are no roads leading to it now. It has no commerce, and there is scarcely a wagon load of produce raised annually within ten, perhaps twenty miles of it."

With the state institutions up and running in Lincoln the capital city was poised to begin building a metropolitan community of businesses, professions and services. Deciding that Lincoln should be incorporated, petitions were

circulated and presented to the County on April 7, 1868 who summarily "declared [the city] a body corporate." After a temporary slate of trustees was appointed the first election was held May 18, 1868 with sixty votes cast. The first trustees elected Dr. H. Gilbert as chairman, who would amount to Mayor. However they failed to maintain the corporation. In fact no record of any meeting survived and the corporation was dissolved by the county.

Another petition was presented April 7, 1869, this time with 189 signatures. The corporate limits were defined as covering two and a quarter square miles and four of the original five trustees were reappointed. The second election chose only one of the trustees as appointed but this time the incorporation "took" and city officers were elected within and by the trustees with Charles Gere as their chairman.

Lincoln had grown sufficiently by 1871 to draw a city charter and be incorporated by the Nebraska Legislature as a City of Second Class. This also meant that, for the first time, the mayor could be directly chosen by the electorate instead of by the trustees. William F. Chapin therefore became Lincoln's first

Overleaf
Lincoln Fire Station #3 was located just west of the southwest corner of 13th and F Streets as shown in this turn of the century photo. Because its exact twin stood at 23rd and O Streets, only the building at the left shows it cannot be the O Street station. Both buildings were replaced with brick buildings and though Station #2 still stands, it no longer serves as a fire station. The oldest extant fire station structure is on the southeast corner of 27th and Pear Streets and has served many commercial purposes.

directly elected mayor although Dr. H. D. Gilbert and Charles Gere preceded him in a matter of speaking.

Nebraska cities with a population of over 5,000 were given the option of "the commission form of rule" wherein only nonpolitical councilmen were elected. The council then elected one of their number as mayor. Lincoln adopted this new plan by a vote of 1,982 to 1,911 and the council elected Frank Zerung as mayor.

In 1935 Lincoln voters approved a modified city manager form of government directly electing Charles Bryan, brother of perennial presidential candidate William Jennings Bryan, as mayor. On May 20, 1963 the mayor-council form of government was adopted making Dean H. Peterson Lincoln's

first full-time mayor. Another first of sorts came in 1979 when, after sixteen years on the city council, Helen Boosalis was elected Lincoln's first woman mayor, defeating "unbeatable" Sam Schwartzkopf.

Before any city offices existed some thought was given to education. The first classes in Lancaster County were held in John Cadman's stone-walled dugout well before the Capital Commission stayed there in 1867. The city of Lancaster owed its original impetus to the Methodist Protestant Female Seminary of 1864 even though evidence suggests no classes

The auditorium of the new high school building is pictured here shortly after it opened January 9, 1873 with students, faculty and presumably parents, judging from the size of the crowd.

were ever held there until 1867 when members of the community approached Mrs. H. W. Merrill whose husband had planned to be one of the seminary's professors. At their suggestion Mrs. Merrill obtained permission from the Seminary Association to teach a tuition graded school in the mainly unfinished building. The Merrill family also received the right to live in the building where classes were offered in a ground floor room with a dirt floor and no glass in the windows which were over-hung with rugs to keep the wind out. The number of students was small and fluctuated as parents kept children out to help in farms or businesses. Then, in the spring, a fire started in a faulty flue causing the wood portions of the stone building to burn and the school closed after hardly getting started.

Later in 1867 the city hired Milton Langdon to build a stone schoolhouse south of "University Square, facing south." The newspaper hoped the school would be ready for students by November 25 and subsequently announced that there would be a fund-raising dinner at the Methodist Church to support the enterprise. "Bring in your turkeys, chickens, puddings, pies and let us have a gay time." For the admission price of $1 guests would get dinner, hear speakers and be entertained with music. The school fund raised $85. The twenty three by thirty foot stone school, just north of the northeast corner of 11th and Q was opened immediately by George Peck who hoped for an enrollment of up to thirty-five students. By the beginning of the following 1868 to 1869 school year sixty-five students

signed up forcing the city to purchase the old frame Methodist Church on the northwest corner of 10th and Q to accommodate the extra students. The stone school building served students only a brief time, later becoming a jail, but it is probable that it survived later as a private dwelling and perhaps its basement and some walls stood and were in use as an apartment until the building was razed. Finally it became a small part of the site of the Lied Center for Performing Arts. In 1870 A. M. Ghost, Lancaster County Superintendent of Schools, reported that Lincoln's two schools were supplemented with one private school and that 236 students attended at least part of the year.

As the city and school-aged children continued to grow in number a $50,000 bond issue was approved in 1870 to 1871 prompting the question as to whether it should be used to build several schools or one central, union school which would primarily serve as a high school.

Charles Gere editorialized that one school was the answer and to those who said it was too far for some students to have to walk, he responded that "the children of Lincoln are not so physically degenerate, that they cannot get to a school located any where near the center of town, without endangering their health or wearing out their youthful energies." The central school carried the day 151 to 60 and for the first time Lincoln had a separate high school building. When completed however it was so far to the east of Lincoln that during winter months when snow covered the ground some parents would not send their children to school, fearing they might be attacked by wolves prowling the city's garbage in search of food. The school's officials too feared the location might be too far away and asked the city council to give them $50 to plant a row of trees around the school as a green belt to protect it from possible prairie fires. The trees were planted and when the site was abandoned with the completion of the new Lincoln High School on J Street it served briefly as a parking lot until 1957 when Pershing Municipal Auditorium was built on the block.

Law enforcement in the village of Lancaster was met with citizen response but in 1864 Peter Billows, a farmer who doubled as a blacksmith, became a sort of unpaid constable partially because he was big enough to handle almost any unruly situation. As the population grew with the coming of the capital, J. H. Hawke was elected Lancaster County Sheriff and Lincoln city constable. Local attorney Milton Langdon, whose cabin was near the corner of 9th and Q volunteered his milk house for use as a jail "when a citizen became a little too 'wild and woolly'" and about 1870 it was reported that Carl Richardson was the official town marshal with three men working for him. A slightly more proper jail was secured in 1871 when Lincoln aldermen rented a room in D. A. Sherwood's real

The first purpose-built U. S. Courthouse also serving as a Post Office in Lincoln was built at 9th and O Streets on what was land then seventeen feet above its present grade. The $200,000 stone building was completed in 1879 and was called the third most imposing post office west of the Missouri River. In 1906 the building became Lincoln's City Hall, serving until the 1960s when the new County-City Building was completed. The restored building, now on the National Historic Register of Historic Places, still houses city and related non profit organizations.

estate office at 11th and O for $15. In 1873 the "old stone school" near the northeast corner of 11th and Q was converted to a jail while Marshal J. E. McManegal asked that the city purchase six sets of ball and chains. City funds being in a state of constant shortage however meant that only four were actually purchased.

In 1885 a new city charter required civil service rules be implemented in hiring law enforcement employees which resulted in a new police department organized from the ground up. Police Marshal W. W. Corder then reorganized the department into seventeen men each of whom worked six twelve hour shifts a week. At this point in time Lincoln had one policeman per 3,000 citizens. The city finally built its first purpose-built jail in 1916 when what had been Market Square sprouted the structure on the northwest corner of 10th and Q though Mayor Charles Bryan said that because as many as seven men were held in ten square foot cells, conditions were "inhuman." With the advent of the automobile the department purchased three motorcycles and two motorcars putting them on the cutting edge of

In 1897 the first high school was joined on the block at 15th and N Streets by the Administration Building to the north or left in this photo. When the third building, McKinley, was constructed on the block in 1904 the three were connected by a "sky walk" on the second floor level.

mechanization. A major drawback still existed in the area of communications however, as the only way an officer could contact the station was by running, borrowing a telephone or finding one of the few, scattered, call boxes.

In 1932 the new Police Department/ Fire Department/County Health Department building was completed at 10th and Q complete with a seventy-eight person jail. Joe Carroll was sent to the FBI academy in 1938 and was made Chief of Police in 1941. One of his early decisions was to appoint Hulda Roper as the city's first policewomen though she refused to carry a weapon. A cadet program started in 1960, police dogs were added in 1961, "Handi-Talkie" radios purchased in 1963, downtown bicycle patrols in the downtown area instituted in 1988 and today nearly all of the patrol cars are even equipped with computers and video cameras as well as up to the minute communications systems.

One of the most pressing problems any growing city quickly meets is the supply of potable water. The first settlers had been able to find adequate water by simply using Salt Creek above A Street as the salt did not leach into it at that point. The state drilled a well on the capitol grounds when the building was constructed and the University met the problem by ordering a well, windmill and two cisterns immediately after University Hall was completed. The first photographs taken from the capitol and university show numerous windmills dotting the city but a central supply for the city was obviously needed.

An early solution proposed was to drill four municipal wells, one on the capitol grounds, one at the university, one at the penitentiary and one at the insane asylum. By connecting the wells with a five inch pipe it was thought twenty to sixty million gallons of water could be collected. The, then insurmountable, problem was how this water could be salt free. In 1881 voters approved a $10,000 bond issue to finance a public water works. An expert from Illinois reported that one, sixty foot well drilled just east of the capitol would produce 800,000 gallons of water a day, enough to supply a city of 50,000 people. Exactly why this proposal was not carried out was never explained but within a year a municipal well was drilled in Lincoln Park near 6th and F Streets and a stand pipe was erected in the park at 8th and F Streets. A sixteen inch water main was then placed from the stand pipe to the northeast to supply the city. When this well proved insufficient in 1887 they simply drilled another well in the middle of 6th Street and connected it to the stand pipe. Unfortunately they were pumping clear water from a roughly twelve inch vein and when the second pump was activated they started pulling water faster than it could flow to the wells. As a result, salt water was simply sucked from the adjacent strata and all the city's water was suddenly saline and undrinkable.

By purchasing land along Antelope Creek wells were sunk along its path and with the addition of the Mockett pumping station on A Street and the Rice station at 24th and N the immediate problem was solved. Unfortunately the city was still growing and even these wells were soon to prove inadequate and water fields at Seward and Ashland were investigated in 1922 at the request of the Chamber of

Commerce. When drought set in during 1930, supplies were strained. Then in July with the temperature at 107° much of Lincoln's water again turned salty. The solution was found in 1932 when a $2,300,000 bond issue allowed construction of a twenty-five mile, thirty-six inch wide pipeline from Ashland. Although water can still be obtained from the Antelope Valley watershed wells, today virtually all of Lincoln's water comes from Ashland and is distributed by over ten pumping stations.

Fires were, of course, a fact of life in early Lincoln just as in any Great Plains village where a lack of water mains and a lack of any sort of real fire department, combined with poorly constructed buildings meant disaster was always just around the corner. Water was a primary problem because at first only Salt Creek and then the few wells delivered the only source of water. Even as Lincoln began to grow in its first few years as capital of Nebraska, little thought seems to have been given to even the most rudimentary volunteer department. With a population of 2,500 in 1871 the city council urged an experiment with "fire engines and other apparatus" and the following year a number of city-owned lots were sold to establish an engine house, purchase two hose carts, a see-saw, hand-operated pump and a Silsby steam-powered engine. The steam engine arrived the next year and was christened Chapin #1 in honor of the Chapin Volunteer Fire Company organized at the direction of Mayor Wm. F. Chapin. In April of 1873 the city hired an "engineer" whose job was to have steam readily available should the need arise and to sound the bell

Probably taken in the 1890s, this interior view of the 13th and F Streets fire station shows the harness rigging hanging in readiness for a summons. It was said the horse-drawn rigs could be completely installed in less than thirty seconds.

call for volunteers when a fire was reported. All of this was to little effect until 1875 when an actual organization finally took place with the hiring of Turnis P. Quick as fire chief who purchased two horses and organized the Phoenix Hook and Ladder Company. Now the city had fifty volunteers trained and ready to respond. The fire equipment was headquartered at Granville Ensign's livery barn at 225 South 11th Street and also gave the volunteers a second floor meeting room.

Lincoln's Fire Department was considered "one of the best… equipped departments in the west; in fact second to none" in 1877 when the city owned three hose carts, one hook and ladder truck, a chief's buggy, supply wagon, three engine houses, nineteen horses, had five paid firemen and an annual budget of $35,000. In 1911 Lincoln's first gasoline-powered truck, an American LaFrance pumper was purchased and by 1919, Buck, the last fire horse was sold.

The first libraries in Lincoln, the Young Men's Library & Lecture Association and the Young Ladies Library & Reading Room Association, were struggling with the drought, grasshopper invasion and general economic recession which began in 1873. The local press urged they combine and on November 1, 1875 the two groups met with several businessmen at the old stone school at 11th and Q to discuss the proposition. By year's end and after several more meetings the amalgamation was perfected and the Lincoln Public Library and Reading Room Association was formed. A call for donations sparked a number of gifts including the impressive Appleton

American Encyclopedia given by Prosper Smith. The new library opened for business on January 28, 1876 with the combined treasury at $321 and collection of 367 books.

Because the directors wanted to keep the library open on Sundays the directors themselves took over as librarians, in alphabetical order, during 1876. By early 1877 the city had approved a request from the library for city funds but this was vetoed by Mayor R. D. Silver "because it would lead to other foolish appropriations…there [was] no provision in the city charter…and he 'did not think the citizens cared to be taxed to furnish a resort for boys and young men inclined to be wild.'" The legislature subsequently passed an act enabling "establishment and maintaining of free public libraries." In July newly elected Mayor Hardy signed a $100 appropriation for the library which in turn signed over all of its assets to the city. Because there were still liabilities amounting to several hundred dollars the library charged $1 a year for membership until 1888 when all old debts had been paid off.

The library moved on several occasions and by 1880 was occupying the second floor of Hurlbut's Clothing Store on the south side of O between 11th and 12th Streets. President Charles Gere reported that the library consisted of 1,700 books, nine daily papers, twenty weeklies and fifteen magazines. In 1888 the second floor of the new Masonic Temple on the northeast corner of 11th and M Streets was rented for what was hoped would be the library's permanent home. Unfortunately on September 16, 1899 the building and library with its 15,500 books

This **1870s** view of downtown Lincoln was taken from the state capitol looking to the northwest. The mostly empty block at the center is the site of the First Baptist Church today.

was destroyed in a fire which consumed most of a half block. Reports, which seem apocryphal, said that the number of books checked out at the time of the fire, which would represent the total collection, was 376—the exact number of books they owned on the opening day!

Mrs. William Jennings Bryan was head of a committee which approached Andrew Carnegie who agreed to grant Lincoln $77,000 for a new building. Local contributions were solicited and amounted to over $10,000 and lots on the northeast corner of 14th and N Streets were acquired. The Omaha architectural firm of Fisher & Lawrie was chosen and the new building's ground was broken on December 1, 1900 with occupancy on May 27, 1902. The collection and Lincoln's population continued to grow and by the early 1960s the shelves, which had been built to hold 33,000 books were home to nearly 200,000 volumes. Bennett Martin Public Library was completed on the sold site and opened in 1960. With expansions and remodeling in 1967 and 1977 Bennett Martin still serves as the headquarters for the Lincoln Library System and its seven branches.

Taken in the 1930s, this photo looks to the southeast and shows the fountain originally built over the salt water well in the center of the block at 9th and O. In this photo it has been moved to the west within the same block to make way for an addition to the second U. S. Post Office. By this point the artesian flow was not strong enough to push the water's flow to the fountain which merely collected rain water and leaves. The back of Old City Hall is in the background.

In 1873 the southwest corner of 13th and O Streets housed the brand new Hallo Opera House. When the 1,500 seat theatre burned in October of 1875, it was replaced by the Centennial Opera House pictured below in 1876. The bridged sidewalk at right was to accommodate a stream which ran diagonally across the intersection to ultimately empty into Salt Creek at N Street.

After being in rented quarters for many years, this building on the northwest corner of 10th and Q, the old Market Square Block, became the first City Hall as well as Fire and Police Department Building until the city government moved into the old federal building at 9th and O Streets. This building was replaced in 1925 with a fire, police and county health department building, the site of which today is the Journal-Star Printing facility.

The 1880 census showed Lincoln with a population of 13,003 but with no paved streets. In 1887 the idea of paving was introduced, the city divided into two districts and contracts let. Little thought had been however given to the manifold problems of grading, draining and burying water, gas and sewer lines as well as replacing streetcar tracks resulting in little more than a mess with the intersection of 11th and P noted as "presenting the appearance of a harbor" when it rained. After examining several cities it was determined to begin paving with red cedar blocks whose advantages were that cedar did not readily rot and resulted in a much quieter surface when interacting with horseshoes and steel wheels. In June of 1888, eighty train car loads of square cedar fence posts arrived and were sawn into workable lengths. By 1889 there were eight miles of cedar paving completed. The red cedar did not prove out as well as hoped, particularly in areas like 11th and P which, because of springs, was always at least damp. This was not a particular problem even though the sand base stayed wet until it rained which surprisingly resulted in the blocks floating. One report said that P Street itself simply floated down to Salt Creek and had to be chased by city workers. A 1915 report showed that Lincoln had twenty-three and a quarter miles of brick, twenty-one and a half miles of asphalt, fourteen and three quarters miles of concrete and one mile of cedar block paving "although there is not much left of the blocks."

The
Railroad
Arrives
and Private Enterprise
Develops

CHAPTER
8

"Nobody will ever go to Lincoln who does not go to the legislature, the lunatic asylum, the penitentiary, or some of the state institutions."

The city of Lincoln and its various state offices were eager for railroad service to be extended to the capital city for, as was well known, until the railroad reached a community, its progress would be slowed and for those who were ultimately bypassed

dwindling prospects, even decline were almost assured. In November of 1867 Lancaster County issued $100,000 worth of bonds to be awarded to the first railroad to reach Lincoln and two years later the state legislature approved grants of 2,000 acres of Nebraska land for every mile of railroad track laid for two years setting aside 500,000 acres for the project.

On May 12, 1869 the Burlington & Missouri River Railroad was chartered in Nebraska to build a railroad from Plattsmouth through Lincoln to Fort Kearney. That year, three other railroads showed interest in the Lincoln route. The Atchison & Nebraska Railroad starting from Atchison, Kansas was offered $120,000 in bonds, the Midland Pacific at Nebraska City was to receive bond proceeds of $150,000 providing they build maintenance shops in Lincoln while the Burlington & Missouri River Railroad was promised $50,000 in county bonds providing that construction began by June 3, 1869 and the road reached Lincoln by September of 1870. That April, the city of Lincoln added $5,000 in bonds to the Burlington for depot construction when they agreed to build the structure just west of the city between O and Q Streets.

Apparently it was becoming clear that the Burlington was going to win the race as on June 12, 1869 Governor Butler, Secretary of State Kennard, State Auditor Gillespie and the Burlington's Chief Engineer Hans Thielsen broke ground near the later depot grounds. On July 4, 1869 construction began at Plattsmouth for the first sixty mile segment with announced hopes that they would reach Lincoln by July 4 the next year. Unfortunately when that date arrived the tracks reached only to a point northeast of Havelock at about Newton so an excursion train with open cars was dispatched from Plattsmouth which stopped at Newton with the passengers transferred to wagons to continue their trip into Lincoln for a celebration. On July 26, 1870 the engine Hurricane arrived in Lincoln at the temporary twenty-four by fifty foot cottonwood depot, though true rail service on the four hour trip from Plattsmouth did not commence for a number of days.

Charles Gere saw the arrival of the railroad as evidence that Lincoln was no longer a mere village and announced that the former weekly Lincoln State Journal would henceforth be a daily paper. Gere also saw the opportunity the railroad offered for the city and knew that what it now needed

In 1912 Lincoln Telephone & Telegraph Co. wrote a $2,293,000 check to the Bell Company's Nebraska Telephone Co. acquiring Bell's interest in twenty-two southeast Nebraska counties. This necessitated building the below three-story structure on the northwest corner of 14th and M Streets, just south of their original building. Two more floors were added to this building before its being razed for a parking lot while the new larger phone company building was erected on the block to the east.

was a second railway to ensure competition which would lead to lower freight rates. To that end Gere and several other local businessmen called a meeting at the 10th Street Methodist Church to be held July 28, 1870. Membership to the group was set at $2.50 per quarter and Gere was elected chairman. Four years later the group was incorporated at the Board of Trade and later became the Lincoln Chamber of Commerce.

State Treasurer James Sweet of Nebraska City was one of the first to see the possibilities of a railroad connecting the Missouri River with Lincoln and met with other businessmen on December 12, 1867 with the intent of creating a railroad to protect Nebraska City's river docks and connections to Fort Kearney and the west. Secondarily the group saw a large profit potential from the land and bond revenue being offered for being the first rail connection to the capital city. The group convinced Otoe County to issue $150,000 in bonds to help finance the project

and ground breaking occurred June 5, 1868, well before the Burlington started work. The plan was not only to connect with Lincoln and thence to Grand Island but to also create a branch from Lincoln south to Fort Riley, Kansas. In 1869 the Midland Pacific's first locomotive arrived at Nebraska City on a steamboat. The plan was then to simply run the Lightfoot down an incline to a flatboat which would take it to the dock where it would be driven onto tracks ready for the ultimate fifty-eight mile trip to Lincoln when the tracks were completed. The incline was apparently just a bit steeper than originally planned as the Lightfoot shot completely over the flatboat ending up in the Missouri River with only the top of its smokestack above water. Fortunately they were able to simply pull the locomotive up out of the water where it awaited the necessary tracks.

By January of 1870 tracks had reached Dunbar but the Burlington arrived in Lincoln well before the Midland Pacific's arrival at their 5th and H Street depot on April 22, 1871 becoming the capital city's second railroad. The Midland Pacific became the Nebraska Railway Company and in 1877 was purchased by the Burlington.

In 1915 Lincoln had the following rail services that were established in the year that follows each:

Burlington & Missouri River Railroad from Plattsmouth 1870
Midland Pacific Railroad from Nebraska City 1871
Atchison & Nebraska Railroad from Atchison, Kansas 1872
Union Pacific Railroad from Valley 1877
Lincoln & Northwestern from Columbus 1880
Missouri Pacific Railroad from Weeping Water 1886
Fremont, Elkhorn & Missouri Valley Railroad from Fremont 1886
Chicago, Rock Island & Pacific Railroad from the Missouri River 1892

Beatrice Butter & Egg Co. moved from that city to Lincoln in 1898 in order to take advantage of better railroad facilities. Buildings at 7th and L and 7th and P Streets were constructed. After first relying on ice but from local ponds and streams, the firm put in a "manufactured ice" plant with enough capacity to supply local demand as well. This ice truck was photographed at the six-story building at 726 P Street about 1920.

The Missouri Pacific Railroad arrived in Lincoln in 1886 giving the capitol city a direct link to St. Louis and access to their 7,000 mile-long main line system. This building at 9th and S Streets provided depot service for The Missouri Pacific as well as the Fremont, Elkhorn & Missouri Valley Railroad, later becoming part of the Chicago & Northwestern. Remodeled in 1953, the depot was razed in the mid 1960s as part of the site of Lincoln's new post office.

Although the first telephone in Lincoln arrived in 1877 when Louis Korty of Omaha obtained a Bell franchise though it was little more than two tin cans on either end of a string as the phones connected only two parties who could only call one another. The first true exchange was organized in November of 1879 which allowed its sixty-five subscribers to contact any of the others by connecting with the exchange. This early phone company charged individual customers $3 or businesses $4 per month. In 1882 long distance phone service began with a connection to Omaha and by 1889 there were 615 subscribers in Lincoln who could communicate with fifty-seven Nebraska and sixty-six Iowa cities and the new Bell Telephone building was finished on South 13th Street just south of the alley. Charles Bills, a Fairbury banker joined his brother, Hon. Judge Allen W. Field in forming a company to compete with the Bell system and because they needed additional financing and legal expertise, they enlisted Lincoln attorney Frank H. Woods to incorporate the business and bring his brothers George and Mark Woods along to provide financing. The new company, named the Western Union Independent Telephone Company was incorporated in 1903 and headquartered on South 14th Street. By the end of their first year 1,800 people had subscribed and were charged $1.75 for residential or $3 a month for business connections. Because the Bell Company was

When a new hotel for the southwest corner of 9th and P Streets was announced in 1890 it was predicted "it would become as unwieldy as an elephant" as there were already too many hotel rooms available. The 233 room, seven-story, 110 by 146 foot, $350,000 stone Lincoln Hotel opened the following January amid rave reviews for its marble-floored, two-story lobby, café and grillroom. In 1911 a $300,000 annex was built to the south. Through the decades the Lincoln Hotel housed royalty and President Wm. McKinley as well as serving as home to several Nebraska governors. After numerous owners, the hotel was razed in June of 1972 for the site of a new hotel, now the Holiday Inn

still operating their own separate exchange in Lincoln, subscribers to one company could not connect with phones on the other company's exchange. Thus doctors, businesses and individuals who wanted full service had to subscribe to two companies and have two phone numbers.

In 1904 Western Union Independent changed their name to the Lincoln Telephone Company and decided to try an almost unproved new technology, the Stowager Automatic Phone. It had a primitive dial system which enabled subscribers to connect with other parties by dialing their number and not having to go through a central exchange operator. The new technology was comparatively expensive forcing Lincoln Telephone to raise prices which enabled Bell to offer a price decrease and even twenty-five year fixed rate contracts. As competition increased Bell started charging rates below their cost to lure customers and law suits commenced. Ultimately the Woods traded their telephone interests in several Nebraska communities and $2,293,000 in cash for the Bell interests in twenty-two southeastern counties. In 1950 LT&T reached 100,000 phones and by 1980 Lincoln Telephone & Telegraph was the seventh largest independent telephone company in the United States with 310,000 subscribers.

In 1889 the Sisters of St. Francis purchased the Buckstaff mansion at 11th and South Streets for $20,000 for use as Lincoln's first general hospital. In 1891 the house, shown at the left in the photo, was supplemented with a two-story brick and stone building then known at St. Elizabeth Hospital. The hospital grew on this site until 1970 when the 265 bed hospital was razed and replaced with the new St. Elizabeth Community Health Center at 70th and J Streets across the street west from the U. S. Veterans Hospital.

Burlington & Missouri River Railroad land agent, J. D. MacFarland acquired the right to operate his Lincoln Street Railway in 1870 but it was not until 1881 when the corporation was granted right of way to lay tracks and 1883 when there was a real line operation with a reported 200 horses and eighteen miles of track. With the 1887 invention of the electric streetcar, horses' days were numbered and Lincoln was in the forefront of the new technology with electrification beginning in 1891. In 1893 Lincoln reported its thirteen street railway companies had more miles of track than any city in Nebraska, Iowa, Kansas or the Dakotas and was thirty-fifth in the nation for the longest track. The new technology was cleaner, faster and more efficient but more expensive which brought about a number of consolidations. Still ridership was high and in 1894 it was reported that 110,000 fares were collected during the week of the state fair.

However the recession caused bankruptcy the following year when the company's assets were sold and in 1898 further consolidation formed the Lincoln Traction Company. The last horsecar in Lincoln closed in 1906 with Mayor and Mrs. Frank Zehrung on board. The lead "horse" was carrying a sign that read "always leave 'em laughing." In 1907 the Woods Brothers incorporated the Citizens

In 1880 Lincoln's population had reached 13,003. Coupled with the laws of supply and demand, ladies of the evening and bawdy houses appeared to compliment the saloons and gambling rooms which were primarily located along 9th Street and P Street.

Mary Wallace, born in Ireland in 1844, arrived in Lincoln as Lydia Stewart about 1880

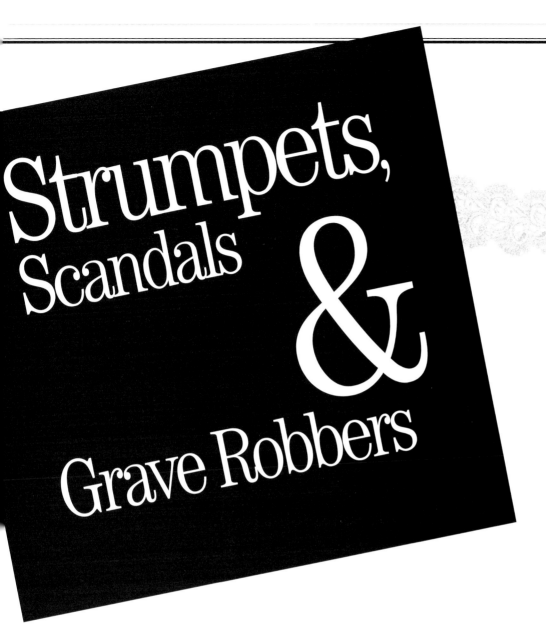

Strumpets, Scandals & Grave Robbers

after a short stop in Omaha. An ingenious arrangement between several somewhat and outright illegal enterprises in Lincoln allowed Lydia to operate her "house" at 124 South 9th Street without harassment by simply remitting $15 per employee and $25 per manager monthly to Police Judge Albert Parsons. By paying the fines in cash, Parsons pointed out that

costly paperwork, arrests and court appearances could be dispensed with which also, unfortunately, allowed funds to be diverted from their intended city coffers.

As Lincoln reached the status of City of the First Class in 1887 virtually all city officers and employees had to be rehired save Parsons, the lone carryover. When the city council discovered Parsons' "oversights," they promptly fired and replaced him. Parsons, out of an obviously lucrative position, claimed the

council lacked jurisdiction and sought a federal restraining order. When the federal order was ignored, the entire city council and the Mayor were whisked off to Omaha to show why they should not be held in contempt. Judge Dundy surprised everyone by finding the lot guilty.

The case ultimately ended up in the U. S. Supreme Court before the defendants were absolved of their crimes and

Continued on page 151

Interurban Railway to aid in the development of their properties along Sheridan Boulevard and to connect downtown Lincoln with the suburb of College View. An early problem of how to have a street railway cross the Rock Island Railroad's tracks was solved by building a bridge on Sheridan Blvd. at about 32nd which also allowed the collection of an additional one cent fare and the crossing was thereafter known as the Penny Bridge. By the end of World War I streetcar lines were being closed in favor of the more flexible routes available to busses. But the beginning of World War II brought a federal law prohibiting the closing of street railways which would bring more busses and an increase in demand for gasoline and rubber tires both of which were rationed. Thus the trolley cars continued in Lincoln until after the second world war and had their last run on September 1, 1945 when the College View and Randolph lines closed and converted to bus service.

In August of 1881 the more-or-less temporary frame Burlington & Missouri River Railroad depot of 1870 was replaced with this new $125,000 masonry building at 7th and P Streets. Shown looking northeast from the first O Street viaduct about 1900. The then two-story Beatrice Creamery Building is at right and just peeking between the two primary structures is the dome of the Missouri Pacific Railroad's depot at 9th and S Streets. The pictured Burlington depot was replaced with the current building in 1927.

Strumpets, Scandals & Grave Robbers

the principal of home rule was reaffirmed. Lydia continued her trade, dying of cancer in 1923 with the newspaper obituary which referred to her trade as "surrounded by the blackness which marks the house of shame, the doorway through which thousands walk to disgrace." The building survived, was added onto and a beer garden completed in 1903. After being closed in a 1907 anti-corruption movement, it became the City Mission and after another enlargement in 1928 became Mission Arts Gallery in 1987.

In 1880 Miss Mollie (sometimes Mary) Hall arrived from England and set up shop in a euphemistically termed cigar store in a two-story, brick building between two laundries at 817 P Street. Upstairs were her living quarters and furnished rooms. On January 2, 1885, eighteen year old Pearl Forcade was found murdered in her "apartment." The story might have ended there had her body not gone missing a few days hence. This too might have been forgotten except the body mysteriously reappeared at a local mortuary. This was too good a story to overlook.

The University of Nebraska Medical College had opened in Lincoln in 1883 with fifty-two students who were promised "abundant anatomical material" in the college catalogue. Even though unclaimed bodies were given by the state penitentiary and insane asylum, the promised "material" proved insufficient and the chancellor recommended the anatomy professor furnish his own specimens. The professor passed the problem on to his students who later admitted simply watching the local newspapers for burials from which they then conveniently borrowed the recently deceased.

When details of their midnight shenanigans were exposed in depth, a hue and cry arose bringing the University's closure of the College of Medicine in Lincoln. When Omaha pointed out that they were not only far more cosmopolitan but larger and hence had adequate supplies of certain needed materials, along with requests from local businessmen, the University of Nebraska's School of Medicine reopened there a short time later.

Lincoln's first newspaper, the Nebraska Commonwealth was actually printed in Nebraska City on September 7, 1867. By its second edition, in November, the paper had moved to the capital city changing its name to the Nebraska State Journal in 1869. In 1881 the remnants of the Methodist Protestant Female Seminary on the northeast corner of 9th and P Streets were purchased, razed and replaced with the pictured three-story building. Over time the paper became the Lincoln Evening Journal in 1945. The Lincoln Star joined the Journal in building a joint printing plant in 1950 with the Star becoming the morning paper and the Journal the evening paper. In 1995 Lee Enterprises, the Star's owners, bought the then 127 year old Journal becoming today's Lincoln Journal Star.

Born in 1871 at 10th and P Streets, the First National Bank built a new building on the southeast corner of 10th and O Streets two years later. After several mergers, that building was razed and in 1910 the nine-story building, shown here in early construction, rose in its place. First National built another new building at 13th and M Streets in 1970 and though both buildings are extant First National Bank & Trust Company no longer exists in Lincoln.

In about 1885 brothers Carlos and Lionel Burr commissioned architect James Tyler to design a six-story skyscraper on the northeast corner of 12th and O Streets. Tenants of the Burr Block, as pictured, included attorneys William Jennings Bryan and later Vice President of the U. S., Charles Dawes and Stephen Pound, father of Roscoe Pound. Security Mutual Insurance Co. purchased the building in 1906 and in 1915 dismantled it, rebuilding it on the same site, four floors taller. The "new" building has had several owners through the years and currently serves a number of commercial and residential tenants.

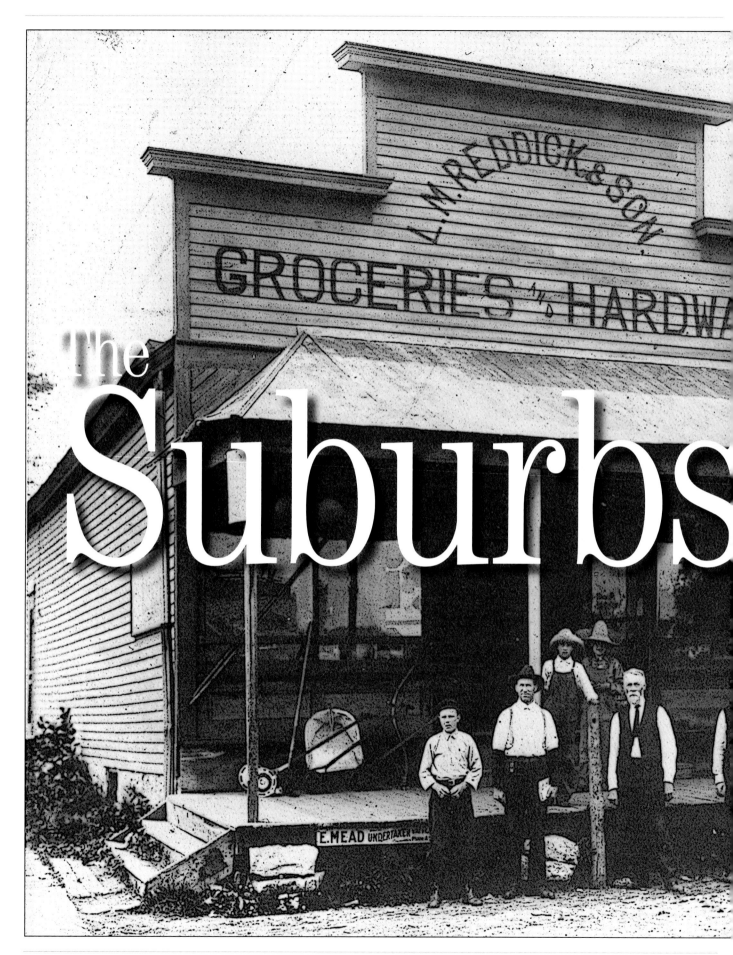

The Suburbs

Form

"Heaven is not built
of country seats
But little queer
suburban streets."

In a manner of speaking Lincoln's first suburb was noted on the original plat as East Lincoln which was simply the area east of 17th Street. Instead of developing as a suburb it almost immediately was platted as Lavender's Addition and no further mention of

Overleaf
Redick's Grocery, shown with the Redick family, stood on the northwest corner of today's North 66th or North Cotner Blvd. and Holdrege Streets. Although the wooden sidewalk had disappeared the building stood until the 1940s when it was razed and a drug store built in its stead.

Rev. Mr. Elisha Mosher Lewis, a Presbyterian minister, banker and businessman, built the French Second Empire house below in 1878 at the corner of Grand and University Place, today 16th and U Streets overwhelmed in the University of Nebraska's Sorority/Fraternity Row. The house was purchased by Dewitt Syford in 1904 and on the death of his daughter Constance in 1965, ended up the property of the Nebraska State Historical Foundation which has announced their desire to sell it.

East Lincoln is ever made. Reverend Elisha Mosher Lewis, DD arrived from Jackson, Michigan about 1863 before Lincoln or even Lancaster existed. Although a Presbyterian minister, it was noted that Lewis obtained a federal land grant intending to establish a Baptist community on the site. The community did not get off the ground but some twenty years later Lewis established the Congregational Church of Salt Creek near the village of Davey. The rather denominationally indiscriminant Lewis did build a house on the northeast corner of Grand Avenue (today's North 16th

Street) and University Place (today known as U Street) which survives today as one of Lincoln's oldest houses at 700 North 16th Street in the middle of the University of Nebraska's campus.

University Place
University Place: "The air is pure, water plenty and perfect, and the haunts of vice and crime are relegated to other places."

Perhaps the first proposal for a Methodist school in Nebraska occurred in 1855 when Simpson University, to be built at Omaha, was proposed. The territorial legislature even incorporated the school whose thirteen trustees included Mark W. Izard and Thomas B. Cuming both of whom served as territorial governors. With less than 300 Methodists in the entire territory and no organized churches, the proposal proved overly optimistic and premature and though nothing came of the incorporation it did show the interest of Methodists in education. In 1858 the city of Oreapolis was created near the mouth of the Platte River with expectations of becoming the eastern terminus of the Union Pacific Railroad and an educational center. Although the railroad chose to locate to the north on the Missouri River, the Cass County University & Oreapolis Seminary formed and built a three-story brick building. Both the

In 1909 Dr. Benjamin F. Bailey built a home on the grounds of his hospital at 5345 South Street. The entire campus, now occupied by Madonna Rehabilitation Hospital, tore the house down in 2005, the last remnant building of either Lincoln Normal University or Green Gables Sanitarium which established the surrounding village of Normal Heights.

school and city failed leaving few traces of ever having existed. The Methodists did not give up, creating the Nemaha Valley Seminary & Normal Institute at Pawnee City in 1864, Peru Seminary & College at Peru in 1866, York Seminary at York in 1879, Nebraska Wesleyan at Osceola in 1879, Nebraska Wesleyan at Fullerton in 1881, Central City College at Central City in about 1883, Mallalieu University at Bartley in 1886 and uncompleted attempts at Lancaster, Wayne, Orleans and Madison.

Real estate developers Brace & Bigelow began developing Lincoln Heights in 1888, twenty years after much of the area was owned by Elder E. M. Lewis who hoped but failed to develop a Baptist colony. As an upscale portion of Lincoln Heights, the firm platted Grandview above and to the north. Here, at 12th and Nance, George Bigelow built the pictured "mansion" to attract wealthy potential home owners who were also clients from Lincoln. The Grand View Building Association failed along with plans for the garden residential development and the house was razed before the current 1950s redevelopment.

Rev. Henry T. Davis and others called for consolidation and unification of the handful of schools still operating n 1886. That December the three Methodist conferences of the state met at St. Paul Methodist Church in Lincoln with that very concept high on their priorities. After considerable discussion, the concept was accepted and cities were invited to present proposals. The first ballot showed Lincoln eleven, York

eight and Bartley four. York's bid offered land, its extant buildings, equipment and donations totaling $190,412.30. Lincoln made two offers, one amounting to $140,000, the other they valued at $293,500 which included a large number of city lots around the proposed campus which they valued at $200,000. Of course the location near the capital city carried great weight but no dollar value. On the second ballot Lincoln carried the voting with fourteen to York's nine.

The site chosen for Nebraska Wesleyan was known at the Pitcher-Baldwin Tract about four miles northeast of Lincoln's post office. The Kansas City architectural firm of Gibbs & Parker was chosen to design the $50,000 building to sit on a forty-four acre campus. The cornerstone laying was planned for September 22, 1887 with a train leaving Lincoln at 12:30 PM for Havelock and returning to the city at 7:00 PM that evening. At Havelock the train was met by a shuttle for the campus provided by Levi Brothers Livery. Counting those coming by private carriages, it was estimated that about 1,000 attended the service. Following the speeches, Benjamin Rhodes held an auction of school-owned lots, selling fifty of the school's 800 lots for a total of over $13,000. The crowd was so enthusiastic that pledges for the school were increased from $50,000 to $70,000. A perhaps apocryphal story includes a conditional gift of $1,000 offered by Lincoln physician Bartlett L. Paine whose will later endowed both Nebraska Wesleyan and Lincoln's St. Paul Church. If the story is correct, Dr. Paine offered the $1,000 if the school was located no more than a specified distance

Bethany Heights "main," south business district on the west side of Saunders Avenue, today's Cotner Blvd. is shown with the Bethany trolley just about to turn toward downtown Lincoln on Holdrege Street. A couple of the pictured buildings, including the tiny brick Bethany State Bank, still stand across the street from the Cotner Center Condominiums, partially built around the old Bethany School.

from Miller & Paine's Department Store in Lincoln. After a careful calculation it was found that the original site for the main building was some fifty feet too far east so the building was resited west to guarantee the substantial gift. Dr. Charles F. Creighton resigned from St. Paul Church in Lincoln to become Nebraska Wesleyan's first chancellor and built a house at 50th and Madison. Construction continued but stopped when a blizzard intervened and lot sales, which were financing the building, faltered. Creighton wired Bishop Henry Warren for help. Warren offered $1,000 but Creighton explained that $10,000 was the required amount. To allow for material costs and completion of construction, Warren ultimately bought $5,000 in school-owned lots at Peck's Grove and near the campus and loaned an additional $5,000.

The building was described as being 168 by 72 feet, three stories of red Milwaukee cold pressed brick and Colorado red granite plus a 9 foot ceiling in the basement. The $70,000 structure was topped by a thirty foot clock tower on a slate roof and faced west into the setting sun. Near the roof line on the south side were the words "let there be light" and on the north side "there was light." The lower level contained eight rooms for chemistry to isolate any odors and the mechanical equipment. The first floor had seventeen rooms for offices and classrooms while the second floor housed classrooms, a library and a museum. The third floor principally contained a 1,000 seat chapel as well as classrooms while the attic could be finished later as needs arose.

The first registrant was Lincoln bookseller Herb Esterbrook who was said to have had to climb a ladder into the building where he paid a $5 matriculation fee and the $10 in-state tuition for the first term. Nebraska Wesleyan opened informally on September 5, 1888 with a few students who gathered in the library which still required use of ladders to enter the building. With all staircases finally completed, the grand opening ceremony was held on October 24, 1888 with speeches including one by Governor John M. Thayer. By year's end the student population had risen from nearly fifty to ninety-five and annual salaries were established; the chancellor made $3,000 and professors made $1,000 to $1,200.

Bishop Warren wrote Jacob Haish of Dekalb, Illinois, who had just given $50,000 to Denver University, asking for a similar amount to build a second structure at Nebraska Wesleyan. Haish responded that he would

Looking southeast from about Cotner Blvd. and Garland Streets Cotner University looms above the village of Bethany Heights in this 1911 photo which also shows the first Bethany Christian Church on the right horizon.

pledge 50 percent of the gross sales of his company's barbed wire in Nebraska for one year up to $25,000 to build Haish Mechanical Institute of Nebraskan Wesleyan University plus a similar amount to provide maintenance and support for the engineering college. The university and the Methodist churches of Nebraska quickly spread the word and advertised "No fence but barbed wire; no barbed wire but Haish…we want Nebraska Methodists fenced in with Barb Wire…[Haish is] Methodist wire…It is a perfect wire." Haish was so taken by the enthusiasm that he pledged to send the money before sales even occurred.

Artemus Roberts, who also designed William Jennings Bryan's Fairview, and Alfred Woods were chosen as architects. In December of 1891 the four-story, $50,000 building with $10,000 in furnishings was dedicated, north and a bit east of the main building. Classes in Haish opened in 1893

but an arsonist doused the main floor with kerosene and set the mainly brick building afire. Because virtually the only source of water to fight the fire was the building's own cistern, it burned leaving only a few brick walls standing. Students and administration rallied, promising to rebuild but when it was discovered that no fire insurance had yet been secured, funding, which was also caught in the national recession of the period, proved doomed. The walls were finally salvaged for use as brick sidewalks and years later Lucas Library was built near the Haish's original site. Apparently the same arsonist tried on two occasions to burn the main building, once while students and faculty were in the auditorium but, though the building filled with smoke, there were no serious injuries and the building survived. The renovated and restored Old Main still stands as the only extant original building on any of Lincoln's universities. Careful examination of the flat area near the top of Old Main's south elevation still reveals the ghost of the old inscription "let there be light."

John C. Jensen of Utica graduated from Wesleyan in 1906 and was offered a part time instructor's position at $250 per year. Jensen ultimately headed the school's Physics Department, retiring after forty-five years of service. Although he was responsible for many campus improvements including the installation of electric generation and later engineering the connection to city power, Jensen is most often remembered for his pioneering work in radio and television. In 1913 his Wesleyan radio transmission has been called the first in Nebraska. Radio station 9YD,

While Bethany's Christian Church was being built on Saunders Avenue services were held in the auditorium of Cotner University two blocks to the northeast. When the above church was completed in 1909 it was a central gathering place for the community and considered one of the largest churches in Nebraska. Destroyed by fire November 28, 1928, the new and current church building was literally built above the ashes of the old even utilizing portions of the old basement.

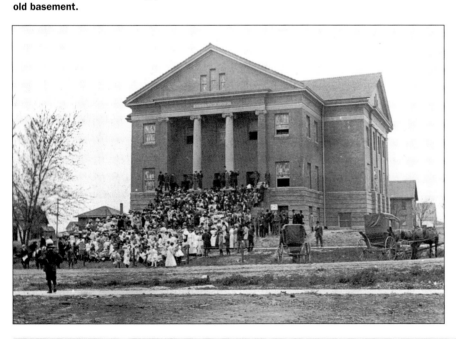

later WCAJ at 590 KC is also mentioned as a contender for the first educational radio station in the United States. For unexplained reasons, when the Federal Radio Commission, predecessor of the Federal Communications Commission, first assigned wavelengths, WCAJ was coupled with WOW in Omaha with WCAJ having one seventh of the combined stations' day. Because Wesleyan was linked with prohibition and WOW was interested in selling advertising to Omaha breweries, WCAJ was sued to remove them from the assigned frequency. A United States Court of Appeals decision in 1932 sided with WCAJ. With the Great Depression, WOW felt it finally had leverage and while Jensen was out of the state, they offered Wesleyan $10,000 for their one seventh interest in the 590 frequency. Chancellor Cutshcall accepted the

offer which figured heavily in saving Wesleyan during the depression though Jensen was understandably, greatly disheartened.

Along with the forty-four acre campus of Nebraska Wesleyan the Baldwin-Pitcher Tract yielded the 400 acre townsite which would build around the school. Although there was no village prior to Wesleyan's creation, the first settler was Agusta Harris who arrived in 1874. While logic would tell us the first church should have been Methodist, in fact there was a frame Baptist church on what would become 47th and Cleveland which was later cut in half and moved to two other sites for small buildings, neither of which survives. Although the first post office, under postmaster W. Gage Miller, was opened February 12, 1889 as Athens, the town had been

On August 30, 1888 a group of over 200 met at what had been the Hawley cornfield to dedicate Nebraska Christian University at Bethany Heights. The men shown atop the building reported being able to see downtown Lincoln and the beginning of Nebraska Wesleyan's first building to the northwest.

incorporated as University Place by Dr. Creighton and forty-four others. The discrepancy in names appears lost in time but on July 30 the Athens post office became University Place and there were enough houses to accommodate the women students, a problem following the early decision not to build dormitories. The city's incorporation specifically forbade saloons, pool halls, horseshoe playing on Sundays and movies unless shown outdoors in the park. A trolley line to Lincoln was soon completed running east on St. Paul Street through sunflower fields west of the village to a turnaround on 49th Street.

Businesses, beginning with a two-story grocery store that was also a post office on the northwest corner of 48th and Madison grew with the development of the village.

The first Methodist church services were conducted by Dr. Creighton on November 18, 1888 for nine women and nine men who met in an unfinished room in Old Main. Lots had been provided for the church across the street from the campus but because the priority was on the school, its construction was delayed. By roofing the basement, what the parishioners jokingly called the Hole-in-the-Ground Church was opened in 1903. Nearly every time additional funds for the church accumulated, a greater need for them arose at the university resulting in a delay in the church's ultimate completion which was December 12, 1909. The 1,500 seat First Methodist Church

was soon noted as having the "largest congregation in Nebraska." The village and the community grew simultaneously until "The Holy City nigh unto Bethany" was annexed with its 4,112 population to Lincoln in 1926.

Bethany Heights

"WITH THESE ARTICLES AS A BASIS OF ORGANIZATION I SEE NO REASON WHY ALL DONATIONS OR GIFTS MADE TO [COTNER] UNIVERSITY SHOULD NOT BE THE SAFEST OF FOUNDATIONS. THEY HAVE A BUSINESS RING TO THEM."

In 1884 the Christian Church of Nebraska established Fairfield College at Fairfield, Nebraska. By its third year the school had an

Chancellor of Cotner University, Dr. William Prince Aylsworth and Mrs. Aylsworth at their home on the corner of Hiram and Maxfield Streets in Bethany Heights.

enrollment of 137, its high point. The school was, as its historian stated, "doomed to failure." At the same time Fairfield's prospects waned, a group of over twenty Lincoln businessmen, who had each pledged from 5 to 85 acres, offered the Baptist Church 200 acres of land east of the city for the development of a denominational school. The plan was supplemented by the incentive that even by giving several hundred acres of land, the adjacent and surrounding property would increase in value many times over the owners' purchase price if the university succeeded and a town developed.

The Baptists however declined as they were already supporting one school and felt a second would be uneconomical. The Lincoln group, which included J. Z. Briscoe and Dr. Bartlett L. Paine, then made a similar offer to the Nebraska Christian Missionary Society. The Christian Church's

The first Bethany Heights School faced west on the southwest corner of then Fairfield and Canton Avenues, now Fairfax and 67th Streets. The entire southwest corner of the block was occupied by the Rowland Lumber and Coal Co.

board, which interestingly included William Prince Aylsworth, President of Fairfield College and J. Z. Briscoe, then received another offer from a separate group which proffered 500 acres of land west of Lincoln at Hawthorne. After negotiations, the original group's offer was increased to 321 acres plus eighteen Lincoln lots which they valued at $4,000. This offer was accepted and what had been the Hawley cornfield five miles east of Lincoln was chosen for the twenty acre campus. The name chosen for the community was Bethany Heights after their church's first American college in West Virginia.

O. C. Placey of Chicago, who had also submitted plans for Nebraska Wesleyan University, was chosen as architect for a fee of $1,000. The basement was excavated and foundation begun by Thomas Price & Co. in May of 1888 with sufficient construction completed that summer that a cornerstone laying celebration could be planned for August 30. The Christian Missionary Board, which was meeting in Lincoln, and many area church members left the downtown depot at about 10:00 AM, some going by private carriage but the bulk taking the Missouri Pacific Railroad to Newman's Station, the closest rail stop, which today would be at the southwest corner of 66th and Vine Streets. Those who took the train then walked a bit over a mile north to the new campus. Some climbed to the top of the uncompleted building where they reported a vast panorama with the uncompleted building of Nebraska Wesleyan to the northwest while others wandered about the campus area. The group then walked about six blocks to the north where there was a small grove of trees for a picnic lunch. This area would later be the east terminus and turnaround for the Omaha, Lincoln & Beatrice Railroad and later still a

A bird's eye view of the village of College View in about 1897 looking to the northwest probably from the hill at about 54th and Pioneers Blvd. The just-completed 1894 Seventh Day Adventist Church is at the left and the four-building campus of Union College is at the right.

transformer site for the Lincoln Electric System. The party then returned to the campus for the official 1:00 PM cornerstone laying. Following the speakers, singing and ceremony C. C. Pace, a Lincoln auctioneer held a lot sale to help establish land prices in the new village and raise funds for the school. Thirty-nine lots, each fifty by one hundred feet, were sold for a total of $8,315. Then E. T. Gadd announced that all lot prices would increase by 20 percent on September 1.

Nebraska Christian University's classes started in the Demarest house on September 30, 1888 with thirty students enrolled. The building was completed about a month later and was described as four stories plus full basement, 135 feet high to the top of the spire and constructed of Milwaukee cold pressed brick and stone. Inside were thirty-two classrooms, seven offices, a 500-seat chapel, library and study hall. Six hundred trees purchased from former Governor Furnas' nursery in Brownville were planted on the grounds, which covered twenty acres or eight square blocks running from today's Aylsworth Street on the south, Cotner Blvd. or 66th Street on the west, Colby Street on the north and 68th Street on the east. Briscoe offered the new university a "chair" in Bible studies, which he would finance with $25,000 in interest bearing securities, Lincoln real estate or sixty-five lots in Bethany at the choice of the trustees. In hindsight their choice of the Bethany lots was perhaps not the wisest.

In 1890 six Lincoln physicians established an autonomous medical college which opened on the University's fourth floor. The medical school soon outgrew the building and was moved to Lincoln as the Lincoln Medical College, ultimately

This turn of the century post card looks west on Prescott Street, named for W. W. Prescott the first president of Union College. To the right is the band shell, later moved east after being struck by a car, a windmill in the center of the intersection sited optimally for fire fighting and a public horse trough. Looking carefully past the windmill St. Thomas Orphanage at 27th and Prescott is just barely visible on the horizon. As noted on the card, this intersection was then known as 11th and L Streets.

Judging by the size of the trees west of
Nebraska Wesleyan's first, and extant, building,
this photo was probably taken about 1890, two
years after the building was dedicated and the
first classes inaugurated. Today only the absent
bell, a bit of the clock tower and considerable
added landscaping would look much different.

graduating nearly 300 physicians. While in Lincoln, the medical college also spawned a dental college which ultimately folded into the University of Nebraska's Dental College.

In 1890 the virtually new school faced a slow down, precedent to a depression and an examination of their finances shows they were operating mainly by selling real estate. When lot sales faltered some of the original purchasers reneged on their payments. At first the board attempted to rent the land out for farming. Samuel V. Cotner, a banker and businessman in Omaha and Briscoe's brother-in-law bought fifty-five acres of land in Bethany for $12,000 which was given to the university, divided into lots and offered for sale at a total of $40,000. In thanks for the gift, which it was supposed would save the university, Nebraska Christian University was renamed Cotner University on April 28, 1890. Up to the time of the Cotner gift, $100,295 worth of school land had been sold. With things looking better, the trustees built a sixteen-room women's dormitory just east

of the campus for $4,373. Pressure from the nation's economy however was bearing down as the recession deepened. Lot sales stopped at the same time $250 lots from two years previous were valued at $25 while crop failures meant parents could no longer afford tuition, causing enrollment to plummet as well. Chancellor A. E. Jennings reported in 1894 that although school property was valued at $312,000, it was useless in paying expenses. Still the depression worsened. The Board of Trustees armed themselves with shotguns in hopes of preventing an Omaha bank from seizing the school for a $50,000 loan upon which they had called. The telephone was disconnected to save the $10 per month bill.

Mr. F. M. Call of St. Louis, who had earlier considered a $50,000 gift, was contacted. After much discussion Call agreed to give the school $50,000 to be secured by all the institution's property and

renaming the school Call University. If the university was then able to raise a separate $50,000 endowment, he would forgive the entire loan and return the property. All creditors agreed but literally at the eleventh hour Mr. Call retracted the offer. In 1896 William Prince Aylsworth accepted the presidency when Cotner's assets were listed at over $313,000 and liabilities at just under $100,000. With only seventy-five students, things did not look bright but Aylsworth proved to be a magician. By convincing most of the faculty to remain for as little as $10 a month, refinancing the numerous loans by one fourth and raising contribution monies, Aylsworth announced on April 1, 1900 that Cotner University had been redeemed.

In 1929, not only had a gymnasium with a removable stage been built just east of the original building, nearly 200 acres of land near Estes Park, Colorado had been secured and buildings completed there for a summer school campus. Of course, 1929 was the best of times precedent to the ruinous

Union College, College View, Nebr.

By the 1920s Union College's Main Building housed offices and gymnasium in the basement, classrooms on the first floor, chapel and library on the second with museum and chemical laboratory on the third floor. Behind the building, to the east, is the then new 100 foot steel, 60,000 gallon water tower which was supplemented by an earlier water tank in the main building's tower.

times to come while, flush with expectations, the school's $35,000 endowment was used for the Colorado expansion. University President, L. C. Anderson issued two announcements in June of 1933. The first was the school's closure to protect its assets and the second was his resignation. Cotner College left its original campus but reopened in 1946 opposite the University of Nebraska's agriculture campus at 35th and Holdrege and later built a new brick building across from Love Library on R Street in 1954. This building was sold to the University of Nebraska with the proceeds used to fund a Chair of Religion in the University's Philosophy Department while the Cotner Commission on Continuing Education live on at 20th and R Streets.

William The Conqueror Sisley's house sits on College Avenue, now South 48th Street, across the street west from the Union College campus. Behind this house, Sisley's barn served as a boarding house for workmen at the school as well as the first Seventh Day Adventist church services. The house was a "demonstration" project for craftsmen and contractors interested in building the new college. Now in its third owner, the house looks much as it did when built in 1890.

With the birth of Nebraska Christian University, Bethany Heights was laid out with its 100 foot wide main street named Saunders in honor of Governor Alvin W. Saunders. Other streets carried the names of Christian universities viz. Drake, Canton, Hiram and Lexington. The village grew around the school and its post office opened January 6, 1890 in what was known as North Bethany three blocks north of the university through which the O.L. & B. Railroad ran. South Bethany, three blocks south of the university also had a trolley car line and in later years would assume the post office in its block-long business district on the west side of Saunders, across from Bethany School.

On March 19, 1925 Bethany, having dropped the "Heights" from its name, signed the contract to pave Saunders Avenue with asphalted concrete in a straight line from Adams south to Holdrege Street. It then took the old mill stream course on a diagonal path to the southwest where the stream emptied into Dead Man's Run in the edge of Bethany Grove, a park made from a corner of Samuel Cotner's fifty-five acre gift to the University. The new paved street opened with a parade on September 29, 1926 and it was announced that they hoped the paving would ultimately connect Havelock Avenue to the north and O Street to the south.

Although Bethany had sought annexation to Lincoln from about 1921, it was necessary to wait until University Place voted to join Lincoln, as annexation over a non-annexed area could not be considered. Thus Bethany's 1,078 population and city assets became a part of Lincoln in 1926 and today is seamlessly surrounded by the capital city on all sides.

Havelock

"IN DRY LINCOLN [THERE WERE] NO CASES OF INTOXICATION AMONG THE STUDENTS REPORTED, EXCEPT A VERY FEW DUE TO HAVELOCK."

Before the city of Havelock existed there was almost a village named Newton. Newton's plat was filed on October 5, 1870 and though some references say this was the ultimate site of Havelock, Newton actually sat astraddle the Burlington & Missouri River Railroad two miles northeast of Havelock at milepost 534, thirty minutes from Lincoln and twenty-five minutes from Waverly. The nearly 1,000-acre, 701 lot townsite was owned by real estate developer and later Mayor of Lincoln, Lt. Governor of Nebraska and member of the state legislature, Robert Emmet Moore. Harrison Johnson's 1880 History of Nebraska rather over optimistically or perhaps confusing Newton with Waverly, said that Newton had "about 200 inhabitants, good school and church advantages, several stores and mechanics shops."

It is quite certain that Newton existed only as a tiny frame depot building and was merely a whistle or "demand" stop on the railroad because in 1875 Newton's plat was vacated under a legislative act that specified no lots had ever been sold. The siding and depot remained however until 1890 when the building was moved southwest and became Havelock's first depot. About the only happening in Newton occurred on the 4th of July, 1870 when the Burlington ran a special train to Newton, the western end of the line. From there the party from Plattsmouth was transferred to wagons and carriages and paraded into Lincoln for a dinner which was hoped to signal the Burlington's arrival at the capital city. Lincoln had to wait three weeks for the tracks to be completed and for the official entrance to the city.

In 1886 Burlington Vice President Albert E. Touzalin of Omaha along

Havelock's Main Street with The Havelock, the first or second business building in the village is shown here as Baker's Pharmacy and today is the site of the Joyo Theatre. The double-brick building to the east was the second post office, the first having been in postmaster George G. Smith's dry goods and barber shop known as The Havelock whose sign still shows as a ghost in this 1900s photo.

EPISCOPAL DIOCESAN SCHOOL FOR BOYS AT LINCOLN · NEB · J.H.CHMMONS ARCHITECT · OMAHA NEB ·90·

Architect J. H. W. Hawkins' rendering for Trinity Hall the building for the Nebraska Military Academy, later Worthington Academy named for Episcopal Bishop Worthington. When completed in 1892 the building's front, as pictured, faced to the southeast.

with Burlington land agents John D. MacFarland and John R. Clark, purchased the Miller Tract and another parcel of land totaling about three square miles bordering on today's 48th Street, Adams Street, 70th Street and Salt Creek. They then transferred the property to the Lancaster Land Co. and filed the plat of Havelock on June 30, 1887. Touzalin, who had immigrated from England as a boy, named the site for his boyhood hero, British Major-General Sir Henry Havelock the hero of the Battle of Lucknow, India. The land company's plan was to then offer the Burlington 300 acres near the center of their land free of charge if the railroad would agree to place a repair facility there which would ensure their surrounding land would be worth many times their purchase price as a community grew around the shops. On June 3, 1890 the original plat was vacated and a new one filed which showed the railroad's roughly sixteen square block site in the center.

Within a few months the old Newton depot had been moved to about 60th and Burlington Streets in Havelock. About the same time George Grant Smith opened a frame dry goods store combination barber shop on the northeast corner of 61st and Havelock Avenue and W. J. Johnson built a hardware store directly across the street on the southeast corner of the intersection. On December 31 Smith opened the Havelock Post Office in his store and it was reported that there were at least five families living in the new city.

As the Plattsmouth, Nebraska shops of the Burlington Railroad became overtaxed and further and further from the western edge of the line, officials began looking for sites for new facilities. With the grant from Lancaster Land Co. the railroad approved $275,000 for construction at Havelock. Ground breaking with

Burlington General Manager George W. Holdrege was held in June of 1890 and the first 400 by 130 foot, two-story, brick and glass-roofed building began. On June 3, 1892 work on damaged locomotives was started along with the construction of two more buildings. By 1898 over 400 men were employed at Havelock and 262 locomotives had been repaired or rebuilt. As more and more work was sent to Havelock the payroll grew apace and by 1908 the Havelock shops were valued at $2.5 million and considered the largest railroad works west of the Missouri River. Over the years many more buildings and employees were added and the railroad became the Burlington Northern & Santa Fe Railway but virtually all of the original buildings still stand and are in use.

In 1922 the Burlington Shops and the city of Havelock experienced a strike which affected both to an unexpected extent, stopping the city in its tracks. With the beginning of WWI all of the nation's railroads were nationalized for the war effort but with the end of hostilities they were returned to their original private ownership. Because railroad wages had dramatically risen during the war the federal government established the Railroad Labor Board one of whose duties was to regulate and adjust pay scales downward to meet the national levels. On July 1, 1921 wages were reduced by 12 percent and time and a half for overtime was eliminated. That December the railroad itself announced that forty hour work weeks would be instituted to avoid massive layoffs. Meantime the nation's coalminers had gone on strike which in turn forced the Burlington to close the shops for ten days. This had an instantaneous effect on the local labor force and Havelock. The unions were quick to react when the railroad did not stop the wage cuts. The unions called for a strike on June 28, 1922 taking a reported 400,000 men nationally and 3,593 in Nebraska out on strike. The railroad responded that the men were striking because the federal railroads were simply enforcing regulations and that the railroad was powerless to act under these federal regulations. They also announced that any employees who returned to work by July 10 would not loose any benefits or seniority but those who did not report back by that date would have no rights or privileges as employees.

As tempers rose the U. S. District Court issued a restraining order preventing railroad employees from interfering with the railroad's operation but rallies and picketing continued uninterrupted. Burlington General Manager W. F. Thiehoff arrived in Havelock for a press conference at which he hinted at the possibility of

Havelock's Ballard Field is shown here October 29, 1929 with the Havelock Engineers playing Teachers' College High School. That night initiated the first electric "lighted stadium west of the Missouri River" and made Havelock the third high school in the U. S. to have night football. With 2,600 watching Havelock squeaked by Teachers' High thirty-one to zero.

Nearly twenty years after Worthington Academy's Trinity Hall exploded in 1898 the then picnic grounds still had huge pieces of stone, thousands of bricks and jumbles of pipe as the lone remnants of the school planned as "a monument that will live forever." Today the rubble survives, much of it covered by decades of grass, trees and underbrush.

One of the last visible remnants of the once vast industrial complex of West Lincoln stood southwest of the current Pfizer Drug Company facility until the land was cleared for potential development about 2000.

simply closing the entire Havelock shop while moving the operation to Denver and expanding it. President Harding saw commerce grind slowly toward a halt and threatened to renationalize the railroads if the conflict could not be brought to an acceptable closure. When the unions again did not agree, a federal restraining order was issued and the possibility of Nebraska National Guard troops being brought in was considered. By September 14, thirty-five of the nation's railroads, but not the Burlington, settled with their employees.

With a large percentage of Havelock's families having no income businesses were pushed to the limit of extending credit and several of the city's churches even folded; still the local strikers refused to return to work. Meantime the brass foundry at Plattsmouth had been moved to the Havelock shops and even though the union had not agreed to anything many had returned to work. The railroad, the newspapers and unions all had varying reports on how many had returned to work. The union said most of the workers were still out on strike while the railroad said that less than seventy-five were still out. Now, some eighty-five years later, it appears the strike was never officially closed and may well represent the longest outstanding strike in the nation's history even though few, if any, of the strikers are still alive.

After the city of Havelock's incorporation in 1893 the balance of the Lancaster Land Company's unsold lots had been purchased by Lincoln's Woods Brothers Company with the intention of developing the city into a major industrial center. To supplement the railroad's large facility and payroll the Woods Brothers Silo & Manufacturing Company approached the A. G. Hebb Automobile Company of Lincoln and offered them a triangular tract adjacent to the Burlington's main line tracks if they would consolidate their three plants

Few photographs remain of the short-lived Lincoln Normal School which stood southwest of the southwest corner of 56th and South Streets. This steel engraving shows the stone and brick building which faced west. Its front door would have been close to the current main entrance to the Madonna Rehabilitation Hospital.

The "Normal Loop" was a circular terminus of the street railway which ran southeast along the current Jim Ager Junior Golf Course, turned east on South Street and terminated as shown at about 52nd and Newton Streets. Barely visible to the south is Union College to which the tracks were briefly extended a few years later.

In November of 1939 the burning of University Place's Jackson High School gymnasium exacerbated the school's already crowded conditions and hastened the need for Northeast High School which would replace it as well as Bethany and Havelock High Schools.

Merlyn C. "Doc" Mayo, who graduated from Nebraska Wesleyan in 1923, opened his drug store complete with soda fountain at 48th and St. Paul Streets the year after he graduated. Within months it became The place for students to gather. After nearly fifty years, the soda fountain closed but lived on when it was given to the new campus Student Union.

into one new building in Havelock. In 1918 Hebb accepted the offer and began construction of a $150,000, two-story, brick, 160,000 square foot factory. In order to finance the building a large block of company stock was authorized. The Woods companies bought a large block and encouraged the people of Havelock to invest as well, predicting the population of the city would increase by 1,000 immediately and reach 25,000 by 1930. The stock was offered to local investors at $50 a share for each $100 of stock, a deal almost too good to refuse. The Havelock Post editorialized that the stock was offered at the reduced price to "distribute some of the guaranteed earnings to people who are in daily touch with its advancement." It was also opined that fifty new houses would have to be built by local craftsmen and the factory would be a natural magnet for even more industry.

Although demand for trucks, which were the Hebb's major product, was predicted to rise dramatically with the end of WWI, quite the opposite occurred just as production began in 1919 on three models. As Hebb became unable to pay its outstanding bills a new corporation was formed called the Patriot Motor Works with new sets of accounts payable constructed at the same time. Many locals as well as suppliers were increasingly skeptical with some original creditors not only uninterested in charging more materials to the old company in new clothing but

several asked the courts to judge both corporations bankrupt. When the bankrupt facility was put up for auction the Woods Brothers Company bought the building for $110,000 with stockholders ultimately recouping about $0.10 on their $1 of investments.

The Woods then began manufacturing their own trucks in the same building. In 1927 the Aircraft Company was incorporated with offices in downtown Havelock and production at the old Hebb plant along side of the trucks. Truck production faltered but aircraft building prospered and by 1929 it was announced that the 700 employees, building four airplanes per day were at work in the largest aircraft production facility in the world! Obviously, 1929 was the best of times and the beginning of the worst of times and with the Great Depression, even though they had orders on hand for 260 airplanes, the Woods realized they would prove unsaleable if built. Production was lowered to about one airplane per month. The main employees kept busy running a welding school in the building while they waited out the depression.

Arrow Aircraft was meantime busy trying to figure out how to build airplanes cheaper so they could be sold to a larger market. In 1935 Lewis Imm and their engineers perfected an airplane incorporating a Ford V-8 automobile engine, mounted backwards and geared down two-to-one, which could be purchased for $57, a fraction of the air-cooled aircraft engines they had been using. The Ford powered Arrow Sport was approved for production by the U. S. Bureau of Air Commerce, the first such approval for an automotive engine

for aircraft. The result was that now an airplane could be sold for $1,500, nearly half the price of the earlier models. Price was the advantage, the disadvantage was the weight of the cast block which tipped the scales at 402 pounds before the liquid coolant was added. Pilots reported the Sport took off and flew beautifully but when the stick was slightly pushed forward the plane took on a "brick-like glide" scarring even the most intrepid until they mastered the small problem. Ultimately they were able to trim nearly 150 pounds from the weight but the problem remained, just on a smaller basis. As the workforce increased the Woods manufactured over 120 of the Ford-powered Arrow Sport V-8 model G planes from 1936 to 1938. The Woods, ever looking for new markets, landed a contract to manufacture parts for the Boeing Company and took on new east coast partners to finance the necessary expansion. When Boeing reneged due to perceived shipping problems arguments ensued with the lenders resulting in yet another sheriff's sale of the property and the end of aircraft production in Havelock in 1940. After leasing the building during WWII the plant, at 4133 North 56th Street, was purchased and expanded by the Goodyear Rubber Company which continues to manufacture products in the old Hebb Truck Company building. It is still readily visible along the east front.

By the late 1920s a group of Havelock businessmen and the local Lion's Club recognized that many of the city's fathers had never seen their sons play in a football game since so many worked days and all of the games were in the afternoon. The obvious solution was to schedule the games at night, a time beneficial to both. All that was needed was a means of lighting Ballard Field. With donations and fundraising, the group was able to purchase ten fifty foot poles lighting the field with over 40,000 candle power. The first game was held at 8:00 Wednesday October 29, 1929 with the Havelock Engineers defeating the Teacher's College High team thirty-one to zero. After experimenting with variously painted balls to make them more visible at night they ultimately decided on dark balls with a spiral of white. To make a dramatic opening to each game an Arrow Sport took off from Sias Field, dropped low over the field and threw out a football. The plane then returned to the airfield where automobiles were parked adjacent to the runways to light their way home. Amidst little fanfare in Havelock it was later discovered that this represented the third high school in the United States to have night football and

the first field west of the Missouri River to be illuminated. The Lincoln Star wrote that Ballard field "has almost everything found in major university plants…enclosed gridiron, public address system,… press box and now floodlights." Coach W.H. Browne of Lincoln High School however refused to let his players participate in games at Havelock as "the night air is bad for youth."

The city of Lincoln had been looking northeast for some time, yearning for the exceptional tax base provided by the Burlington Railroad as well as other industrial businesses. It was said that the tax base available for the Havelock schools was as high as any city its size in the U. S., another point not missed by Lincoln. Local polls showed Havelock thought nothing could be gained by joining Lincoln but many were impressed by the promises of better police and fire protection as well as lower taxes.

After months of squabbling brought on by University Place businessmen and Nebraska Wesleyan administrators who feared students would be wooed by Havelock's taverns, the two communities were linked together and to Lincoln by completion of a trolley line in July of 1898. Here the trolley is shown coming back from Havelock, headed south on then Warren Avenue, now North 48th Street.

A trial ballot published by the Times-Post showed the annexation question failing but over 400 petitions were signed asking that the question be put to an official vote. On April 1, 1930 annexation was approved 1,063 to 663 by the Havelock voters and, as was then the law, the voters of Lincoln approved the merger on September 15, 1930. At the last Havelock City Council meeting they approved destruction of portions of the city's official minutes by the City Clerk and the council was "adjourned forever" by Mayor Paul Karnes.

Almost at once Havelock changed while the Times-Post urged citizens to "put forward their best foot and remember good manners…when we go to live with Auntie Lincoln." Someone should have asked Lincoln to do the same. At noon on October 15, 1930 all Havelock city property including the schools, parks, fire department, police department, cemetery, library and records were transferred to Lincoln. As changes started a petition asked the Lincoln City Council to "do what they know the city of Havelock would have done" and not put a water well in the Havelock city park. On December 4 a contract was let for the well without comment from the City Council. Havelock was also astounded to watch as the new park department coolly arrived and dismantled the lights from Ballard Field, moving them to the city tennis courts on South Street and even, according to some reports, a few to the Lincoln High School Oval. The Lincoln Board of Education also announced in December that "the playing of football games at night is contrary to the Lincoln Board of Education…night football is out as far as Havelock is concerned." Even the usually even-tempered Times=Post was infuriated pointing out that nearly 100 percent of the town had been showing up at

home games. Havelock High School responded by announcing that it would play Jackson (University Place) High School the following Friday night. Absolutely no response came but the game did not take place and it is safe to assume that if the annexation question had arisen at that point there would not have been one vote in its favor.

Within months the long-standing and promised beat policeman in Havelock had been removed to be replaced with an off-duty officer paid for by the Havelock businessmen. The post office closed and reopened as a branch of Lincoln; the street names were replaced with Lincoln's grid system; an occupation tax was implemented; the high school had been stripped of much of its chemistry and physics equipment; questions were ignored by the Lincoln city council and the streetcar lines were abandoned.

The Joyo Theatre began life in 1912 on the south side of Havelock Avenue. The Lyric, shown below, was built on the northeast corner of 60th and Havelock Avenue (then 12th and O Streets) in 1928 by my great uncle Volney Headrick. In 1936 the owner of the Joyo bought the Lyric and moved his theatre and its name to its present location. Although the barber shop, ticket booth and marquee have been altered and recreated, the auditorium is little changed.

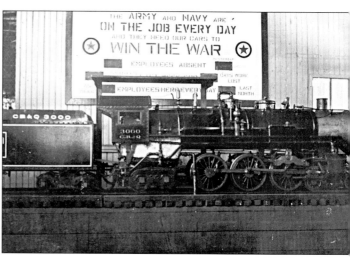

The "temporary" gymnasium at Nebraska Wesleyan was built in 1911 just southeast of the smokestack which still stands. The barn-like board and batten structure seated 600 and even had electric lights. Shown here about 1920 the gym also served doubled duty as a tabernacle where revival meetings were held every summer. The temporary gym served, with enlargements and a brick veneer, for over forty years.

During World War II the employees of the Havelock Shops recorded production, attendance and war work progress on a board behind a scale model steam locomotive.

The Lancaster Block was built in 1890, three years before Havelock was incorporated, by the Lancaster Land Company as a show of confidence in the village's success. The street level stores had a variety of tenants, one of which was usually a grocery store. The second floor, later apartments, had a dance floor, sometimes used for roller skating and the Union Hall which was the headquarters for striking Burlington employees in 1922. Renovated in 1988, the building is on the National Register of Historic Places and is in the heart of the Havelock Neighborhood, also listed on the Register.

Havelock's citizens openly talked about seceding while knowing it was obviously an impossibility.

The ink on annexation was barely dry when Lincoln began discussing the possibility of a new high school incorporating the old systems in Bethany, University Place and Havelock with one obvious intention of drawing the former communities together and making them more a part of Lincoln. With the exception of Havelock the other two high schools were badly overcrowded and in need of replacement. The Lincoln Superintendent of Schools announced in 1931 that a new high school, equidistant from the three existing buildings would be built on a thirty acre tract at 63rd and Adams which would also provide unrestricted areas for football, baseball, track with spectator seating and adequate parking. A flyer was circulated to students at all three schools asking them to submit ideas for the new high school's name which could not feature a person associated with one of the former suburbs,

a street name or a name that "merely suggests its location, as north [or] east." An area minister suggested HUB High school with H for Havelock, U for University Place and B for Bethany. Cooler heads prevailed and the students came up with Pershing High School, a name associated with Lincoln but none of the villages. The city declined saying that their intention was to honor General Pershing by naming the new city auditorium, which would replace the one destroyed by fire in 1928. The new Pershing Municipal Auditorium did not come into being however until 1958. Meantime the board ignored their own dictates and took on the naming themselves using Northeast High School, almost exactly the name they said they "would not be likely to give favorable consideration."

Years went by as the new school was discussed and plans refined. In 1938 federal officials urged Lincoln to apply for a 45 percent, $270,000 grant from funds appropriated by Congress and allocated through the Public Works Administration.

Literally thousands of letters, wires, phone calls and trips to Washington ensued culminating in Lincoln voters approving a bond issue to pay the local portion. In March the PWA returned the request "without approval." Even with the apparent loss of federal funding the firm of Davis & Wilson was chosen as general architect and a second bond issue was approved April 9, 1940. Contracts were let on September 24, 1940 and Olson Construction Company began almost immediately with an estimated completion of August 15, 1941, scarcely a year hence.

At about 2:00 PM on October 17, 1940 each of the three existing high schools sent their bands marching towards the construction site for the official cornerstone laying ceremony. After a decade in the planning, Northeast High School was ready for its first class of 1,037

This 1900 northward view of the Havelock Shops shows the erecting shop at left and blacksmith shop to the right, virtually the entire facility at that point in time. Both structures are extant.

students on September 1, 1941 even though adjacent streets were unpaved and no sidewalks had been constructed. As predicted the new high school was instrumental in bringing the three suburbs into Lincoln and bringing about a community spirit between them.

College View

"MAKE YOURSELVES AT HOME. STAY UNTIL YOU REALLY KNOW WHAT LINCOLN IS, AND IF YOU DO NOT DECIDE THAT THIS IS THE BEST POSSIBLE LOCATION FOR [UNION] COLLEGE, YOU ARE AT LIBERTY TO CARRY AWAY THE DOME OF THE STATE HOUSE TO ORNAMENT YOUR FIRST BUILDING, WHEREVER YOU MAY CHOOSE TO PUT IT."

Like the communities of Bethany Heights and University Place the suburb of College View was born with a denominational college. The first Seventh Day Adventist exposure in Lincoln occurred in 1885 when a tent meeting was held. Then in 1887 a four-story, fifteen room mission building was erected four blocks south of the state capitol, perhaps about where a Seventh Day Adventist church was later erected at 1505 E Street and replaced with an extant church at 1020 South 15th Street, though not now occupied by the Adventists.

The first Adventist school in the region opened in a Minneapolis church basement at 4th and Lake Streets in 1888 with four teachers and eighty students. As this site became cramped, what was first called the Western School and later, as suggested by W. W. Prescott, Union College, was proposed as a joint venture, or union, to build a school to serve the area between the Mississippi River and the Rocky Mountains. The specific proposal was first published with the new name on February 4, 1890. The committee immediately received offers from Des Moines and Atlantic, Iowa, Wichita, Kansas and the Nebraska cities of Lincoln and Fremont and although Omaha later stated they were interested, no bid was forthcoming. Through balloting the list was pared until only Lincoln remained, partially because the offers from the community were perceived as better and additionally because the diversity presented by the several existing colleges and normal schools were felt to extend a more open accceptance of a denominational educational institution and religious community. Four sites near Lincoln were initially considered: The May Site or Walton Farm to the southeast, the Taylor tract about where Eastridge would later develop, the Oyler Farm near Yankee Hill and Cushman Park west of Lincoln on A Street. The Taylor and May sites were visited and the 280 acre gift which included the Walton farm, also the May site which was given by J. H. McClay, was accepted. At that time, although sited, nearly all of the streets did not exist but were mere farm land. The only indication of where 48th Street would be placed was a locust hedge. One of the proposed land gifts was from Lincoln clothier, David May and his wife Tillie who intended a gift of twenty to thirty acres from their one hundred sixty acre tract to the west but wanted as much of their land, which lay directly east of the proposed campus, to face the school. The solution was for them to give a strip of land twenty feet wide and a half mile long running from Calvert Street on the north to Pioneers Blvd. on the south which explains why today's 48th Street jogs to the southwest at Calvert and back to the southeast at Pioneers to incorporate the May property.

The intention that land given to the school would cause adjacent property, still held by those who gave it, to increase in value held true. Within months of the college opening land which had sold for as little as $25 an acre was suddenly selling for as much at $3,000 after the college opened. The land cartel also promised the school that they would build a street railway to connect the school and village with Lincoln and that it would be in operation by school opening in September of 1890 but later extended to January 1891.

In 1889 the school hired William the Conqueror Sisley, an Adventist who had already worked on the construction of Battle Creek and Walla Walla Colleges, to prepare proposals for the new campus and buildings. Sisley, whose salary was not to exceed $3.30 a day, arrived in Lincoln, set up an office in the Burr Block at 12th and O Streets and moved into the Lincoln Hotel while he got initial plans ready. Joined by Enoc Jenkins, Sisley hired Mr. L. E. Koon to survey and draw the plat for the new village of College View which would surround the campus. As soon as John Gardner and John Morrison began selling lots Sisley bought property on the west side of 48th Street opposite the campus at what would today be 3919 South 48th Street. On the back alley behind this lot he built a barn which was completed about April 1, 1890 where he brought his family. It was

in this barn that Sisley lived and the first Adventist church services were held. Community meetings were held in the barn and many workers stayed until more houses were built. In order to determine the skills of various local builders and craftsmen Sisley invited them to demonstrate their trades by digging the basement, laying a foundation and ultimately completely building and finishing the two and a half story house which still stands as a sort of pattern house. The plan worked to perfection for Sisley as he not only ended up with a house which to this day is said to have no foundation cracks but cost him very little.

As the barn was built the Burlington & Missouri River Railroad constructed a siding spur and depot at about 49th Street for the college's use and within weeks ten carloads of stone had arrived for Sisley's use. In April and May of 1890 construction of the college's main building and South Hall were begun with anticipated completion scheduled for the end of the year. The 147 by 73 foot, three-story plus sunlight basement main building was dedicated on September 24, 1891 with a program attended by nearly 600 people and classes begun on the 30th of the month with 73 or 74 students which grew to about 300 by year's end. The school day opened in the chapel after which forty-five minute classes began as the students marched from the chapel, reportedly in silence.

The original proposal called for four separate schools within the college, each offering basically the same classes but in English, German, Swedish and Danish (Norwegian) in segregated

classes. The students were living in equally separate dorms, eating in separate dining rooms, even attending separate chapel services. This concept was carried out in the construction of North Hall as well which had Scandinavian and German sections which later were used as a sort of early day, coed dorm with the girls on the first two floors and the boys on the upper floors with separate staircases so that there was no actual connection between them. The top three floors had the famous rope tied to a radiator fire escape plan. Although the intent was to promote each group's culture and language while they were assimilating into English, it was not popular with students and dropped in the fifth year.

A five foot, 1,400 pound bell was purchased from Montgomery Ward for $85 and slowly the campus took shape. During the first year or two there were so few chairs that each student had one for his use and had to carry it from his room to the dining area and back. In 1894 electricity generated in the school's power house east of the main building replaced kerosene lamps but all electricity was shut off at 10:00 PM when lights out really meant it.

From the beginning students were expected to work at least one hour a day to help defray costs of room and board in addition to the paying $73 per month for tuition. This led from working in the dining rooms and laundry to college-owned industries starting with a broom factory in the basement of North Hall and expanding into a bakery, print shop, bindery, furniture factory and even the sale of a cereal known from its inception at Union College as Granola or

Dextro depending on where on the campus it was produced. By 1893 the school claimed that 90 percent of its students were working in one of the college-owned industries.

The recession of 1893 hit Union College just as it virtually closed Nebraska Christian (Cotner) University and Wesleyan and Union's enrollment dropped to 278. With North Hall nearly empty Union College leased the building to the Nebraska Sanitarium which had been located on the northwest corner of Bancroft and 49th Streets across the street from the campus. In 1905 the sanitarium, whose board included Dr. John H. Kellogg of Battle Creek, MI, purchased the hall for $17,000 but as they too faced hard times, ultimately sold it back to the school in 1921 for $65,000 and then became a girls' dormitory for the balance of its existence. Still things were tight and in 1923 the entire campus was offered for sale for $325,000 but there were no takers.

Obviously Union College has succeeded well beyond the dire expectations of 1923 and today the four-year coeducational college has nearly 1,000 students.

As the first lots were sold for $100 and up, the village of College View slowly took shape. And though, like Lincoln, there were virtually no trees with the exception of the locust hedge along the west edge of the campus and a few isolated cottonwoods, trees were planted. One of the first things the Lincoln group promised was to have a street railway running by the time the first classes were in session. In order to accomplish this, the line which ran east on Sumner was extended south on 30th Street to Prescott where it served St. Thomas Orphanage before turning east towards College View. Unfortunately there is a deep ravine at about 36th Street and the weak electric motors could not adequately get back up the east hill. The line did run in the summer of 1891 fulfilling the promise but it was far from what was expected. The following year the Normal Heights line which ran east on South Street to 52nd to serve Lincoln Normal University extended from its loop to Van Dorn then west to 48th Street and continued south into College View ending at the exact center of the original land grant at 48th and Prescott. This was termed the Low Line and when finished ended service on the old Prescott line to the west. In 1908 the Woods Brothers Citizens Interurban, also known as the High Line, was laid south on Sheridan Blvd. down the median of the boulevard serving the homes being developed along the top of the level ridge. When the cars got to the Rock Island Railroad overpass at

about 32nd Street those wanting to continue on into College View had to deposit an additional penny fare and the bridge became known as the Penny Bridge. This line then met Calvert Street and turned east, then south on 48th Street and also turned at 48th and Prescott. The Normal line ceased service in 1919 and the High Line along with the Randolph Line which connected Lincoln with Tabitha Orphanage at 46th and Randolph were the last two trolley lines in the city and terminated service on September 2, 1945.

Although Sisley's house and barn are usually conceded to be the first house and barn in the city both Mr. Jenkins and C. W. Miller claim to have built the first homes. The first store building in the village was Zalmon Nicola's store which also served as a post office, meeting hall, and church. In the back of the building, was Nicola's home first built on the southwest corner of 48th and Prescott. He knew that the business district would congregate around the trolley line and the center of the plat. In 1889 College View, named for the school and for the view from the hills, was incorporated as a village with first mayor honor going to either A. R. Henry, Joe Sutherland or J. D. Morton depending on how you define the office of mayor. The village library opened in Nicola's store in 1901 but the building and entire collection burned on the first day of service. A new brick building was then constructed on the northwest corner of the same intersection and because the old building had been insured, a new library was again tried in the back of the store. Sadly two years later another fire again destroyed both operations. This time, although again covered by insurance, it was thought more prudent to approach the Carnegie Corporation. In 1916 the new stone library on the southwest corner of the campus was opened with a gift of $7,500 from Carnegie with the provision from the college that the building and land would revert to the college should the building no longer be used as a library. With the building of Gere Library on 56th and Normal Blvd. the old Carnegie library was abandoned and reverted to Union College where it became the studios of radio station KUCV before it in turn became the flag ship station of the Nebraska Public Radio Network.

By March 13, 1893 the city had grown to over 1,000 allowing its reincorporation as a City of the Second Class. Sometime before the turn of the century vegetarianism became a popular tenant of the Seventh Day Adventist Church and among others Dr. Kellogg promoted the peanut as a source of protein to substitute for meat. Also it soon became a popular Sunday activity to take the trolley from Lincoln or even Havelock, Bethany or University Place to College View where a local merchant offered bags of roasted peanuts for a nickel. From these beginnings the village earned the sobriquet of Peanut Hill which can still be heard occasionally today. In 1919 College View claimed a post office, Carnegie Library, cemetery, waterworks, fire department and city hall. Still, the question about annexing with Lincoln had begun to be a topic of conversation. The college administration was opposed and voters did not approve the idea in 1923, 1925 or 1927, but in 1929 annexation carried the day 538 to 511 amidst the question of whether students who were realistically not permanent citizens, but agreed with annexation, should be able to vote. Still the vote held and on April 27, 1929 Lincoln voters approved and the 2,905 citizens of College became a part of Lincoln. Union Avenue became 48th Street to conform to Lincoln's numbering system and College Avenue became Prescott in honor of W. W. Prescott, Union College's first president.

Like Bethany, Normal Heights and University Place, College View has now been not only surrounded by the city of Lincoln but is almost absorbed. The campus, church and Adventist schools are the only islands noticeably extant.

After a decade of planning, but less than a year of construction, Northeast High School at 63rd and Baldwin Streets was opened for its first class of 1,037 students on September 1, 1941. This photo is probably dated about 1950 as the landscaping had begun to develop and the clock above the front door is visible.

[NORMAL] " IS…ONE OF THE MOST HEALTHFUL LOCATIONS…OF THE COUNTY…AN ABSOLUTE FREEDOM FROM FOGS, WITH ALMOST PERPETUAL SUNSHINE…ONE OF THE GARDEN SPOTS OF THE EARTH [WITH] A MARVELOUS SUPPLY OF PURE, SOFT WATER COMING FROM A GREAT DEPTH IN THE GROUND."

About 1890 the normal, or teacher's training school, at Shenandoah, Iowa burned to the ground. Fortunately at about the time the locale was saturated with teachers. J. F. Saylor, who had been associated with the school, joined with Franklin F. Roose who had twelve years of educating teachers to his credit, to form a new institute on thirty-five acres of land which had been secured east of Lincoln. E. R. Sizer and John McClay of Lincoln assisted in the project and platted a village they named Normal Heights to be established around the campus. Parts of the site were given by farmers like Artemus Roberts whose 160 acre farm was purchased for $2,880.00 from the Burlington & Missouri River Railroad in 1870 as the northwest quarter of Section 33 with four blocks in the new village donated to the scheme by each of four owners in May of 1892. When it appeared that the school idea would fail, Roberts gave an additional square block of lots which may have been matched by other donors but at any rate the project proceeded at that point. On today's map the area of the village would be approximately bounded by 40th, 48th, Sumner Streets with Normal Blvd. on the south with the business district centered at 56th and South Streets.

The architect for Lincoln Normal University was the same Artemus Roberts who had given land to the project. He would also, a few years later, be the architect for William Jennings Bryan's, Fairview which is still standing, almost completely surrounded by Bryan LGH East Hospital. William Jennings Bryan, of course, is Normal's most famous son. The foundation for the school would alone cost a staggering $20,000 while the main building is reported to have totaled $86,000 and built of stone from Colorado and Wisconsin and brick. By the time the school opened for its first classes in September of 1892 there were four buildings on the campus including the main building, a dormitory with dining hall, water, heating and electric plant. The college was advertised as covering "more floor area than any other normal," and offered forty different courses and departments and had room for 1,000 students. The basic course was for eight weeks which cost students only $24 and after which they were accredited and issued a state teacher's certificate. There was an obvious need for teachers in the still young state of Nebraska and the school reported that 700 students had signed up for the first term. In order to provide access to the school and village a street railway was extended from 27th and Sumner to South Street, then to 52nd Street in Normal Heights where it turned south and made a loop before returning back to Lincoln. In later years the track was extended to the south to connect with College View.

At 2:00 AM on December 1, 1898 a fire broke out in the main building and because the fire trucks from neighboring communities were unable to gain immediate access due to snow, the building was a complete loss by morning. Amidst rumors of arson, the administration promised classes would resume in the remaining buildings and the main building would be rebuilt as soon as possible. It was not to be, however.

Dr. Benjamin Franklin Bailey of New Hampshire arrived in Lincoln in 1886 and had his office and hospital in his home at 1347 L Street. By 1895 he had set up a hospital in a building erected by private interests at 1441 U Street as a dormitory but it proved too far from the campus and was secured by Dr. Bailey after a brief attempt by others to establish a boarding school there. In 1901 Dr. Bailey incorporated and purchased twenty-five acres of land which had been the old Lincoln Normal University. He then razed the skeleton of the main structure. What had been the Men's Dormitory and dining hall on the southwest corner of 56th and South Streets became the main hospital for Green Gales Sanitarium while a "rest cottage" for mental patients and those with communicable diseases was built to the southwest.

The new hospital, which could serve up to fifty-five patients, opened for business July 15, 1901 and had a staff of thirty-five with twenty-five nurses, some of which were enrolled in a nurses' training class and several staff physicians. Fees were quite simple: primary examinations were $5 to $10, rooms were $20 to $35 a week and visitors could stay in unoccupied patient rooms for $2 per day. There were also a number of rules which were strictly enforced including patients must furnish their own hot water bottles, bath robes and towels; guests known to gossip about other guests or staff would be immediately asked to leave and lights were turned out promptly at 10:00 PM. Dr. Bailey advertised "cheery evenings, music, library...not a hospital, not a hotel, but a home." In 1909 Dr. Bailey built a bungalow at about 54th and South and in 1936 some of the graduates from the old normal school asked him to give them the capstones from the building which he had used as garden ornaments in his garden. These stones were set in Roberts Park with a brass tablet and though the tablet is long gone, the carved stones still stand just southeast of the picnic shelter in the park as a monument to the school.

In 1942 the nursing school closed and after Dr. Bailey's death the 119-bed hospital, other buildings and campus were sold to the Benedictine Sisters who established the original Madonna Home, now Madonna Rehabilitation Hospital. The year, 1977 saw the last of the college buildings leaving only Dr. Bailey's bungalow and barn. Then in 2005 Dr. Bailey's house was razed leaving only the stones in Roberts Park as remnants of the original school, sanitarium, once described as the "largest, best-equipped and most beautifully furnished institution of its kind in the west" or Madonna site. Although the old Methodist Church at 54th and South, grade school on the southeast corner of 52nd and South and all of the business buildings are gone, about a dozen of the original administration and faculty houses can still be seen, extant in the area while street names like Saylor, Roose and Lillibridge serve as reminders of the old university.

In 1890 William Jennings Bryan purchased five acres of land at about 48th and South, near Normal Heights, the first of several tracts he would own in the area. Although he complained about having had to spend $250 an acre for the initial plot he said it was worth it being $100 for the scenery, $100 for the climate and $50 for the soil. About seven years later he bought thirty acres just north of Normal Heights and his wife Mary began conferring with Artemus Roberts about building a home on the "gently rising knoll" at about 49th and Sumner Streets. The Queen Anne brick and stone house cost nearly $20,000 and was described as being three stories high with twenty-five rooms and an entrance featuring two lions, "Radicalism" and "Conservatism." After living briefly in the barn while Fairview, sitting in its 350 acre farmstead, was completed, the family moved in on October 1, 1902, the Bryans' seventeenth wedding anniversary. Tours are now scheduled on an occasional basis or by phoning for opening hours.

In 1903 Artemus Roberts' son, James, who had graduated from Lincoln Normal University, purchased fifty acres of land on the north side of South Street, started a small dairy at 6200 South Street and began a milk route. The original farm was then used first as a fruit juice facility, then a cheese factory after transferring the property and business to Roberts Dairy. The farm building later served as a church, branch YMCA and lodge facility which was razed in about 2005 for a small subdivision of homes. Artemus' other son, Barton bought twenty-five acres along A Street for a truck garden about where Holy Trinity Episcopal Church now sits. A portion of the original Artemus Roberts property was given to the City of Lincoln as Roberts Park. In 1919 Normal, having quietly shed the "Heights" portion of its name, was uneventfully annexed adding its unrecorded population to Lincoln.

The Second Capitol is Built and Lincoln Becomes a

City
of the
First Cla

"The grinning imperfections of the [new] capitol are a perpetual illustration of the contractor's lively sense of the propriety—and privilege—of preserving congruity between the moral standard of letting, and the mechanical standard of performing the contract."

SS

Lincoln's first means of transportation was limited to foot and horse power but in 1870 J. D. MacFarland's Lincoln Street Railway was incorporated and in 1881 finally given right of way to lay rails for a horse-drawn railway. On November 1, 1883 Mr. Durfee was

busy breaking bronco ponies for the railway by training them to pull Car #4 up the hill from the depot to the Arlington Hotel on the southwest corner of 9th and Q, the steepest hill they would encounter when actual service began the following day. Suddenly riders were, for the price of a nickel, riding in comfort up Q, past the Arlington all the way to 13th and O Streets. At the end of 1883 there were 200 horses and thirty-seven street railway cars operating over eighteen miles of track in Lincoln and by 1887 there were three competing horsecar lines.

In 1887 an electric streetcar was perfected which received its power from a wire above the tracks, suspended from poles along the right of way. This clean, quiet, efficient development was introduced to Lincoln in 1891 by the Lincoln Electric Railway Company which still had horse-drawn competition from twelve other lines. The advantages of electricity quickly brought competition which in turn brought fierce protection as the cost of putting the new service into operation was considerably higher than horse-drawn systems. Battles arose where competing tracks crossed each other; tracks were sometimes laid by moonlight to avoid confrontation. Electricity supplied by Lincoln Traction Company was occasionally terminated without warning, and

bricks and stones were thrown between competing cars and the public began to agitate for consolidation. After carrying 110,000 passengers during the state fair week in 1894 the consolidation question became an easier decision as a depression set in with street railway failures closing lines which were bought up and the number of competing lines reduced. The primary heir was the Lincoln Traction Company which also built the Terminal Building on the southwest corner of 10th and O Streets in 1915 to 1916. The headquarters of the electric trolley lines with its bay window projecting above the north entrance from which lines running east and west on O Street as well as north on 10th Street could be monitored.

The last horsecar in Lincoln was the Lyman Street Railway which served the Belmont community and ended service in 1906. Busses, with their ease of changing routes with changing demand, began to appear in the 1920s and would have probably ended trolley service by the 1940s had not World War II prompted legislation forbidding the closure of electric trolleys during wartime when rubber tires and gasoline

Overleaf
Virtually no photographs exist of the early construction of Nebraska's second state capitol. This photo of the north entrance, probably taken in early 1888, shows the central section just completed with construction material still scattered around the grounds.

were strictly rationed. With the end of the war however the Sheridan Blvd. to College View and the Randolph line to Tabitha Home ceased service and the day of the bus had arrived.

Although the first state capitol was scarcely two years old in 1871, Governor Butler sent a message to N. K. Griggs, President of the Senate asking him to convey the message to both houses that if any of the elected were particularly stirred by the speeches of their compatriots, under no circumstances should they applaud or stamp their feet for fear the building might collapse. Amid claims that during heavy rains it appeared the supposed limestone was most probably nothing more than sandstone and was dissolving, new cries for removal of the capital to a more central site became more vocal. In 1873 repairs were approved in the amount of $5,897 to repair the roof and fix other deficiencies overlooked by the original contractor. Some claimed that because of "jobbery and corruption which had attended the state government and the construction of state buildings" that we got what we paid for with a capitol literally built from want-ads. Because "the University will fall down next year anyway; the capitol should be donated to Lincoln—the lower part for a livery stable." By 1875 several removal bills were even introduced with many cities and counties eager to get on the bandwagon; one provided that the new capitol should cost no more than $175,000 and governor's mansion no more than $25,000 with both sitting on land donated by the anointed city. The list of counties suggested boiled down to Adams, Buffalo, Colfax, Hall, Hamilton, Kearney, Merrick,

In 1915 William Sharp had consolidated the electric street railways in Lincoln. He then partnered with Charles Stuart, H. E. Sidles and others to build the Terminal Building for the new transit company. The ten story building, which took only nine months to complete, also housed a bank and an interior shopping center with fourteen store potentials on the first two floors facing an interior court area. This postcard is probably from the 1920s era.

Terminal Building,
Lincoln, Neb.

Platte and Polk but one by one the proposals failed or did not even get reported out of committee. Because the original building, though thought too large in its original plan, was also crowded an 1877 bill suggested a west wing be built but partially because of the existing problems an addition was felt inappropriate.

In 1879 Governor Garber noted that "for some time past the outer walls of the capitol had been considered unsafe" and an architects' report suggested the north wall was "in danger of falling down." After $777.98 was expended to temporarily rebuild the failing wall, the 8th Legislature then provided $75,000 to build a new west wing of a new capitol with William H. Wilcox hired as architect to be paid 1.5 percent of the contract price. Though uncompleted in 1881 the legislature granted an extension to September 1 of that year and authorized $100,000 for an east wing. Bids for the east wing were submitted by Butler & Krone, $98,490, Robert D. Silver, $86,400 and W. H. B. Stout, $96,800. When Stout was awarded the contract, J. Sterling Morton and the Democratic Party argued that by not awarding the contract to the lowest bidder it was "explicable only on the ground of corrupt political preference [because] his (Stout's) leased convict labor competed with free, honest labor."

By 1883 both east and west wings had been completed with the old building sitting "book ended" between the new construction which would have made an interesting photograph but if any were taken, none has ever been found. Wilcox's plans for the central section were approved at a cost not to exceed $450,000 and J. S. Gregory received salvage rights on the old building...if anything was worthy of salvage. On July 9, 1883 W. H. B. Stout won the completion bid for $439,187.25 with stone provided and cut by Mr. Tyler who had furnished the stone for the original 9th and O Street post office and his home at 808 D Street which, like the post office and old City Hall combined, still stands as a tribute to the quality of the new stone. The bid also contained the provision that the building be completed by December 1, 1889 which was financed by a three quarter mill levy for the years 1887 and 1888. Apparently Stout's bid was again not the lowest and Silver asked that the courts award him the contract but he was denied. A newspaper reported that "the best and worst that may be said is the denial of the writ met public expectation."

The new building was completed in 1889 and unlike the previous one, faced north and was centered on the original four-square-block tract which the legislature appropriated an additional $5,000 to hire a landscape gardener "to beautify." The engineer's report said the building was of masonry construction with wooden office framing and wood floors with the exception of the basement which was tiled with black and white marble laid up in a checkerboard pattern. Another reporter described the building as "of the Chicago or Minneapolis style of architecture... mixed with a little Greek." As well built as the legislature thought the new building was, by February of 1907 the northeast corner of the building reported settling which in turn caused plaster to fall, windows to break and the fear that this building too might be flawed.

The Nebraska Legislature appointed a five-person Abraham Lincoln Memorial Association in 1903 with a state-sponsored $5,000 challenge grant to design a suitable memorial for the president. Employing Matthew Brady photographs, New Hampshire sculptor Daniel Chester French's clay sculpture proposal was selected. In 1912 the bronze statue was dedicated and sited on the west side of the second capitol. Bertrand Grosvenor Goodhue, architect of the present capitol, suggested moving the statue to a plaza on the north side of the new building however it still sits at the west entrance of the present, third, state capitol as one of only three remnants of the previous building.

In 1887 the population of Lincoln had grown to 25,000, the point at which it could be reincorporated as a "city of the first class" as defined by the Nebraska legislature. One of the results of the reincorporation was the necessity of electing all new city officials even rehiring all of the city employees including the police department. The only exception was Police Judge Albert parsons who still had one year left on an unexpired term. Parsons, however, had incurred the wrath of a group of gamblers and ladies employed in what might be euphemistically termed associated businesses which technically and legally "had no right to exist." It was their contention that Parsons had been routinely "fining" them what might more accurately be called payoffs. These fines were collected in cash on a monthly basis with no bookkeeping or paper trails which, according to Parsons was an expedient which also saved court appearances, arrests and unnecessary paperwork. Of course there was also a lack of knowing exactly how much was collected, from whom and where the funds ended up. Specifically their claim was that $329 had been pocketed by Parsons instead of going into the proper city coffers.

The city council assigned a committee which agreed with the claim although Parsons alleged it was a mere oversight on his part due to a misunderstanding of the law. The council saw it differently and on September 29, 1887, declared the office of the judge vacated and set about hiring a replacement. Mr. Parsons, obviously out of a lucrative position, hired Lincoln attorney L. A. Burr, who applied to Hon. David Brewer, circuit judge of the U. S. Circuit Court in St. Louis, for a bill in equity. The court agreed that the council did not have

the proper authority to dismiss Parsons and issued a restraining order to stop the council. The council queried the city attorney G. N. Lambertson for guidance and they were assured that they were within their rights to fire the police judge and at the attorney's suggestion, they simply ignored the federal order. On October 8, 1887 Mr. Parson's attorney quite naturally informed the federal court of the city's intention to ignore the federal order. The court, like Mr. Parsons, was unamused. The federal response was to order the mayor and entire city council to appear at the U. S. Courtroom in Omaha before Judge Elmer S. Dundy On November 15 to show why they should not be held in contempt. Arrest warrants were issued for Mayor Andrew J. Sawyer and councilmen: L. W. Billingsley, Lewis Pace, Granville Ensign, William Cooper, Joseph Z. Briscoe, James Dailey, John Fraas, Robert Graham, Henry Dean, Fred Hovey, John M. Burks and Nelson C. Brock. The band appeared at the

This winter time view of the 10th and O Streets intersection, looking northwest, shows the then City Hall at left and the 1909, first third, of the new Post Office which was also the Federal Courthouse at right.

Omaha court as ordered and, after hearing both sides representation, the judge stated his court did have jurisdiction and although there was a small defect in the bill and some points in mitigation, heavy fines and not incarceration were in order against the council. Mayor Sawyer and councilmen Briscoe, Burks and Cooper were fined $50 each. The other eight were fined $600 each with all to be committed to custody until paid. Although councilman Ensign, confident they would be held blameless, had earlier promised to pay all fines personally, he was found to have only $10.13 in his possession.

The now not so merry band was marched to the sheriff's office and "Hotel De Bastile." The city's attorney Lambertson took the next train to Washington D.C. to make application to the U.S. Supreme court for a writ of habeas corpus. Jail proved to be the sheriff's own apartment but they were "held." The group, however, dined out and even attended plays in Omaha as the days passed. Mr. Lambertson meantime approached U. S. Attorney General Garland who, amazed that the entire council were incarcerated, put the prisoners in the charge of the U. S. Marshal's office and after six days imprisonment, released them on parole and the entire group was escorted back to Lincoln by a special train. Governor Thayer also petitioned President Cleveland who assured the governor he would intercede should the court find against them. Finally, on January 10, 1888 the mayor and council's actions were exonerated. The lower court was found to have acted without jurisdiction. The Democratic principal of Home Rule stood with great relief, not only in Lincoln, Nebraska but in every other local government across the nation.

Although Lancaster County had existed since 1859 little thought was given to having an actual courthouse on the block set aside for the county in 1867 between 9th, 10th, L and M Streets. What business the county transacted was housed, first in rented rooms, then the Hardenberg-Benadom two-story, cottonwood house at about 9th and Q Streets which the county purchased for $800. The jail, when one was needed, was housed in Langdon's milk house behind his 9th Street home. In 1871 a petition asked the county to issue bonds and build a proper courthouse and jail. Through the following years bond issues were approved and mill levies passed with no action. Finally, in 1887, the commissioners toured courthouses in five states and that July they settled on plans drawn by E. E. Myers & Sons of Detroit, Michigan. Bids were let but refused when the cost was more than intended. In May of 1888 Omaha architect F. M. Ellis' plans were approved and the bid of contractor, W. H. B. Stout was accepted. The jail, on the northwest corner of the block was completed first and on November 1, 1888 and the cornerstone for a 150 by 100 foot Berea, Ohio, completely fireproof building was laid. The only wood supposedly used was in window and door frames, doors and the cupola which held a statue of Abraham Lincoln at its peak. Sadly the supposedly copper Lincoln statue was found to be of lead and with the deterioration of the cupola both were removed, about the only changes in the building before it was replaced by the County-City Building in 1969.

In 1885 the unsuccessful experiment of M. C. Bullock of Chicago ended the attempt to commercially extract salt from the basins northwest of Lincoln, it had become far easier and considerably more economical to simply mine salt from caves in Kansas. The land in the old salt flats northwest of the now thriving city of Lincoln sat idle and forlorn as the high saline content made the land unusable for anything which might require vegetation growth from farming to housing. About 1890 Edward Bignell, Superintendent of Burlington Lines West however saw the inexpensive land adjacent to the Burlington right of way and acquired a large tract in the area. By damming Oak Creek a nearly 1,000 acre

Taken from the second Nebraska State Capitol, this photo looks northwest over downtown Lincoln about 1890. The First Baptist Church is shown on the northwest corner of 15th and K Streets while the then First Christian and today's St. Mary's Catholic Church is at the right. The tiny white building left of the Baptist Church is the Swedish Lutheran Church now renamed First Lutheran and relocated at 1551 South 70th Street.

An electric trolley is shown on K Street looking north with the Lincoln Electric Street Railway Building to the left and chimneys from their electric generation facility behind.

six foot deep lake was formed and the surrounding land named Burlington Beach. The prospectus also called for a $15,000 electric railway to be built connecting Lincoln with the "pleasure resort." The ever-zealous brochure even said the sandy beaches would attract "boat racing and regattas in which the university will take a greater interest than it now does in football." A decade earlier when Chautauqua came to Beatrice, Nebraska a dam on the Blue River attracted a boat ride on the Queen of the Blue which was a two-deck steam boat which took passengers on $1 cruises up the river a bit over two miles with unsurpassed scenery while a band played on the lower deck. Despite rave reviews, the excursion boat was not a sufficient success enabling the owners of Burlington Beach to purchase the steamboat and move it to Lincoln on Burlington flat cars.

The boat, lake and grounds proved a great escape for Lincolnites and in 1896 it was claimed that 150,000 people had visited the park and included a visit from President McKinley who gave a rally there. In 1906 the park was reincorporated as Capital Beach though some of the group's own advertising used Capitol causing much confusion. In 1907 Lancaster County straightened and channelized Oak Creek and Salt Creek removing the unauthorized dam and draining the lake forming more of a marsh. In 1918 the owners simply built a new dam, again without asking permission. Thousands of trees were also planted and a new direction charted for the park. During the 1920s Capital Beach featured salt water bathing, dancing, band concerts, canoeing, picnics,

vaudeville, cafes, shooting galleries, balloon ascensions and began building a midway with a Ferris wheel and circle swing. In the 1930s a giant wooden jack rabbit or roller coaster was built on the west end of the midway and a roller skating rink added with a dining room and the beach's advertising claimed they were the "most sanitary resort in the country." A movie theatre, merry-go-round, children's train and King's Ballroom were added and a concrete swimming pool and sand beach built on the east end of the midway with salt water pumped from the old salt flats while guests were assured the drinking water furnished was the "purest in the Missouri or Mississippi valleys [so one could enjoy a visit] without any thought of germs of any kind." Unfortunately the county again discovered the illicit dam and removed it leaving the Belle of the Blue to slowly languish and rot away on a former shore. This time the dam would not be reconstructed and with the more elaborate Peony Park in Omaha Capitol Beach, like the steamboat, slowly slipped away, closing in 1962. When the park and grounds were purchased by the Copple family, permission was obtained and a third dam built but this time it was not to divert Oak Creek water but to simply form a new, larger, lake fed by runoff produced by the many rooftops and streets constructed as the area was developed for housing. In 2003 the new lake was drained for dredging and among the interesting things uncovered were the old wooden pipes used to divert salt water from the old wells under the lake to the new swimming pool. Today traces of the old amusement park are limited to tree lines and small valleys as apartments and homes completely cover the once prosperous Coney Island-like resort.

Shortly after the end of the Civil War the Grand Army of the Republic suggested that they would provide fundraising to erect a statue of Abraham Lincoln on the University of Nebraska Campus. Although the idea bore no fruit, in 1895, John Currie, a Lincoln stone sculptor promoted a Lincoln statue with himself as the sculptor. To that end he set himself up in a downtown store window and began making a plaster model using a Lincoln life mask. Through this he hoped to establish a fund to place his Lincoln statue in the artesian fountain just north of the post office at 9th and O Streets. Currie even persuaded the state of Tennessee to furnish marble for the project. The stone arrived by freight car and Currie set up a shed on the northwest corner of the capitol grounds for the project apparently with no permission from anyone. Sadly, though a good stone mechanic, Currie seemingly had no sculpting talents and though he continued to chip away at the marble block the State Journal referred to his lack of skill by calling him "Lincoln's assassin." Public pressure stopped the project and Currie was amazingly even granted $200 for the "work" accomplished but no trace of the marble block ever surfaced.

The legislature approved the Abraham Lincoln Association in 1903 and appropriated $10,000 in the form of a challenge grant to produce a Lincoln statue. This board announced in 1909 that they had appointed Daniel Chester

French of New Hampshire, to produce the statue. A portion of the financing was proposed to come from Nebraska's school children who would give nickels to the project which would remunerate French a total of $22,000 but would also need to raise a bit over $16,000 to build a foundation, base and lighting. When the necessary funds could not be obtained, French settled for a partial payment and the right to cast twelve maquettes which he would sell.

In 1912 the Kimball Monument Company set the foundation on the west side of the capitol and on September 12 the completed 270 centimeter figure was dedicated with speeches from William Jennings Bryan, Governor Chester Aldrich and committee head Frank Hall. With the present, third capitol, architect Bertrand Grosvenor Goodhue planned to build a plaza on the north side of the new building for the statue but the statue remains today on the west side as one of only two items retained from the second building.

The first fair in Lincoln was the Lancaster County Exhibit in October of 1870 but Nebraska hosted a fair in territorial days at Brownville in 1859, the only territorial fair ever held in the U. S. Despite trying economic conditions and its loosing money, the fair was deemed a success with awards including $355 in cash, a gold watch, a saddle and bridle and "a goodly number of diplomas." After statehood the next two fairs were held in Nebraska City in 1869 and 1870, then two in Brownville with Lincoln not getting the nod until the sixth and seventh state fairs which were held at the Lancaster County Fairgrounds. Basically the fair moved annually or every

two years going to the community which offered the largest donation and the best accommodations. With the 1898 Trans-Mississippi Exposition in Omaha there was no state fair and the 1899 state fair was cancelled when Omaha left its commitment unfulfilled.

Charles Gere and John D. MacFarland championed Lincoln for a permanent site for the fair and on March 30, 1899 the state purchased the Lancaster County Fairgrounds for $18,000. In 1901 the legislature approved constructing permanent buildings on the new location to be "within three miles of the capitol" and the fairgrounds we are familiar with today came into being. Although it was originally illegal to hold horse races within a half mile of any Nebraska fair, the first horse track and grandstand were completed in the 1890s and seated 12,500 which was replaced in 1929 for $250,000 and again in 1977. With attendance slipping and buildings in need of maintenance the viability of the State Fairgrounds in Lincoln is being debated with an uncertain fate hanging over what was for decades the "biggest show in Nebraska."

On February 12, 1900 the Lincoln City Auditorium opened on the southeast corner of 13th and M Streets with a program by Paderewski, perhaps the most sought after performer in the world at the time. The building was a curved-roofed structure with the stage on the east end and a floor which could be used for seating, banquets, dances or even roller skating. The University of Nebraska's Kosmet Club Review was an annual show which ran for several days. Late in the night after their last performance for the 1928

show, on April 15, a fire destroyed the building and endangered several nearby structures. With the ashes not even cool the city announced plans to rebuild, then it was discovered that virtually all of the fire insurance was owned by the American Legion in favor of the county, who owned the lots it sat on, not the city and although the legion was interested in rebuilding on the site they had no funds. Voters approved a bond issue but it proved unsaleable. Discussion began as to whether the building might not be moved to Roger's Tract on the southwest corner of 33rd and O Streets.

After lengthy negotiation the 13th Street property was purchased by E. M. O'Shea who built the extant Union Bus Terminal there in 1930 and a privately owned auditorium was built on the southeast corner of 10th and M but was never a financial success. When the square block at 15th and N Street which had been the site of the old High School was acquired by the city in 1941 voters again approved a bond issue. This time WWII intervened and then the Nebraska Supreme Court had to enter the fray to negate other site possibilities. Finally on March 10, 1957, nearly thirty years after the fire, Pershing Municipal Auditorium was opened.

Partially in response to the 1874 opening of the Lake Chautauqua, New York assembly in 1874, the Epworth League of the Methodist Church of Lincoln began meetings in a large tent at Lincoln Park while their new facility at 1st and Calvert was being constructed. Their first season in their new park was so successful that president L. O. Jones announced that from their $10,000 gross profit, they would donate "$800…to worn out preachers and $1,000 to Nebraska Wesleyan." In 1911 the huge open air, roofed pavilion which seated up to 5,000 was opened and with the large donut-shaped Epworth Lake at the center. Large crowds arrived from all over the Great Plains for the two-week assemblies. Because as many as 2,500 spent the night for the two week period hundreds of wooden based tents were erected along named and numbered streets which allowed the on site post office to make daily mail deliveries. Also on the grounds were hotels, a rooming house, restaurants, a sixty bed YMCA and a grocery store. Activities ran all day long with classes for adults, activities for children and the evening Chautauqua which featured orators, musicians, entertainers and drama from the leading performers of the world from Billy Sunday, Booker T. Washington, Theodore Roosevelt, Howard Taft, Enrico Caruso, Swiss Bell Ringers, dog acts, William Jennings Bryan and the U. S. Army Band. With as many as 8,000 tickets sold streetcars and trains lined up after the performances to take people back to the city. The radio, motion pictures and the automobile brought the end of Epworth Park and Chautauqua nationwide but the real end came with floods in 1935 and subsequent years which virtually wiped the hundreds of buildings away like a giant eraser. Now what was advertised as the "largest gathering place in North America" is the north portion of Lincoln's vast Wilderness Park.

Although the first purpose-built U. S. Post Office and Federal Courthouse combined at 9th and O Streets was felt sufficient for Lincoln's use as far as their projections could imagine, by the beginning of the 20th century it was quite obviously outgrown. The first step to alleviate crowding was

to establish three substations, then a 1902 act provided for a $200,000 addition to the existing structure but this was shown to be inefficient. In March of 1903 the U. S. Treasurer was authorized to build a new post office also acting as a governmental office building for Lincoln on the empty north half of the 9th and O Streets block. When completed the old building was to be offered to the city of Lincoln for use as a city hall or other city offices for $50,000. The new, nearly 100 percent larger, building was on the northeast corner of the

block and allowed the remnant of the then downtown park and old artesian water fountain to remain, just east of the structure. In 1915 an addition to the west of the new building doubled its size and required moving the fountain to the west end of the alley. Unfortunately the force of the artesian flow was insufficient to move the salt water that far and the fountain gathered rain water and leaves. The Lincoln Chamber of Commerce began lobbying for the construction of the final third of the building in 1938 which was

Assurity Life Insurance Company

Building on a Rock-Solid Foundation
From three Lincoln landmarks to a single, unified company.

Assurity Life experienced a major milestone in 2007. Three century-old life insurance companies founded in Nebraska—Assurity (formerly Woodmen Accident and Life), Security Financial Life (Security Mutual Life) and Lincoln Direct Life (the Royal Highlanders, later Lincoln Mutual Life)— were united under a single Lincoln-based financial services organization, Assurity Life Insurance Company.

We value and maintain the principles on which our original companies were founded—working for the best interests of our policyholders and an unrelenting commitment to financial strength and stability. We also focus on creating value for our customers by cultivating lasting relationships and fostering innovation in our products and in the way we do business.

At Assurity, we are committed to delivering service that's among the best in our industry.

We're Helping People Through Difficult Times.

South Location	Downtown Location
4000 Pine Lake Road	1526 K Street

800-869-0355 / 402-476-6500
www.assurity.com

Assurity®
Life Insurance Company

completed at a cost of $850,000 in 1941. With the construction of the new post office at 7th and S Streets, the old building became surplus federal property and after private ownership, then city use it has now been sold and converted to commercial property on the ground floor with condominiums and apartments on the upper floors. Meanwhile the first post office, later City Hall, was nearly vacated with the construction of the new County-City Building on South 10th Street but in order to live up to the contract with the federal government, at least one city office has always remained occupied. The building was placed on the National Register of Historic Places and with the help of the Lincoln Junior League, Kawasaki Motor Corporation and others, it has been restored and continues in use as not only city offices but other community-based entities as well.

In 1897 the first Lincoln High School building was supplemented by a new, larger $25,000 structure to the north with the old building renamed Science Hall. Even with the addition, crowding was still in evidence and it was suggested that the auditorium be converted into classrooms...a distinctly unpopular idea. By 1905 the buildings which were designed for a maximum capacity of 850 had 1,200 students but only discussion seemed to ensue. Two separate high schools became a topic in 1909 but it was pointed out that the old buildings were in such disrepair they would need to be replaced at any rate. The School Board then suggested

Nebraska's second state capitol is shown looking to the southeast probably about 1915 judging from the size of the trees on the grounds.

four potential sites for a new high school: 14th and A, the existing block at 15th and N, the Davenport Tract at 22nd and J and the Davis Tract at 17th and K Streets. The 14th and A was dropped without comment but the three had both positive and negative facets.

The existing block was too near to disruptive businesses, noise and traffic. There was no room for adequate playing fields and it would require renting quarters to house classes while a new building was constructed.

The Davis Tract at 17th and A would be expensive to acquire and was in a high traffic and noise area.

When Lancaster County spun off from Cass County in 1859 the records were kept at the clerk's home while the treasurer's records resided in the room above the Sweet & Brock Bank on the northeast corner of 10th and O Streets. The Hardenberg/Benadom cabin near 9th and Q Streets was then purchased as what may loosely be called the first courthouse. Petitions and plans floundered until 1887 when the architectural plans of E. E. Myers & Sons of Detroit were approved for a proper courthouse on the block given by the state of Nebraska to Lancaster County for that use at 9th and J Streets. The plans were refused as being too expensive but the following year Omaha architect F. M. Ellis' drawings were accepted and a contract let for construction. Although the statue of Abraham Lincoln and the tower were subsequently removed, the F. M. Ellis designed building in the photo below was utilized until replaced by the first portion of the current County-City Building in 1968.

In 1884 economical generation of electricity allowed replacement of horse and mule drawn street railway cars. By 1893 Lincoln claimed to have more miles of street railway tracks than any city in Nebraska, Iowa, Kansas or the Dakotas. The 1895 depression brought the Lincoln Traction Company's ultimate buy out and combining of the several competing, failed lines. Though buses were introduced after World War I, electric trolley service continued until September 1, 1945 when the Randolph and College View lines closed bringing an end to Lincoln trolley service.

The Davenport Tract at 22nd and J was virtually in a swamp, had a bad reputation as the site of traveling circuses and tent shows. It was too far east and south of the current student body and it was next to the Rock Island Railroad. There was no bridge over Antelope Creek which could flood the area at any time. On the other hand it was near the center of the city's new population growth, was away from the noise and disruption of downtown, had plenty of room for growth and playing fields and it was near Antelope Park.

The parents voted in favor of the roughly ten acre Davenport Tract and on May 2, 1911 bonds were approved which would ultimately build not only Lincoln High School but Whittier Junior High (the first purpose-built junior high school building in the U. S.) and Bancroft Elementary School. The cornerstone, the gift of the classes of 1909 and 1911, was laid June 20, 1913 and the school was open for classes in September of 1915. The 1,200 student "Palace of Learning" was a 300 by 200 foot, cream-colored brick, four-story building which included the wished-for cafeteria, swimming pool, large library, two gymnasiums, auto repair shop, a 1,300 seat auditorium and over 100 rooms.

In 1920 the students borrowed $21,000 from the Stuart Investment Company which was guaranteed by forty local businessmen who pledged $500 each and construction was begun on The Oval. The Oval was a half mile track and football field which featured sod and could seat from four to five thousand and was said to be larger and better than the University's. In February of 1928 the Oval's loans were paid off by student fundraising without having expended a cent of taxpayer funds, the only such high school facility of its kind in the U. S.

Pioneers Park and Pinewood Bowl

John F. Harris, son of Lincoln pioneer and Burlington & Missouri River Railroad land commissioner George S. Harris, contacted his boyhood friend George Woods and asked him to find land suitable for a large park to be dedicated to his parents. Woods suggested a 500 acre tract southwest of Lincoln bordered by today's Calvert, Van Dorn and Burlington Streets which had been considered for several projects through the years and was adjacent to Haines Branch and Yankee Hill Brickyards.

Lincoln Mayor Verne Hedge accepted the gift in 1929 though there were many who predicted the park would never be used as it was too far from the city. Hedge assured the public that the park, now to be named Pioneers Park in honor of all pioneers rather than just Harris' parents, would be connected to the city by a boulevard from Cornhusker Highway and U.S. 34.

A golf course was one of the first designs off the drawing board and the balance of the park was soon planted with thousands of trees, with much funding provided by the WPA, NYA and other federal projects. The artificial forest was first watered by windmills which proved to pump saltwater which necessitated almost immediate replanting. Much of the design which is still evidenced came from Park Superintendent Chet

Ager and landscape architect Ernst Herminghaus. The park and "temporary" golf course were dedicated May 17, 1930.

Through the Lincoln Chamber of Commerce's Women's Division and a local ministerial organization the apparent need for a large gathering place for non-denominational Sunday services was addressed in 1939 through the formation of the Pinewood Bowl Committee. Originally designed for the men and women stationed at the U.S. Army Airfield northwest of Lincoln it was continued after the war with a more community-based approach. Through the years the park has been expanded to over 800 acres and Pinewood Bowl modernized with staging, lighting and sound enhancement and continues as a popular summertime venue for musicals, plays and community concerts as well as occasional high school graduations. Although disease and drought have cyclically taken their toll on the man-made forest, it has been replanted several times with a now much broader mix of evergreen and deciduous trees and is quite obviously not in the least too far from Lincoln to be used.

Pioneers Park and Pinewood Bowl are sponsored by

RUNZA

Partner In Progress

The first municipal auditorium opened as pictured above on the southeast corner of 13th and M Streets on February 12, 1900 with a sold-out concert by Ignace Jan Paderewski. The building was planned to be as flexible as possible with the stage at the east end and removable seats which allowed banquets, dances, rallies and even roller skating. The University of Nebraska's Kosmet Klub Review was among many groups who used the auditorium. After the last performance of their annual show, a fire in their props literally burned the timber-framed, brick-clad structure to the ground.

Although the city announced its intention to rebuild, it was soon discovered that the $11,000 fire insurance policy was held by the American Legion but paid in favor of Lancaster County, not the city of Lincoln.

The Legion could not raise sufficient funds to rebuild and though voters approved a ten year bond issue, they proved unsaleable. Through time E. M. O'Shea secured a ninety-nine year lease on the real estate and in 1930 completed the three-story Union Bus Terminal. As discussions proposed other locations, including 33rd and O Streets, the city finally settled on the old High School block at 15th and N Streets in 1941 and a second bond issue was passed. Questions about sites pushed the concept to the Nebraska Supreme Court then the Korean War further delayed construction.

Finally, March 10, 1957, nearly thirty years after the fire, Pershing Municipal Auditorium with its huge mosaic west façade opened. Today, fifty years later, many are calling for its replacement with a larger, more parking-friendly location.

The only problem mentioned was parking—the 2,200 students had sixteen cars and from two to six of the faculty drove to classes!

A group of Lincoln businessmen formed the Lancaster Hotel Company in 1923 with the intention of building a major hotel in the city to attract more and larger conventions. The site they hoped to develop was the east half of the block on the west side of 13th Street between L and M Streets. The site, Block 89, was then occupied by First Congregational Church on the south and First Presbyterian Church to the north with both on land given to them by the state of Nebraska in 1867 in order to insure the new capital city had a diverse population of church denominations. Both congregations agreed with Lincoln Mayor Sawyer transferring his home at 17th and F to the Presbyterians as a new site while First Congregational merged with Plymouth Congregational Church and moved into their building at 17th and A while they planned a new building for the combined churches at 20th and D Streets.

The consortium completed the ten story, 300-room red brick and stone hotel which was first referred to as the Lancaster then the Community and ultimately opened as the Cornhusker Hotel in 1926. On the south half of the property was a parking lot and service station. The hotel was leased first to Harry Weaver, then in 1930 was purchased by Charles Schimmel whose family also owned the Blackstone Hotel in Omaha. A. Q. Schimmel was then sent to Lincoln as the manager. The hotel soon became the preferred stopping place in the city as well as a favorite place to eat in its Teepee, Powwow, Landmark and Georgian Room restaurants. The Cornhusker was sold to the Radisson Company, ultimately closed in 1978 and sold to First National Bank. As civil defense sirens blared, Lincolnites watched in awe as the solid building was imploded on February 21, 1982. The site was then chosen by David Murdock who began construction of the ten story, 304 room hotel, convention center and office tower still known as the Cornhusker. With ownership now with the Marriott Hotel Company, the Cornhusker is still a premier restaurant and hotel destination and sharp eyes can still find the old carved stone American Indian heads from the original exterior, now salvaged and remounted in the atrium between the hotel and convention center which is also the office building.

Lied Center for Performing Arts

We believe the ARTS are integral to humanity.

Since 1990, the Lied Center for Performing Arts, Nebraska's Home for the Arts, has brought the world's finest performing artists to our state for Nebraskans to enjoy and learn from. Each year more than 200,000 people are impacted by our performances and activities.

Our stages have been filled with varieties of music, vibrated with the energy of dance, and been charged with the electricity of ideas in plays or the words of distinguished speakers.

Through our AdventureLIED and Arts Across Nebraska programs, we also share artists with citizens across the state in public performances and school activities.

In this age of instant messages and video downloads, there is still something thrilling about live performances. When artist and audience share the same space, magic happens.

For more information on Lied Center performances and educational programs, visit us online at liedcenter.org.

Lied Center for Performing Arts
301 N. 12th Street • Lincoln
402-472-4747 • www.liedcenter.org

LIED CENTER
FOR PERFORMING ARTS

Nebraska
UNIVERSITY OF
Lincoln

The University of Nebraska–Lincoln does not discriminate based on gender, age, disability, race, color, religion, marital status, veteran's status, national or ethnic origin or sexual orientation.

Lied Center programming is supported by Friends of Lied and grants from Association of Performing Arts Presenters, National Endowment for the Arts, Mid-America Arts Alliance, Nebraska Arts Council, New England Foundation for the Arts, and Lincoln Arts Council. All events in the Lied Center are made possible entirely or in part by the Lied Performance Fund, which has been established in memory of Ernst F. Lied and his parents, Ernst M. and Ida K. Lied.

The
Third Ca
is Built and
Lincoln Becomes a
Metropo
City

CHAPTER

11

Capitol at Night

pitol

itan

"You may say a
mere building
can't change a
city…but this
building has done
so…Beauty does
that to people, to
cities, to states,
when it is above,
about, and of,
them."

As early as 1901 reports began to circulate that the second capitol's east wing was beginning to sink, with fears that it would soon prove little better than the first building which was said by many to have been built "from want ads." In 1907 it was claimed that the

sinking was in fact due to the Superintendent of Education's area having been built above an excavation which had never been properly filled or that a lower level vault in the first capitol had been built over and had collapsed. Discussion of a possible new capitol began in 1914 but World War I and several seasons of poor crops, eliminated any thoughts of a new building. As the capitol continued "its downward career," window glass began breaking and cracks appeared in the plaster and masonry repairs were initiated.

Within a few years the observation dome was closed to visitors as being "unsafe except for the most active climbers." As talk continued, the 15th and J Street location was even questioned by some outstate newspapers, one of which urged consideration of 27th and O Streets as a new site.

In February of 1919 the legislature passed House Roll 3 which created a five-man unpaid Capital Commission consisting of the Governor, Secretary of the Highway Department and three other citizens of the state as appointed by the Governor. Their charge was to investigate and plan construction of a new state capitol to occupy the current ten acre site. The building was to cost no more than $5 million, paid as construc-

tion occurred, and financed by a six year 1.5 mill levy. It was to contain at least 7,500,000 cubic feet of space, be practical and inspiring and "accomplished without scandal, friction, extravagance or waste." This was a giant charge for a committee for which only one had even the slightest training. George Johnson, the Nebraska State Engineer, was empowered to contact Omaha architect Thomas Rogers Kimball who would, it was hoped, act as consultant in finding an architect. Kimball had been the general architect for the 1898 Transmississippi Exposition in Omaha, was active in planning the 1904 St. Louis World's Fair, had designed many significant buildings in Nebraska and in 1918 was elected president of the American Institute of Architects. Kimball answered that he was uninterested in the position and said he would furnish a list of local AIA members who would be good candidates for the advisory role and that he would be pleased to suggest a few architects as well. The committee simply ignored his refusal and in June of 1919 chose him as official advisor.

The committee, under Kimball's reluctant guidance, first contacted fifteen Nebraska architects explaining that the new state house would be designed by a contest with the first designs supplied by Nebraskans, then opened to a select few nationally from which an ultimate winner would be chosen. From this beginning Ellery Davis of Lincoln, John Latenser & Sons and John & Allan McDonald of Omaha were chosen to represent Nebraska designs. In January of 1920 thirty-two national architects were solicited from which seven preliminary designs were selected for final consideration. The Capital Commission set up shop in the third floor ballroom of the Governor's Mansion south of the capitol and first reduced the ten to six, then four and ultimately three designs as submitted by Bertram Grosvenor Goodhue, John Russell Pope and McKim, Mead & White all of New York. Of the three final jurists, who would make the ultimate choice, one was chosen by the final group of architects, one by the commission and one by the other two jury members.

Of the final ten designs, eight followed the U. S. Capitol's federal design and though Nebraskan Davis' featured a tower, Goodhue's tower was strikingly different. On July 1, 1920 the jury announced that Goodhue's design had won them over, "we all ran over to the design with the tower. It took all of us right off the bat…it was the easiest judgment of my experience." Although modified slightly, the initial design featured a 400 foot square base with a four acre footprint and an 80 by 80 foot tower with a height of 400 feet. Two economic considerations favoring Goodhue were that 72 percent of

Standing on Hildreth Meiere's mosaic of the sun, looking south from the main, north entrance's vestibule of the Nebraska State capitol, down the foyer to the rotunda. The floor shows three of Meiere's round mosaics symbolizing mineral, vegetable and animal devices. In the Guastavino ceiling are three central Meiere full-color polychrome mosaics representing the past, present and future. Dependent from the polychrome Guastavino dome of the rotunda is the 3,500 pound, 136 bulb, bronze chandelier reportedly the largest single bronze casting created up to 1930.

Lee Lawrie's nineteen foot tall, 15,000 pound, seven eights of an inch thick bronze casting of the Sower was shipped from the east coast on an open railroad flat car. Moved to the site on the state-owned H Street Railway, the statue sat on the grounds for days allowing hundreds to climb over and around him. On April 24, 1930 the Sower was hoisted to the 15th floor, the chalk graffito BOZO'S PAL removed and coated with a protective coat of bee's wax where he was stored out of harm's way till he could be bolted to the twelve and a half foot base atop the gold-tiled dome. The Sower also serves a utilitarian function, protecting the environs in a radius of about a half mile, as a lightning rod.

In 1926 W. E. Sharp and A. O. Faulkner's Fraternity Building on the southeast corner of 13th and N Streets was razed. Sharp then partnered with Charles Stuart to build the sixteen story, $1,250,000 Sharp Building in its place. Although most of the building remains intact, for unexplained reasons, the new owners destroyed the amazing lobby frieze and ornamental ceiling in 2005.

the building's 10,000,000 cubic feet were useable areas meaning it was an efficient plan and because the new building could be built around the old one, it was not necessary to rent outside office space while construction proceeded. Groundbreaking occurred with Governor Samuel McKelvie and French Marshal Joffre Commander of Allied Forces in WWI turning a furrow on April 15, 1922 and the cornerstone, which was placed adjacent to its predecessor, laid on Armistice Day, November 11, 1922.

In March of 1922 another cost-cutting feature of construction was instituted when a standard gauge railroad track was laid up from the Burlington Railroad's yard so stone and other building materials did not have to be unloaded from railcars onto trucks, transported to the building site and then unloaded yet again, a plan which ultimately saved the state over $100,000. Because there was considerable argument from the neighbors and others, it became necessary for the state to build and operate the electric-powered Capitol and H Street Line, H Street Railroad, Capitol Commission Railroad or simply the Haitch Street Railway which, on its completion, became the only state-owned railroad in the U. S. Without a doubt the most interesting passenger on the railway was The Sower, a 15,000 pound, seven eighths of an inch thick, nineteen foot tall, bronze casting designed by Lee Lawrie representing an ageless sower of the seeds of life. When bolted atop the fourteen carat gold-plated Guastavino tiles on

the capitol's dome, the Sower also became a lightning rod protecting buildings in a half mile radius around the building.

Goodhue died April 24, 1924, some say partially due to the almost ceaseless attacks on Goodhue's judgment on selection of costs, materials and artists, by George Johnson, a "self-appointed watchdog over an essentially bare bone." Because the state was forced to let bids for each portion on the contract to avoid debt, progress continued, albeit sometimes a bit bumpily. The offices were removed from the old building and moved into the completed quadrangle in December of 1924 allowing the removal of the old building through a gap in the west face that spring. In 1934 the $10,021,836.69 building was, for most intents, completed. With landscaping and other details however, work continues to this day partially because Goodhue felt art work and other minor details should be completed slowly. Formal dedication occurred as a part of Nebraska's centennial celebration on June 14, 1967. When completed, Nebraska's capitol building was deemed the only state house to be paid for when finished, one of the most inexpensive capitols ever built in terms of cubic foot costs, one of the twenty-five best built buildings in the world, one of the ten most beautiful buildings in the world and in 1948, 500 leading architects worldwide declared it "the fourth architectural wonder of the world."

On the eve of the Great Depression Lincoln was in the midst of what the Chamber of Commerce termed "a new skyline every day." Projects included the third Nebraska State Capitol, First Plymouth

Congregational Church, Gold's Department Store and the Stuart Building.

The Stuart family arrived in Lincoln in 1860 and established the Stuart Investment Company. In 1927 Charles Stuart commissioned Ellery L. Davis Sr. and Walter F. Wilson to design a thirteen floor, quarter square block office substituting as both a theatre and retail building for the southeast corner of 13th and P Streets on a site occupied by the Stuart's Nebraska Buick Company and the Lyric Theatre. The blueprints, dated 1927, show a Gothic, Italian Romanesque building with Moorish and Spanish interior features and the only structure in Lincoln to have gargoyles. The first floor exterior spaces were designed for retail stores, half of floors one through six were filled with a theatre, offices occupied floors two through ten with eleven and twelve used by the University Club as dining and meeting rooms while the top floor had a racquetball court, showers, locker rooms, etc. All interior halls were finished with Vermont brocadillo marble. Olson Construction Company, whose slogan was we "built the city of Lincoln," was chosen without bid to be the contractor on September 17, 1927 in a single-spaced, one page letter which was basically a cost plus agreement which pretty much stated, you build it and I'll pay for it.

Amazingly the Bedford limestone building was completed in less than a year with some of the offices occupied in November of 1928 and the opening of the University Club February 1, 1929. One well-advertised feature of the $1,200,000 building was the "weather factory"

When Bankers Life Insurance Co. made the decision to move to the northeast corner of Cotner Blvd. and O Streets from downtown Lincoln, one of the suggestions made by Chicago-based city planner Frank Shagrue was that they buy enough adjacent land to be able to choose their neighbors. After their initial seventeen acre purchase in the late 1950s Bankers Life added two more parcels totaling thirty-five acres to the east along O Street. Although their plans did not envision a shopping center, Gateway was ultimately developed and owned by them for several decades. Although now under new ownership and renamed Westfield Gateway, its development definitely shaped a new direction away from downtown shopping and even influenced where people wanted to live.

This aerial view looks to the northwest showing Gateway before the addition of Sears or Brandeis/Younkers or the enclosure of the former open courtyard.

The south side of O Street looking east from 10th Street in the 1950s shows that downtown was still very much the place to shop in Lincoln at that time. Not a single one of the pictured businesses still operates today.

which was a "giant air-cooling, washing and drying plant" not unique but one of the earliest such systems in Lincoln.

Without doubt the principal feature of the building was the Stuart Theatre portion whose auditorium with main floor, loge and two balconies seated 1,856. The beamed and coffered ceiling held six chandeliers, the two largest being sixteen feet tall, weighed two and a half tons each and required 450 light bulbs each. The terra cotta walls and side balcony, fire escapes were designed to give the appearance of an Italian palace. The curtain within the proscenium held what was described as the "largest all-over appliqué and embroidered curtain ever made…of rich Italian red with antique green and gold lattice. The fleur-de-lis panels are of peacock blue." In the basement were dressing rooms for eighty. The Stuart Theatre opened June 3, 1929 with Eli Shire paying $500 for a gold-plated ticket later turned over to the Nebraska State Historical Society while the balance of the audience paid from $0.60 to $0.75 for a program which featured the "100% talking-singing movie 'The Rainbow Man,'" several shorts, news reel and two theatre orchestras, one of which claimed to be the largest theatre orchestra west of Chicago. Not only were the auditorium and building considered the second most architectural significant building in the city but the theatre won the Western Electric acoustic award for the year.

On April 30, 1972 the theatre, which had been leased to the Cooper Foundation, closed and was released to Dubinsky Brothers

Theatre Company who set about reducing the size of the auditorium by partitioning off the stage for Barrymore's Bar, removing the seats from the two balconies leaving 900, tearing off the side balcony and fire escapes, covering the proscenium, pulling the chandeliers up above a false ceiling, sealing off the dressing rooms, lowering the ceiling and covering the terra cotta walls with carpeted draperies. Theatres nationwide were being forced to do similar shrinking remodeling to make it possible for economical operation though the

Orpheum Theatre in Omaha took a different approach and renovated their somewhat larger auditorium to the tune of $2,000,000. In 1977 the James Stuart Sr. family gave the theatre and first five floors of the building to the University of Nebraska Foundation who initiated a feasibility study to see if enlarging or adapting the theatre was a practical proposition. The study found that with the stage and seating capacities, it would not be an economical venture and in 1986 a new concept for the building, headed by Larry Price,

NEBCO, part of Nebraska's history for close to a century, traces its roots to Abel Construction Company, founded in 1908 by George P. Abel, Sr. Today, NEBCO is a third generation, family-owned and operated business that employs close to 1,000 employees and is one of Nebraska's largest privately owned firms.

NEBCO supplies the construction industry with materials needed for buildings & bridges, streets & highways and homes & hardscapes. Over the years, NEBCO has expanded its operations to include commercial and residential real estate as well as recreational endeavors including a baseball team and a golf course for Lincoln and its surrounding communities.

With 100 years of history, NEBCO demonstrates how being part of a strong, supportive community creates an environment for businesses to thrive.

NEBCO is proud to call Lincoln home.

ABEL FOUNDATION
CHRISTENSEN CONCRETE PRODUCTS
CONCRETE INDUSTRIES
CONSTRUCTORS
KEARNEY CRETE & BLOCK
KERFORD LIMESTONE
LINCOLN SALTDOGS BASEBALL
NEBCO INTERMODAL
NEBCO REALTY GROUP
NEBRASKA ASH
OL&B RAILWAY
OVERLAND SAND & GRAVEL
PLAINS POZZOLANIC
QUARRY OAKS GOLF CLUB
READY MIXED CONCRETE
REIMERS KAUFMAN CONCRETE PRODUCTS
TRAFCON
U-MIX CONCRETE PRODUCTS
WATKINS CONCRETE BLOCK
WESTERN SAND & GRAVEL

Construction
Real Estate
Recreation

NEBCO
CONSTRUCTION ■ REAL ESTATE ■ RECREATION

1815 Y Street ■ Lincoln, Nebraska 68508
www.nebcoinc.com

Building Nebraska…Since 1908

In the winter of 1924 to 1925 the old power plant south of the second capitol is seen in full force in this view looking to the northeast. Clearly visible are the spur rail of the H Street Railway which brought stone and materiel up from the Burlington rail yards.

As the quadrangle was built for the new state capitol, it was business as usual in the second building, which remained until 1925 when the offices were removed from the old to the new building.

condominiumized floors two through ten. In 2000 the theatre itself was purchased by Doug Deeter who set about restoring the auditorium, rebuilding the balcony and fire escapes, exposing the terra cotta walls, converting many of the dressing rooms to a kitchen, removing the false ceiling and lowering the chandeliers. The result was the amazing Rococo Theatre which reopened in June of 2001. Although the building is now more correctly called University Towers, the cognoscenti still refer to it as the Stuart Building.

In 1928 John F. Harris, prominent New York City broker and son of Lincoln pioneer George S. Harris contacted his boyhood friend George J. Woods and asked him to seek out a potential site for a park to be given to Lincoln in honor of his parents. Woods found a 500 acre tract on Haines Branch, southwest of the city which had been proposed as a potential shoe manufactory powered through a dam on the creek. Although the dam had been built, no factory followed and despite a stockyards and brickyard having been built to the south and east, no real development of the land itself had ever transpired. In January of 1929 the deed was mailed to Woods who delivered it to Mayor Verne Hedge. However Harris had, in the meantime, decided he did not want the park named Harris Park but instead that it should be in honor of all pioneers, hence Pioneers Park. Hedge immediately assigned City Engineer D. L. Erickson to draw a topographic map of the area,

architect William Tucker began plans for a twenty-seven hole golf course and Ernst Herminghaus invited three bids to design the park itself. The mayor sought to offset what he thought would be complaints about the location, which some thought was so far from Lincoln it would never be used and called for the construction of a "boulevard around the city [connecting] the Cornhusker Highway and the S.Y.A." (Seward, York, Aurora Highway now U.S. 34).

Herminghaus, apparently not impressed with any of the three proposals, drew his own design which has primarily been instituted. Some original ideas, mostly not Herminghaus,' included a cave where young people could be taught geology and American Indian lore and an arboretum. The Civil Works Administration (C.W.A.), under the direction of Chet Ager, planted two to four foot Scotch and Austrian pines on the west and Black Hills and Colorado Blue spruce on the east. Because the trees were all grown in the city nursery the total cost of the plantings was only $3,000.

On June 2, 1929 a formal dedication was planned with dignitaries and a concert by Paul Whiteman's band. A week of rain culminated with Whiteman's arrival at the Burlington Depot where he gave an impromptu concert, got back on the train and left while the festivities were "postponed till July or indefinitely." On May 17, 1930 the park and the full-sized, bronze bison statue, set near the east entrance and sculpted in Paris by M. George Gaudet, donated by John F. and Gertrude Upham Harris, were officially dedicated. With the dedication

The Stuart Building on the southeast corner of 13th and P Streets, like the state capitol, was built just before the Great Depression was felt in full force in the Great Plains. Designed by architect Ellery Davis and Walter Wilson, the cost plus, stone office building was completed in late 1928, less than a year after it was begun.

Harris was so taken by the park and plan, he also gave an additional 100 acres adjacent to the original tract.

By 1932 it was noted that nearly 75,000 shrubs and trees had been planted on the once barren farm land. Nineteen thirty-five saw the completion of the twenty-seven hole Pioneers Golf Course which was completed with the aid of the C.W.A., Nebraska Emergency Relief Administration (N.E.R.A.), and Works Progress Administration (W.P.A.) Because of drought the course was reduced to its present eighteen holes in 1938. The north entrance was completed by purchasing additional land in 1946 and the following year Pinewood Bowl amphitheatre was opened. A Bicentennial project saw the pillars which once stood at the U. S. Treasury Building in Washington DC and given by Cotter T. McBride as an entrance to what was first known as Municipal and later Antelope park at 23rd and O Streets, relocated and placed near a pond at Pioneers Park. The now nearly 900 acre park has been placed on the National Register of Historic Places and is one of the city's primary parks in a total scheme which has been said to have one of the largest ratio of park acres to population of any city in the world.

The Ganter Block on the northwest corner of 12th and O Streets housed the Lincoln [State] National Bank in 1930. On September 17, 1930 the first employees arrived to do preopening work at 8:00 AM with the bank opening for daily business at 10:00 AM. At two minutes after 10:00 four men left a black Buick sedan at the curb on the east side of the building and entered the bank carrying

four brightly colored pillowcases or cloth bags. A fifth man was left with the car running at the curb and another stood by as a runner to take word back and forth to those inside. The outside watch was overseen by Homer "Big George" Wilson who waited patiently with one foot on the car's running board while cradling a submachine gun. Only one customer approached the bank and immediately saw that something untoward was happening and she quickly walked across the street and phoned the police station from a shop. The desk sergeant, thinking the call was a

prank, simply dispatched unarmed juvenile officer Peter Meyers and patrolman Forrest Schappaugh who had only a .38 caliber pistol, to the scene. When the two policemen approached, perhaps intrigued by the machine gun, "Big George" simply told them to "scram" and since between them they had only one handgun, they prudently scrammed. Because they had no better way of communicating with the station, the two headed for police headquarters. "Big George"

Novartis Consumer Health, Inc.

Novartis AG (NYSE: NVS) is a world leader in offering medicines to protect health, cure disease, and improve well-being. Our goal is to discover, develop and successfully market innovative products to treat patients, ease suffering, and enhance the quality of life. Headquartered in Basel, Switzerland, Novartis Group companies employ more than 100,000 associates and operate in over 140 countries around the world. For more information, please visit www.novartis.com.

The Novartis Consumer Health division has one of its largest production plants in Lincoln. The primary focus of the Lincoln facility is to produce high-quality over-the-counter products for distribution within the United States. Products manufactured and/or packaged at this location include EXCEDRIN; BUFFERIN; THERAFLU; the TRIAMINIC line; MAALOX Liquid and Tablets; the TAVIST line; and LAMISIL Cream.

Over 600 associates are employed at the Lincoln Novartis facility, located on over 420 acres of beautifully landscaped land on Highway 6 between Lincoln and Waverly.

Partner In Progress

The southeast corner of 13th and P Streets housed the five-story Nebraska Buick Co., which was owned by the Stuart Investment Co. and the Lyric Theatre on the same quarter block, to the south.

Block 29, which was originally set aside as the Historical Block, between 9th, 10th, Q and R Streets, first served as Market Square in 1870, City Hall/Fire Dept./Police Dept./Municipal Scales/Municipal Gasoline Station by the 20th century, Fire Dept./Police Dept./County Health/City maintenance Block in 1925, city parking lot and now, the site of the Lincoln Journal-Star Printing Co. plant.

sent his runner into the bank with instructions to act quickly.

As the four men entered the bank they first asked for H. E. Leinberger whom they inexplicably knew had the key or combination to the inner safe which was supposedly still locked even thought the outer vault door was open and then instructed the employees to lie down on the floor. Vice President E. H. Luikart was certain that, even though the employees had been in the inner safe previously, it had been relocked. He explained that Leinberger was away from the bank and that no one else could open the safe but when he demonstrated that it was still locked…it proved in fact to have never been relocked. This error allowed the foursome to relieve the bank of some $2,775,395.12 in cash and Liberty Bonds in just eight minutes. Schappaugh returned with armed reinforcements by 10:10 but it was too late. The Buick had already made its escape with four pillowcases containing what was soon announced as proceeds of the largest cash bank robbery in the world.

Confusion reigned as the witnesses tried to put the events back in order, many various and colorful theories were reported. One idea had the Buick going around the block to P Street where the car was simply driven into a moving van which proceeded around the corner in front of the bank whereupon it left town. Another told of the Buick simply heading east on O Street where they summarily had a flat tire. A farmer who stopped to help was a bit bemused by the machine gun in the back seat but bought the explanation of their being on a duck hunt. In actuality the most probable

scenario, recounted by Assistant U. S. Attorney Robert Van Pelt, had the robbers simply heading south for Kansas, spending the night in Milan, Missouri and then into the Ozarks.

Late in 1931 Dewey Berlovich was arrested in Chicago when he was caught with $10,900 in Liberty Bonds in his possession which he was attempting to broker to New York attorney F. P. Ferguson. Ferguson had already sold some $15,000 of the bonds but claimed to have come by them legally. Van Pelt, along with Lancaster County Attorney Max Towle, felt that Berlovich had probably not been a participant in the actual robbery but knew more details than he was willing to divulge. Van Pelt then contacted Leonard Keeler at Northwestern University, who had been developing what he called a "lie detector" to bring his apparatus to Lincoln for use on Berlovich. Berlovich, obviously petrified of what else they might learn from him, convinced the Lincoln officials

Looking west northwest through construction phase II of the present, third state capitol which began in the summer of 1925. In this photo the second capitol has been removed, a hoist tower has been built and tower footings have been begun.

that he was in Iowa during the robbery and said he would furnish the names of those involved if they would not use the machine on him.

Meantime Gus Winkler, one of Al Capone's lieutenants, had been taken to a Chicago hospital after being injured in an automobile accident where he began to mutter about a bank robbery as he regained consciousness. This attracted the attention of a group of Chicago businessmen who were working to remove the scourge of the Capone Gang whose intimidation and bribery had many of the city's law enforcement officers and elected politicians in his control. Colonel Robert I. Randolph, spokesman for the "Secret Six," the balance of which he refused to identify, put up a total of $1 million to aid federal authorities in their investigation of organized crime. The group then sent their attorneys to Lincoln to aid in the robbery investigation which seemed to have obvious ties to the Capone Gang.

With Berlovich's identification of Thomas O'Connor as one of the robbers and the Secret Six's help, Thomas O'Connor, Jack Britt, Edward O'Hara, William McQuillin, Howard "Pop" Lee and Tommy Hayes were arrested in East St. Louis and were brought to Lincoln for trial. O'Connor and Lee were found guilty while Britt was released after two deadlocked jury decisions. Winkler was brought to Lincoln on September 16, 1931 but released on bond. Because Winkler thought his alibi in Buffalo, New York, though true, might be difficult to prove, he communicated to Towle that he would find and return $600,000 in securities along with a letter saying the balance had been destroyed in exchange for a dismissal of the charges against him. Although Towle was highly criticized by many, he accepted the exchange and in January of 1932 a suitcase was left, leaning against a Chicago lamppost at 2:00 AM, with $584,000 in bonds inside.

The Lincoln National Bank closed its doors and was absorbed by the Continental National Bank but with the recovered bonds and the efforts of W. A. Selleck over nearly fifteen years, five Lancaster County correspondent banks and all of the bank's depositors and stockholders were paid in full. Both Winkler and Berlovich were killed in gangland executions in 1933 and years later a list of what was thought to be the actual robbers was released. One observer noted that those who had been imprisoned were, though perhaps not the robbers of this specific bank, indeed guilty as bank robbers. This may not have been a great endorsement but one which had satisfied local critics at the time. It also surfaced that some months before the robbery an unidentified man had showed up at the bank and offered to do an appraisal of the bank's security

PERFORMANCE
JEEP · DODGE

Performance Jeep-Dodge is a certified Chrysler Five Star dealership with a huge inventory of high quality new and pre-owned vehicles. The team at Performance Jeep-Dodge believes that customer service means making your vehicle buying experience an enjoyable one.

Since 1993, we've been known as Nebraska's Dodge Superstore, volume selling Dodges… and now we have the same philosophy with Jeeps. Best of all, when your vehicle needs service, we have a full staff of factory certified technicians.

As part of the Performance Automotive Group, we are truly Driven to Be the Best.

6601 Telluride Drive
I-80 & North 27th street (exit 403), Lincoln
402-477-3777

performancejeepdodge.com

This Nebraska State Capitol photo was taken in 1967 for the back cover of *The Nebraska Centennial First Lady's Cookbook.*

The southeast corner of 13th and O Streets housed the Nebraska Savings Bank in 1890 and stood on land owned by later Vice President of the U. S. Charles Dawes. In 1902 the property was purchased by Morris Weil for his Bank of Commerce which opened on August 4 of that year. Two years later a federal charter changed the name to the National Bank of Commerce. In 1924 Weil bought the northwest corner of the intersection, again from Dawes, and moved the bank to a new seven-story building on that property. The building pictured then served as a fruit market, then Sartor Jewelers until it was razed in the early 1940s to build the Walgreen Drug Store which still stands.

systems while in fact he was evidently casing the situation and was the one who furnished the details of Mr. Leinberger's having the "key" to the inner safe.

In the ensuing years the 1950 Brink's robbery resulted in a larger cash robbery but it was not from a bank and though there have been larger bank robberies, they were not in cash. Thus Lincoln has managed to hold on to its dubious record of having hosted the largest cash bank robbery.

On August 10, 1941, just months after the U.S. created the first peacetime draft, the Army Air Corps arrived in Lincoln for a secret survey of the 160 acre

Lincoln airfield. That November an unpublicized agreement with the city promised that an army airfield would be built on the site. In February of the following year the plan for a mechanics' school was announced by the Lincoln press and in March a complete survey was finished. Lieutenant Perly Lewis, a Santa Fe Railway engineer in civilian life, arrived and began plans for what was promised as a $25 million construction project to be completed in eight months. The training facility would employ 15,000 locals, a figure capped by federal restriction which said that no more than 3 percent of the area's population could be so employed to prevent an unwarranted impact on the local employment market. Working with the city, the Chamber of Commerce and numerous individuals and corporations, a lease on the existing airfield and the purchase of over 2,000 additional acres was instituted. Amazingly, only five months later 1,070 buildings and four new, mile-long runways had been completed—two months ahead of what seemed an impossible goal.

The first 5,000 troops arrived in July of 1942 and less than a month later the first classes began. By the war's end over 25,000 aviation mechanics had been trained and an additional 40,000 men processed through the facility. In July of 1945 Lincolnites were allowed to visit many of the sites within the base which had before been classified and on December 15 the Lincoln Army Airfield was inactivated leaving 1,500 Lincoln civilian employees out of work and 12,800 military employees about to be transferred. In 1948 the base reverted to city of Lincoln ownership.

Reactivation was sought in 1950 but when it seemed unlikely, Mayor Victor Anderson proposed moving low income local families into the base housing which would be shared with returning servicemen in a community nicknamed Huskerville, though some wags referred to the area as Cardboard City. In 1952, with the Korean War, $29 million in federal government funds along with local government dollars and private donations were employed to straighten and channelize Oak Creek so that runways could be lengthened and many buildings constructed. Another result of the financing was moving civilian air traffic to the 360 acre Union Airport at Havelock. Huskerville was replaced with 1,100 Capehart housing units and the community renamed Arnold Heights. In June of 1952 a lease was signed, the Strategic Air Command formed two B-47 Stratojet bomber wings

The Old Line Bankers Life Nebraska Insurance Co. had several downtown locations before moving to this imposing five-story, stone building on the southwest corner of 14th and N Streets in 1911. With 220 employees, the firm reported $31 million of insurance in force at that point. When Bankers Life moved to the northeast corner of Cotner Blvd. and O Streets in the 1950s the building pictured was razed and today is the site of a surface parking lot.

and Lincoln Air Force Base was reactivated at an expense of about $29 million. As the Korean conflict wound down the city began developing the adjacent municipal airport featuring flights from United and Frontier Airlines while the base became the local headquarters for Atlas and Nike missile installations.

In 1966 the Lincoln Air Force Base was closed prompting the U. S. Air Force's offer of selling Arnold Heights, 1,600 hangers and buildings, what was termed the 7th longest runway in the world and 640 purchased acres to the city at a bargain price. The city, however, noted that the lease provided that the federal government return the land to the city in its original farmland status. The cost of razing all of the buildings and improvements was considerable with the end result of the government agreeing to simply give everything to the city at no cost. The 1959 Lincoln Airport Authority suddenly found itself with a gift hard to comprehend which has allowed the authority to operate the airport with virtually no tax funding by selling, leasing and renting the many buildings and houses as well as a total of 2,750 acres of land abandoned by the Air Force.

In 1887 the Old Line Bankers Life Insurance Company was incorporated by several Lincoln businessmen in the Richards Block on the northeast corner of 11th and O Streets with its primary goal of keeping insurance premiums in Lincoln rather than sending them to one of the coasts. In the first eight months 281 policies with $344,000 worth of insurance had been sold but in 1890 the firm was acquired by another group of locals with the desire to take the business into the Great Plains area. By 1892 they had over $2 million of insurance in force but in the depression of the 90s they, like other insurance companies, struggled and at one point even had to call a board of directors meeting to determine how best to handle a $5,000 death benefit payment. Recovery was swift and after a couple of moves they occupied a new purpose-built, five story stone building on the southwest corner of 14th and N Streets.

By the 1950s it was again obvious that the firm needed a new and larger home office. Board member George Cook was at first a lone voice in seeking a location outside of downtown Lincoln but after World War II the city had begun growing to the east and what had been a dirt lane became North 48th Street which had grown so rapidly and successfully it was known as the Miracle Mile. Cook presumed that not only could a large tract of land be easily acquired east of the city but that it would be far less costly. Five sites were originally considered including the southwest corner of Cotner Blvd. and O, the north side of 52nd and O and the northeast corner of Cotner Blvd. and O Streets. Although Cook was even threatened by some if he pursued moving Bankers Life outside the downtown core, he was ultimately able to convince the board of the wisdom of the move. The seventeen acre site on the northeast corner of Cotner Blvd. and O Streets, whose primary occupant was the Ranch Market, was purchased for $4,600 an acre. Consultant Frank Shagrue additionally urged that more land should be acquired so that they could control their neighbors and to that end, thirty-five additional acres of farmland and an unfinished outdoor movie theatre site were added along O Street.

Service never goes out of style.

← Original
B&R Store in 1962.

Russ's Market
Today →

Serving Lincoln Since 1962.

www.RussMarket.com

Offering Five Star Service
Employee Owned

Although Bankers Life had no original intent of going into the shopping center business, the additional land afforded an excellent economic incentive as well as giving the neighbor protection urged by Shagrue. What was to become Gateway Shopping Center was then proposed on thirty-one acres just to the east of the insurance company's new headquarters. The $3.5 million, twenty store, 250,000 square foot, plaza shopping center was to be anchored by Montgomery Wards which would occupy about half of the total square footage. One downtown merchant predicted it was "inviting foreign merchants into Lincoln." John Lawlor headed the first Downtown Development Committee "to preserve property values and fight the traffic problem." In the 1970s the Conant laboratories, lake, grass airfield and home were purchased by a separate group which built the east extension to Gateway with Sears Roebuck as well as several stores and a strip shopping center on O Street.

The Stuart Theatre's auditorium on May 28, 1929 looking south from the top balcony to the stage. Visible is the orchestra pit and theatre organ which was hydraulically moved up from the basement level.

Within two decades downtown shopping was eclipsed by Gateway Shopping Center and with the new millennium, Gateway and east Lincoln had almost totally reshaped not only where Lincolnites shopped but also lived and the former Lincoln greats of Miller & Paine's, Golds, Hovland-Swansons, Magees, Lawlors, Ben Simon & Sons and Wells & Frost were but memories of "the good old days". In 1985 even Gateway Shopping Center was sold to non-Nebraskans…the threatened "foreign merchants" had indeed arrived.

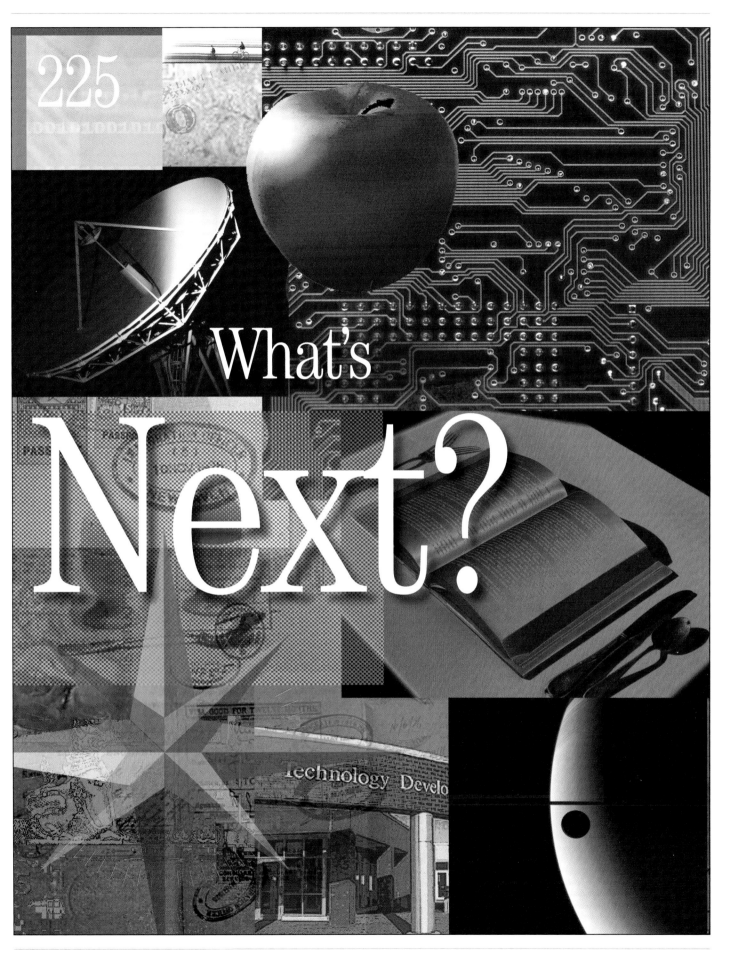

225

What's
Next?

The
Future
of Lincoln

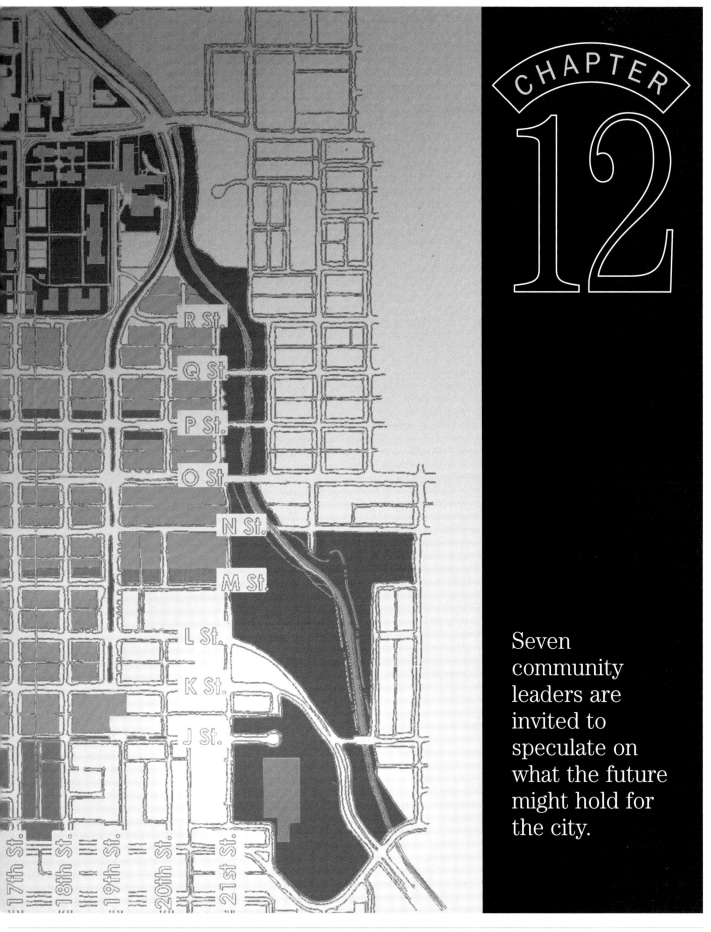

CHAPTER

12

Seven
community
leaders are
invited to
speculate on
what the future
might hold for
the city.

Cindy
Lange-Kubick

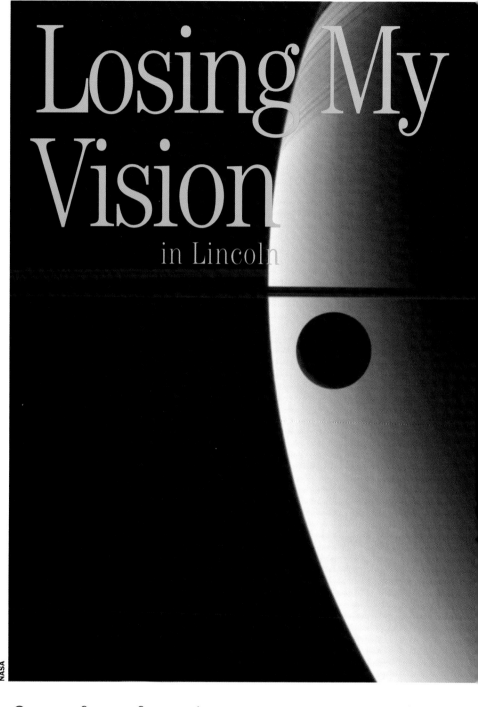

Losing My Vision
in Lincoln

NASA

One of my favorite grocery stores in Lincoln is the Hy-Vee in Williamsburg, a neighborhood where the houses have triple garages and the banks have white pillars and the streets have names like Leesburg and Potomac. It's the one place I know for sure I can find Lorraine Swiss cheese when I need it, and, if I'm lucky, a retired truck driver the kids call the Lollipop Man handing out suckers in the checkout line.

I like to shop at a store called B & R too, a neighborhood institution just off a busy one-way street, enveloped by frame houses with front porches, and boxy apartment buildings with dirt patched yards and a nearby row of antique shops and quirky stores that smell like patchouli. It's the one place I know for sure I can find interesting people who don't always share my skin color or speak my language, and that makes me happy.

I live between these two microcosms of my city -- two grocery stores that sometimes feel worlds apart.

Ten years from now, I'd like to see those worlds collide. Or at least share an orbit. I'd like to see the refugees and working class people who populate B & R and the affluent Hy-Vee shoppers have more in common than infrastructure and Nebraska weather. I'd like to see the New Americans chip away at the dream and get a foothold in the suburbs and I'd like to see the people of privilege on the edges come closer to the city's core, building the city up in the middle without pushing people out. Not gentrified, integrated. Not a planning policy, a people's policy.

And what about the people here? We're a strange lot. I'm mixed up with the immigrants from Germany who should know about settling in new places and forging community, because it's in our blood, even if some of us have forgotten how. This worries me. Sometimes Lincoln acts like it's an exclusive club with membership dues and secret handshakes. Being on the fringes of the old-timers club, you don't always notice, but I've had enough

newcomers tell me to know it's true. We need to work on that. If we want to live in a place where the people are good and our neighbors are friendly, we've got to be good people and friendly neighbors. I say we go beyond our summer festivals and holiday parades and just start talking to each other. Build houses with porches again. Take One Book – One Lincoln to the next level: Maybe a community-wide eating event, One Pizza – One Lincoln!

I've always lived here, long before Williamsburg grew up and the city spilled into the farmlands beyond it. And I've always been a bit sensitive revealing this information. It lacks the cachet of saying you've returned to raise your kids after spending your twenties on the Gold Coast, or West Hollywood.

Spending your whole life in Lincoln is a bit like being in a marriage that has made it past all the lust and has settled into cuddling and arguing about who's turning the thermostat up again instead. Even if you're committed to that better-or-worse-thing, there are still days when you just want to hock the ring, pawn off the kids, move to the Cayman Islands with your feet in the sand and someone else's money in your off-shore account.

Then you look around at where you are and what you'd be giving up, the history you share and the mortgage and those children, and in the case of Lincoln, the friendships and the parks and the short commutes and the wonderful autumns and places like Open Harvest and Blue Orchid and wild Wilderness Park, and weighing it all, you decide to stay.

After all, you know enough people who came here voluntarily. People who left the Gold Coast and West Hollywood and El Paso and Manhattan and Minneapolis and said "I Do" to Lincoln precisely because it wasn't all those things you now lust after. That's the irony. We fly to Chicago and spend a day at the Art Institute but never think about walking in Sheldon's front door. We covet Broadway and ignore our own theaters.

In September 1960 my parents carted me home from the hospital to a small stone ranch with a picture window and a fenced-in yard on Worthington Avenue, just off the highway skirting the edge of town. Twenty-two years later, in the months before my first son was born, by a happy coincidence in the rental market, my husband

the street, a little boy approached and asked if I knew where Dunn Avenue was. I told him I did. He lived there, he said in a quivering voice, but he couldn't find his way home. So we walked together in the dark, talking about small things – how old he was and how many kids I had – and in a few minutes we came to his street, then to his house, where I told him good-bye and never saw him again.

Heading home, and for the longest time afterward, I thought about that boy. How innocent he was and how sad it felt that children couldn't always trust grown-ups, but how Lincoln, for the most part, felt like a place that was safe for kids. I still feel that way. And I hope twenty years from now little boys can still

Lincoln needs a good agent, too. An ad campaign. Someone to start some buzz on the Internet. Not too much buzz, of course. And that's the rub: keeping Lincoln the same and letting it get its groove on in the new century.

and I found ourselves living on Worthington too, just a few blocks from the place I called home.

Old-timers on the avenue still remembered me from when I was small and asked after my parents, while my newer neighbors welcomed us and our son, as if we'd never left. We planted a twig of a red bud tree in the yard and grew corn in the garden. And one summer night walking near the playground of the grade school up

ask ladies out walking after dark for directions home, and know the ladies will make sure they arrive home safely.

I worry about the trade-offs of Lincoln growing up. More people, less quiet, more roads, fewer open spaces, more crime, less congeniality, more Applebees, fewer El Ranchos and Tastee Inns.

And because I like familiar things -- the down comforter on the bed I share with my husband, the one our old dog Higgins used to nudge onto the floor and curl up on to sleep, the frayed white T-shirt I wear to the gym, the original Valentino's on North 33rd Street -- it's jarring to see Home Depots across from Wal-Marts across from IHOPs where a two-lane highway once took Lincoln families to Nebraska City and all those apples.

So I have to keep reminding myself that sometimes change is good -- a new and improved Sunken Gardens, a bigger, fancier Children's Zoo, a town burgeoning enough for a Baby Gap at the mall and coffee shops on nearly every street corner.

Lincoln has always seemed the perfect size, as if it grew with me, both of us getting used to the idea of stretching out and taking up more space in our parallel worlds.

Now it's big enough for "Cabaret" to play the Lied Center and for Lucinda Williams to sing at a grand old theater someone had the good sense to restore – and it's still small enough that you're bound to run into someone you know when you go to the movies or the mall.

More than anything else I hope it feels that way to my kids when they have kids, and when their kids are parents after them.

Lincoln isn't perfect. It needs more flowering crab trees and fewer concrete medians, more downtown grocery stores and fewer downtown bars, more cheap movie theaters and fewer check cashing joints.

Lincoln needs a good agent, too. An ad campaign. Someone to start some buzz on the Internet. Not too much buzz, of course. And that's the rub: keeping Lincoln the same and letting it get its groove on in the new century.

Because I work for a newspaper, I meet all kinds of people. I know that this medium-sized city in the middle of the country is one of the country's largest refugee resettlement areas, home to thousands of families displaced by war and poverty and in a generation they will change the city. They already have. With bakeries that serve baklava and restaurants called Sinbad's and tailor shops named Emsud's. And, with children who go to school together, hearing the syllables of familiar words in foreign tongues, while their parents share benches at soccer games and PTO fun nights.

Lincoln needs to do right by those people as it grows. One person's vision is another's nightmare. Just ask all the poor folks who lost homes and neighborhoods when the city decided to build a radial through the guts of the north side 25 years ago. People without clout lost faith and the city needs to prove its honor over and over again.

These days I don't live on Worthington Avenue. We outgrew the little house, and moved our kids to a bigger place on a long block of duplexes and single family homes, where college students rent and old people have tended their homes since back in the day a mass murderer named Charles Starkweather was rumored to live in a ratty place they tore down ten years ago to build a four-plex.

From my house on Dakota Street I can walk three blocks and find a grocery store and a bank and a tattoo parlor and a Chinese restaurant, a Laundromat and a barber shop and a bar and a McDonalds. It's the way neighborhoods should be designed, the way I hope the sub-divisions of the future come together, small

pockets of people and commerce and community inside a bigger bulls eye, rings of parks and bike paths in concentric circles to the center.

For the moment our house is pretty empty. Higgins died four years ago and we planted his ashes under a chokeberry bush in the backyard. The kids went off to college and one of them has even decided he's grown up enough to be married this summer to a sweet, smart hometown girl. She's a teacher now, helping students from far off lands learn English. My son has an engineering degree and because they both love Lincoln he's getting a business degree too, so he can find a good job, right here, buy a house and stay put. Who knows, maybe he'll end up on Worthington Avenue?

I hope to stay put too, and grow into a cantankerous old lady here. I hope to be a good neighbor to the people who come and go on this street, raising their kids or finishing college. I hope I won't just wax on about the old days in Lincoln, but love it the way it has grown up into a fine, decent, mid-sized city with great grocery stores, and all the best people, and a mind of its own.

Barbara Bartle

Lead

with the
Boldest of
Dreams

Photograph © Visual Communications, Inc.

Lincoln, Nebraska is the heartland of the country. Famed Nebraska pioneer and author, Willa Cather, wrote about this heartland in *My Antonia*, "There seemed to be nothing to see; no fences, no creeks or trees, no hills or fields. If there was a road, I could not make it out in the faint starlight. There was nothing but land: not a country at all, but the material out of which countries are made."

Today, Cather's vast barren prairie has become a vibrant state. We enjoy calling the state capital, Lincoln, our home. While we look to the past with pride in the pioneer spirit upon which this city is built, we muster this same inherited grit and determination to help us shape the character of our community as we grow and evolve.

The face of Lincoln is changing. For many of our children, memories of the "home place" may lie within the rolling Sandhills or the refugee camps of Sudan. Lincoln's Community Learning Centers are part of this evolution to meet the needs of children and families. Our children are the "material" out of which Lincoln will be transformed. By placing the child in the center of our community development, we are endowing a vibrant future for Lincoln.

What is the need for Child-Centered Community Development?

Lincolnites are proud of their public schools. A large percentage of young people attend public schools and overall academic achievement is high. Lincoln is also home to many refugees from all around the world. Over 32 percent of the students in the public schools come from low income families.

Imagine a child coming to school with several heavy bags filled with homelessness, sickness and hunger. The child looks up at the adult in the hallway and says, "Can someone help me with these bags? I'm late to math class." This is the case concept for Lincoln's Community Learning Centers or CLCs.

Schools cannot accomplish this work alone. Richard Rothstein, in his 2004 book, Class and Schools: Using Social, Economic and Educational Reform to Close the Black-White Achievement Gap, argues that reforms aimed at education alone are doomed to come up short, unless they are tied to changes in economic and social policies to lessen the gaps children face outside the classroom. In Chicago, a court order to empty public housing projects, which dispersed families and children into the suburbs, led to a rise in children's academic achievement. "The evidence is pretty clear that the better their housing, the better kids do on tests," said Jack Jennings, president of the Center on Education Policy.

Lincoln's CLCs are guided by the philosophy that schools and communities must work together to provide what children and youth need to be successful. The goals are to: 1) improve student learning and development; 2) support and strengthen families; and 3) support and strengthen neighborhoods.

The CLC service delivery model requires partnerships which create a community underpinning to address a myriad of issues, such as safe, affordable housing, affordable quality childcare, workforce development and accessible health care. Children are at the center of this community development work. By building strong families and healthier neighborhoods, the youth in our schools will experience a better opportunity to succeed academically, socially and physically. Put simply, when we improve the lives of our children by focusing on their needs, the impact radiates concentrically, like a pebble in a pond, and builds stronger families, healthier neighborhoods and a brighter future for Lincoln.

Lincoln Community Learning Centers are Efficient and Effective

Much of the success of the Lincoln CLC initiative results from its seamless integrated design. The work brings about systems change, which defines, implements and institutionalizes new ways for organizations to work together to achieve goals.

Currently there are over twenty CLC sites managed by more than a dozen site supervisors. The community-based lead agencies hire the site supervisors who, in turn, broker and oversee the delivery of an array of programs and activities provided by over seventy community partners. One school principal described his lead agency as a "business partner" able to deliver assets and resources to the school that the school could not otherwise tap. The lead agencies can provide long-term commitments. The site supervisors work where the rubber meets the road. They, along with the citywide co-coordinators, are the adhesive that cements the complex collaboration of lead agencies and program partners. This is not new programming, but the purposeful integration and coordination of accessible neighborhood services which provides value added impact and outcomes.

The governance and planning is both grasstop and grassroots.

At the community-wide level, the CLC Leadership Council is a diverse group of community stakeholders whose primary role and responsibility is guiding the development and long term financing. Their goals are to develop Lincoln's capacity to implement shared partnerships and to mobilize resources to assure that CLCs are a fundamental part of the community fabric.

Each CLC site or pair of sites has an operating School Neighborhood Advisory Committee or SNAC. SNACs are the cornerstone of CLC governance. They are composed of parents, youth, educators and other school personnel, neighborhood residents, concerned citizens, community-based organizations and service providers. Their primary function is to assist with planning, communication and oversight of the neighborhood CLC.

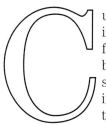

urrently the initiative is financed from a blended funding stream which includes contributions from 21st Century federal grants, Family Service, Lincoln Housing Authority, YMCA, Foundation for Lincoln Public Schools, the City of Lincoln, Lincoln Public Schools, Public Education Network, Title I, the Nebraska Investment Finance Authority, Woods Charitable Fund, Lincoln Community Foundation, Gallup, Chamber of Commerce, J.C. Seacrest Trust, Realtors Association of Lincoln, Woods Bros. Realty

Foundation and the following banks: Lincoln Federal Savings, Pinnacle, TierOne Foundation, US Bank, Wells Fargo and West Gate. That is the simple version! The partnerships have been woven together into a seamless infrastructure which turns reform work into the new way of doing business everyday with the child at the center of our community development.

So what difference have the CLCs made in Lincoln? Here are a few reasons to celebrate:

- 76 percent improved class participation by students;

- 71 percent improved student attendance;

- 69 percent improved their ability to get along well with other students;

- 69 percent improved their homework completion rate; and

- 90 percent had fewer than three school behavior referrals per year.

- CLCs are also making a difference in mobility. Mobility is a variable in student achievement, family development and neighborhood stability. The mobility rate at Elliot Elementary is 40 percent. Of the 222 Elliott students who participate in CLC only thirteen or less than 6 percent moved.

- The Lincoln Chamber of Commerce passed a resolution recognizing the importance of the CLC initiative to economic development. The long range city plan includes Community Learning Centers as a model for neighborhood delivery of services.

Pioneering Work Leads to National Accolades

Lincoln's CLCs have received local and national recognition from Neighbor Works, Coalition for Community Schools and from the National School Boards Association. In addition, articles about the model in Lincoln have been published in national media for the Public Education Network, Education Week and the American School Board Journal. These awards and publications are a tribute to the tireless effort of so many volunteers and professionals in this community. Lincoln has the capacity to lead the country in this new model of placing our children in the heart and center of our community development.

What does child-centered community development look like?
"The CLC has been a lifeline to me." This was what one Mom active in one of the Lincoln CLCs recently shared. Her family is low-income with many challenges. She had a history of alcoholism. At one time her children were wards of the state. The children are now living with their Mom and step-dad. There are two children in the family. One is a fifth grader and the other is in first grade.

Madonna Rehabilitation Hospital

Healing Through Mind, Body and Spirit

Madonna Rehabilitation Hospital was founded in Lincoln by the Benedictine Sisters of Yankton, South Dakota, in 1958 as a long term care facility. In everything we do at Madonna, we work to help the mind, body and spirit heal together … and heal one another. This approach goes beyond traditional therapy and helps nurture within patients the most critical element of recovery: hope.

- Intensive inpatient programs, including brain injury, stroke, spinal injury, neuromuscular diseases, amputation, cardiac and cancer rehabilitation and pediatrics.

- Exceptional extended care through the St. Jane de Chantal program. Memory support care is provided through The Arbors, an assisted living facility; and St. Anthony's for those who require a secure residential setting.

At Madonna … now you can.

Madonna Rehabilitation Hospital

Lincoln, NE   402-489-7102   www.madonna.org

Partner In Progress

Family Goals in Partnership with the Family Support Team

1. An initial goal for Mom was to find treatment for her alcoholism. She completed a program through Lutheran Family Services, achieved sobriety, and has been sober for the past year. She continues to attend weekly AA meetings. Achieving this objective enabled her to have her driver's license reinstated.

2. The CLC provided before and after school care for the children. The CLC encouraged the family to spend time together and made some activities available by providing free passes to the zoo and other Lincoln venues.

3. Another goal for Mom was to learn budgeting skills. CLC staff helped her develop and follow a budget. Other goals for Mom included the capacity to foster leadership skills and to improve her self-esteem.

Results

1. Improved Student Learning & Youth Development:

The children have participated in CLC enrichment clubs and attended the summer camp on CLC scholarships. As a result, the children did not lose ground academically and were 'ready to go" when the school year began.

2. Strengthen and Support Families:

The family benefited from accessing services for household goods, clothing, and grooming items, but the family also donated goods and used clothing to other children. In addition the family received the Lincoln Journal Star newspaper, given daily to CLC families, which provided literacy opportunities. The family participated in and provided volunteer service during the CLC Family Nights.

3. Strengthen and Engage Neighborhoods:

Mom has become an active part of the CLC School Neighborhood Advisory Committee (SNAC). While attending SNAC meetings and two SNAC Summits, Mom has developed leadership skills. She organized a family night at a local fun center. This involved planning the evening for approximately thirty-five people.

.The services and support of the CLC buoyed this family and helped Mom maintain her sobriety and assisted in building her self esteem.

Leading with the Boldest of Dreams
The vision for the future includes not only capital infrastructure but also the vision to build the human infrastructure. The plans need not be separate but integrated with the child at the center. The Community Learning Centers, developed and implemented with their broadest vision, will be located in every neighborhood. These centers will become the child-centered community development planning hubs for economic development, health and human services, the arts, workforce development and education. When we plan from the child to the family to the neighborhood to the community, we will be developing more successful children, stronger families and a healthier community.

Johnnetta Cole, former president of Spellman College wrote in her book, Dream the Boldest Dreams, "leadership comes not only from growing up in a place called home, but from growing out into

NET launched its television service more than 50 years ago, beginning simply with borrowed cameras, microphones and studio space in Lincoln. Today NET operates four statewide public television networks, Nebraska's public radio network and a satellite and fiber optic network to support our technology and learning services.

Yet despite great change and progress, we remain true to our mission: *to enrich lives and engage minds, connecting communities and celebrating Nebraska with services that educate, entertain and enlighten.*

NET Inspires the Extraordinary. From the perseverance of the pioneers to the grace and beauty of the Sandhill cranes to the boundless enthusiasm of our athletes, NET strives to showcase examples of the best. We spotlight stories of beauty, bravery, intelligence and spirit that inspire Nebraskans to strive for their fullest potential – to embrace new experiences and discover the extraordinary within the ordinary.

unfamiliar places." The work to develop Community Learning Centers in our home, Lincoln, has pushed our community to new and unfamiliar places. Our children are still carrying too much baggage that impedes them from learning and becoming successful adults.

By placing the child in the center of our community development, we will be endowing a vibrant future for Lincoln. We need to look into our hearts personally and collectively as a city, and decide what kind of community we want to be. That is our challenge. That

is what keeps pushing us to lead courageously with the boldest of dreams.

NET Foundations for Television and Radio

Inspire Nebraska through NET

NET Inspires Action. Nebraskans are inspired to approach the world differently because of what they have experienced through NET.

Via our broadcasts, educational resources and outreach initiatives, NET explores complex issues that are important to the livelihood of our state, and then brings Nebraskans together to deepen the impact of that knowledge.

NET Inspires Curiosity. Children have a natural sense of curiosity about the world, and NET nurtures that love of learning through trusted

television series and innovative educational programs. And learning doesn't stop with graduation – Nebraskans of every age turn to NET for entertainment and education.

NET Inspires Expression. In a time when opinion is offered as fact and life's big questions are diminished to sound bites, public broadcasting offers art – the space to ponder, question, explore and find peace. That moment may be captured in the soaring strings of Bach, in the profound humanity of drama, in the quiet contemplation of a novel or in the complexity of a question.

NET recently launched the *Inspire Nebraska Campaign*, a five-year fundraising initiative that will ensure Nebraskans will always have the opportunity to experience the extraordinary, take action, nurture their curiosity and embrace expression.

Together Let's Inspire Nebraska.

This ad is sponsored by Joel Sartore Photography: www.joelsartore.com.

netNebraska.org

Partner In Progress

Crandall Arambula

Polly McMullen

Downtown by Design

By any measure, the last decade has been a period of remarkable progress for downtown. There has been a continuous stream of major public-private redevelopment projects, beginning with the Burnham Yates Conference Center expansion at the Cornhusker Hotel in 1996. The opening of both Embassy Suites and Haymarket Park in 2000, the new Lincoln Children's Museum, the conversion of both the Lincoln Building and Old Federal Building from offices to downtown housing and the opening of the wonderful Grand Theatre in 2004 are further examples of downtown's continued growth.

During this same period, our much-loved Haymarket

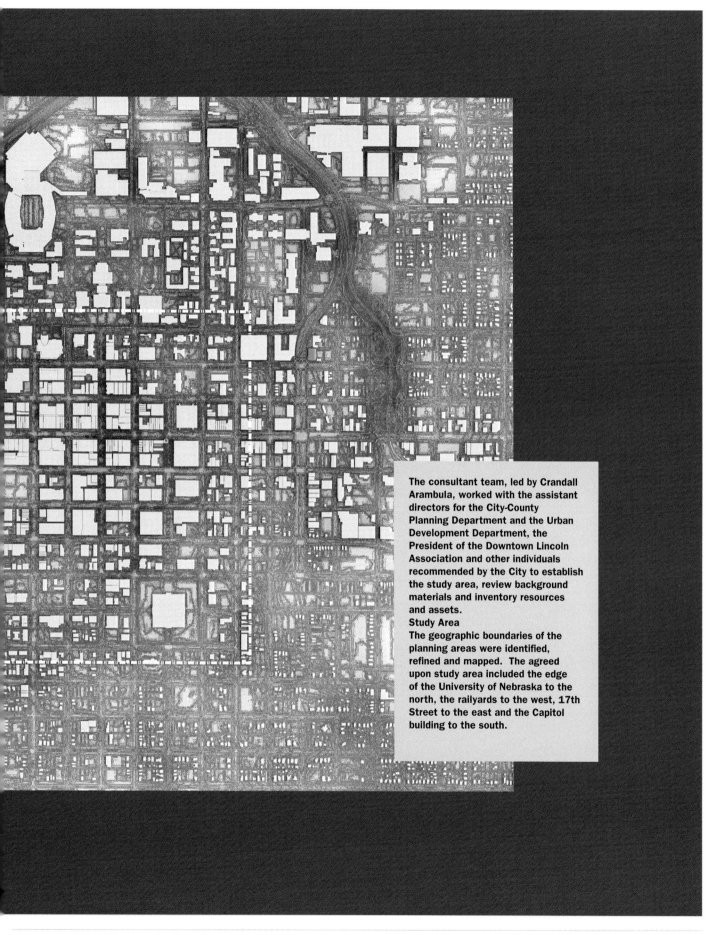

The consultant team, led by Crandall Arambula, worked with the assistant directors for the City-County Planning Department and the Urban Development Department, the President of the Downtown Lincoln Association and other individuals recommended by the City to establish the study area, review background materials and inventory resources and assets.

Study Area

The geographic boundaries of the planning areas were identified, refined and mapped. The agreed upon study area included the edge of the University of Nebraska to the north, the railyards to the west, 17th Street to the east and the Capitol building to the south.

district has flourished and work is underway on the $270 million Antelope Valley revitalization effort. Today, the Haymarket district is a favorite destination for Lincolnites and tourists alike, who flock to its diverse array of restaurants, coffee shops, art galleries, performing arts venues, unique shops and Saturday Farmers Market.

Antelope Valley is an ambitious 20-year blueprint to revitalize a blighted 600 acre area east of downtown and the UNL campus. The vision includes removing these blocks from the flood plain and creating an open waterway and green space to attract residential and commercial development and more UNL research facilities like the Beadle Center.

In addition to these public-private redevelopments, Lincoln's corporate community has stepped up in a big way in downtown. NEBCO, the major local company owned by the Abel Family, completed a beautiful new building on Lincoln Mall and Ameritas purchased the Wells Fargo Center to ensure this treasure would remain in local ownership. TierOne Bank acquired the former Centel Building at 12th and N and transformed this building into a corporate headquarters for their rapidly growing company.

National Research Corporation purchased the former Gunny's Building at 13th and Q for their corporate headquarters and Nelnet, one of Lincoln's fastest growing businesses, now owns the former Miller & Paine building at 13th and O and is expanding into the Gold's Building as well.

Downtown is a thriving arts and cultural center for both the performing and visual arts. An increasing number of galleries, and venues for the performing arts are joining the Lied Center and Sheldon Gallery in bringing art lovers downtown.

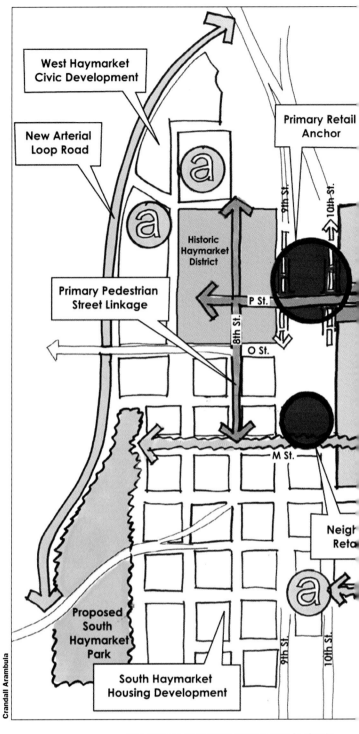

The Lincoln Downtown Master Plan is simple in its essence; it is based on a few proven concepts intended to ensure the long-term vitality and viability of the downtown. The plan builds on Lincoln's recent downtown successes and strengthens its established downtown areas, the central business district and the Historic Haymarket District. It recognizes the importance of making downtown more "people-friendly" – for pedestrians, shoppers, residents, tourists, motorists, and investors alike.

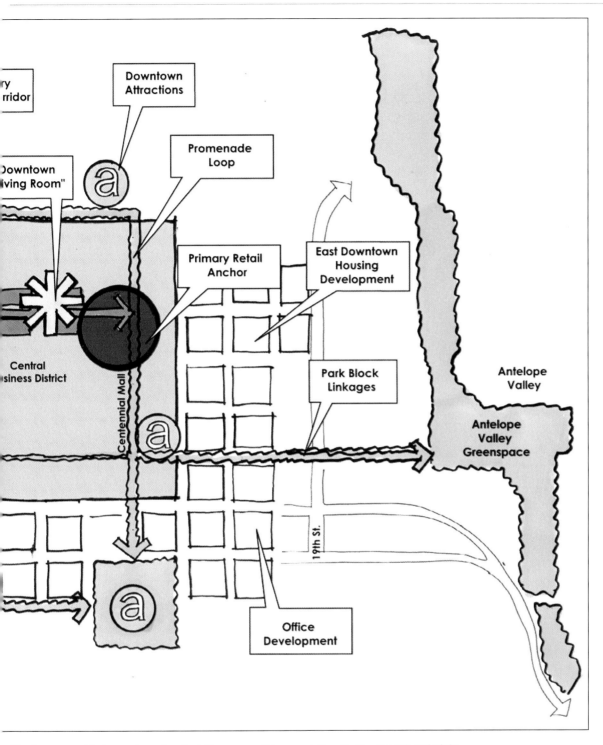

ry
rridor

Downtown
Attractions

Downtown
iving Room"

Promenade
Loop

Primary Retail
Anchor

East Downtown
Housing
Development

Central
usiness District

Centennial Mall

Park Block
Linkages

Antelope
Valley

Antelope
Valley
Greenspace

19th St.

Office
Development

The key concept is to create a clear "retail corridor" – a pedestrian-oriented street on which anchor retail and attractor uses are strategically-located at each end. This retail corridor links to a local network of equally pedestrian-friendly streets, greenways and open spaces leading to and providing amenities for adjacent districts and neighborhoods.

The Lincoln Master Plan strengthens   P Street as the primary retail corridor. Destinations on the five-block P Street retail "string" include:

- The City's "living room" – Civic Square – a new, centrally-located public open space.

- Primary retail anchors – at each end of the blocks of core retail.
- P Street also serves as the pedestrian-friendly connection between the Haymarket and central business districts. By strengthening this connection, the Master Plan reinforces the uses in each district.

The plan also capitalizes on the proximity of these established districts to adjacent potential development areas –   the "emerging" and complementary West Haymarket, South Haymarket and east downtown/Antelope Valley districts.

Because of all this new development and business expansion, downtown vacancy rates are currently the lowest they have been in over 25 years. In one of the most promising happenings for downtown Lincoln and the future of downtowns across the country, young people and young entrepreneurs are flocking to downtown. The generation that grew up hanging out in shopping malls is now embracing the authenticity, history and energy which only a downtown offers.

Downtown Lincoln is blessed with young entrepreneurs like Robert and Will Scott, who are purchasing and redeveloping properties in downtown and Haymarket, Bradley Walker of Nanonation, a growing technology firm, Charlie Hull of Archrival a Generation X and Y branding firm with national and international clients, and so many others. They are our future and DLA is doing all we can to welcome and encourage them and attract more of them.

Several years ago, it was becoming apparent that downtown was ready for a longer-term vision to guide our future so the city and DLA joined forces to undertake the first Downtown Master Plan in over 30 years. The plan was completed a year ago and unanimously adopted by the city council. It is a bold and attainable blueprint for the next 20 years!

The master plan first proposed redevelopment of the rail yard area west of the Haymarket as the site for a much-needed arena in close proximity to Memorial Stadium and Haymarket Park. As you may have read, a task force appointed by the mayor reaffirmed this location and is laying the ground work to make it happen.

The plan also calls for over 2000 additional housing units over the next 20 years to address

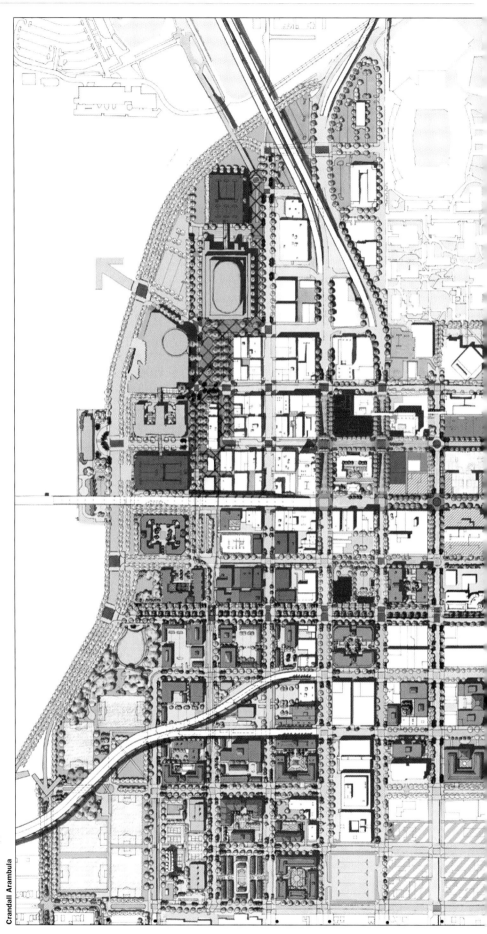

Crandall Arambula

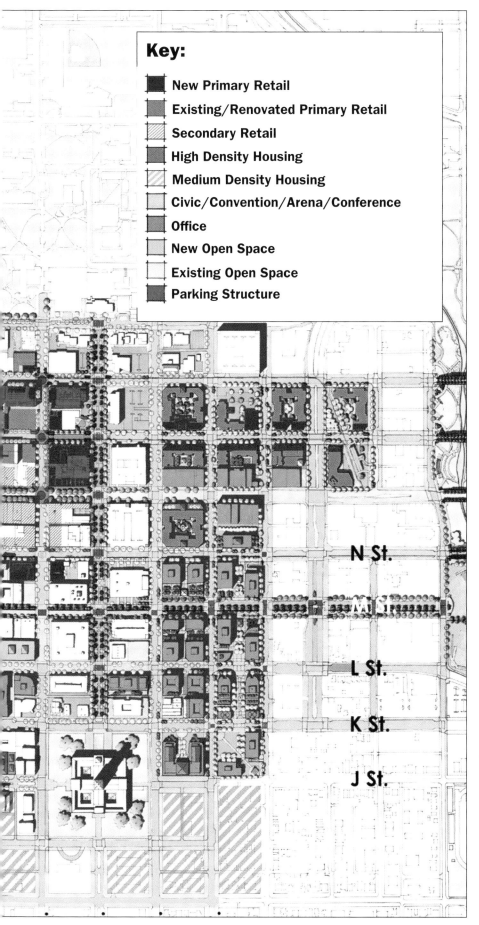

Key:

- ■ New Primary Retail
- ■ Existing/Renovated Primary Retail
- ▨ Secondary Retail
- ■ High Density Housing
- ▨ Medium Density Housing
- ☐ Civic/Convention/Arena/Conference
- ■ Office
- ☐ New Open Space
- ☐ Existing Open Space
- ■ Parking Structure

N St.

M St.

L St.

K St.

J St.

The capacity diagram is a snapshot of the character and intensity of development that could occur in the future. It is not intended as a literal illustration of proposed projects and facilities. Rather it serves to paint a vision of how the plan's concepts could be realized and to aid in calculating the long-term development potential of downtown.

A Vision for Build-Out
The diagram illustrates design schemes and development intensity that are realistic and economically feasible. The diagram is based on:
- Market research that identifies the potential for new development.
- Fundamental requirements necessary to attract investors, including proximity to public amenities and availability of parking.
- The public's desire to stimulate economic development while improving community livability.

How the Diagram is Used
The capacity diagram is used to identify potential development investment in the downtown. New private investment for retail, office, residential, and support services can be generalized from this analysis diagram. Public improvements required to stimulate private investment are also considered and can be used to determine the likely "return on investment ratio."

New Development Capacity Summary
- Retail: 900,000 SF.
- Residential: 2,800 units
- Office: 4,900,000 SF
- Parking structures: 12,400 spaces

the growing interest in living downtown. Both Antelope Valley and the area west of 9th Street and south of "O" to "K" Street in the Haymarket are envisioned as future urban neighborhoods with a variety of housing products for downtown dwellers of all ages and income levels. While not ready for development today, these areas include industrial properties which could convert to new uses or be removed to make way for new development over the next 20 years.

Retail plays a prominent role in the new master plan, especially the 'P' and 'Q' street corridors which connect the Haymarket, downtown, the campus and ultimately, Antelope Valley. The centerpiece of this retail area is a civic plaza to be built at 13th and 'P', envisioned as downtown's "living room" and gathering space.

Downtown's next public parking garage will be built at 14th & Q Streets and a city Request for Proposal (RFP) to pursue development atop this new garage and along the east and north edges of the proposed civic plaza at 13th and P drew two strong proposals. Both proposals envision a mix of office, residential, hotel and retail development on this key block bounded by P and Q, 13th and 14th Streets.

As our community looks to what the next decade could mean for downtown, it is likely that it will hold even more promise and potential than the past decade has delivered. National trends underscore a re-emergence of downtowns and the recent news of Vision 2015, a private sector leadership group committed to strengthening Lincoln, especially UNL and the downtown area, has brought excitement and momentum for downtown's future.

Key:

- Retail
- Marketplace
- Restaurant/Entertainment
- Office
- Government/Office
- New Parks and Open Space
- Existing Parks and Open Space
- New Parking Structure
- High Density Housing
- Medium Density Housing
- Education/UNL
- Arts/Cultural
- Civic/Convention/Arena/Conference
- Festival/Event Spaces

Crandall Arambula

The Land Use Framework provides a practical, proactive guide outlining the preferred community vision for development of downtown Lincoln. It is intended to attract both new users and maintain and strengthen existing desirable uses.
The Framework is realistic and achievable, addressing and meeting the market outlook for Lincoln over the next twenty years, as projected in the Long Term Market Analysis and Preliminary Retail Strategy prepared by Economics Research Associates.

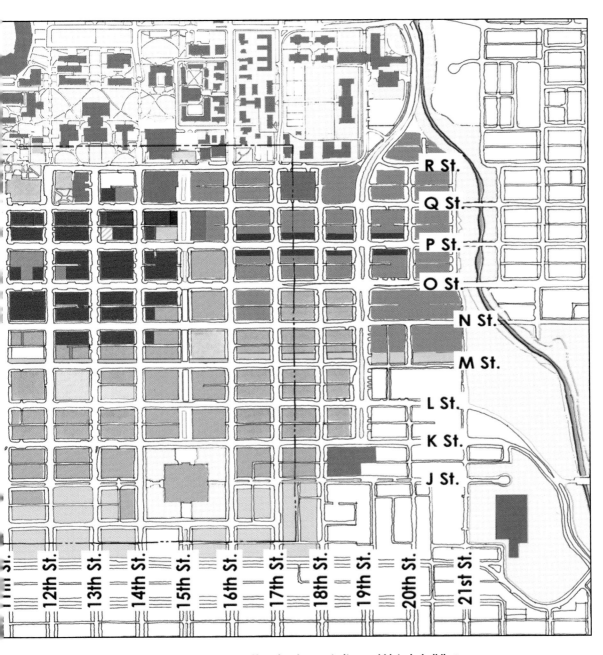

R St.

Q St.

P St.

O St.

N St.

M St.

L St.

K St.

J St.

11th St.
12th St.
13th St.
14th St.
15th St.
16th St.
17th St.
18th St.
19th St.
20th St.
21st St.

A Mix of Uses
The land use framework promotes a mix of uses, both vertically and horizontally. For example, mixed-use buildings with housing on upper floors support the retail uses on their ground floors, and benefit from nearby transit services.

When parcels contain a vertical mix of uses, the color shown on the Land Use Framework typically indicates the predominate or most important ground floor use; or in some cases, as with parking structures or housing, the predominate use can be the upper floors which make up the bulk of the building, even when ground floor uses differ.

New development sites and historic building renovation opportunities are identified for local and national retailers and businesses. Development should be transit- and pedestrian-friendly and employ sustainable practices for construction and habitation.

Illustration by Holly Pepper

Marilyn Moore

Through the Eyes of Children

Matthew makes his way carefully to the front of the Board Room. He is seven years old, and he's about to finish first grade. He and seven other first-graders, all of whom have completed Reading Recovery, are going to read to members of the Board of Education. He clutches his book, a poetry anthology, as he sidles up next to the person to whom he will read.

Then, he climbs on her lap, and carefully opens his book to the poem he has prepared to read. He reads it flawlessly; he and his teacher have practiced this many times. When he finishes reading, he pages through the rest of the book, and glances up at the woman who has been listening to him read. "I can read all of the rest of them, too," he says quietly, but with confidence and pride. Matthew knows he's a reader.

One of the most important tasks charged of adults teaching primary children is teaching them to read. In fact, it's so important that nearly half the day in kindergarten, first, and second grade is devoted to reading and literacy. We know that if children are competent readers by the end of third grade, they will likely be quite successful in the rest of their school years. Likewise, if a child is struggling with reading at the end of the grade, those struggles are likely to continue. Grade level reading by the end of third grade is a strong predictor of future school success.

Reading Recovery is a program designed for the 20 percent of first grade students who are having the most difficulty in learning to read. Matthew was in that group as a first grader, and he, like nearly 85 percent of the students who complete the Reading Recovery program, finished first grade as a grade level reader. He is well prepared for that important third grade step.

Because of Reading Recovery, and a host of other interventions and supports for children as they learn to read, about 85 percent of Lincoln Public Schools' (LPS) students are reading at or above grade level. Support continues for those children who are below grade level in subsequent grades.

Thanh is from Vietnam. She and her family came to Lincoln when she was not yet in school, and she entered kindergarten speaking no English, which made her a Level I English Language Learner. By the end of second grade, she spoke, and wrote, English fluently. In an essay about being an American, she wrote about freedom in this country, and about her parents' good jobs (they work for a food processing plant, hard and demanding work), and about how much she likes to go to school. She concluded, "I am glad to be an American."

Thanh is one of nearly 2000 students in Lincoln Public Schools who are learning to speak English, along with learning math, science, history, and all the other subject areas. We say that on any given day we have children from fifty-five countries who speak fifty-five languages. Many are already multilingual when they come to the United States; they just need to learn English. Many have not been in school at all when they come to the United States, having spent months or years in refugee camps. All share a desire to learn English. They work hard, as do their teachers. Some, like Thanh, learn quickly. For others, it takes longer. Generally, a student is fluent in speaking and listening within two to three years; reading, and especially writing, will take longer.

I stand with the principal on the front step of the school as he greets children and families on the last day of the school year. The children represent the faces of the neighborhood, the community, and the world. There are many ethnicities and cultures represented, by dress, language, and custom. Universal across all of them is an obvious love and pride

on the parents' faces as they greet the principal and give their children a last-minute hug. The principal calls the children and their parents by name, and he checks with a child about a field trip, with a mom about a new baby, and with the bus driver about her summer volunteer plans. On the front step of the school, within about fifteen minutes, the phrase "learning community" comes to life.

There are thirty-six elementary schools, ten middle schools, and six comprehensive high schools within Lincoln Public Schools. In addition, there are four high school focus programs, an alternative high school, and several specialized program sites. The schools range in size from an elementary school of less than 200 to a high school of nearly 2000. Each school is its own "learning community," with its particular demographic and economic make-up, some quite diverse, and some not nearly so. In common, they hold the goal of creating a community, to which each student and adult belongs, and for which each student and adult is responsible. Knowing names, knowing families, is important in each. In a recent parent survey, 98 percent of the parents reported feeling welcome at their child's school.

It's the week before Thanksgiving, and the students at Irving Middle School are engaged in their annual canned food drive for the Lincoln Food Bank. It's a competition among the first period classes, and the prize for the three classrooms that donate the most pounds of food is a special breakfast, catered by a local company. There are some daily prizes, too, and Irving's VIP Wells Fargo joins in the effort. When the drive is completed, the school as a whole enriches the supply at the Food Bank by more than 8000 pounds.

Each year, Lincoln Public Schools' (LPS) students, and their teachers and other staff members, contribute to the community in which they live in a myriad of ways. There are drives for the Food Bank, generally totaling more than 65,000 pounds of food. Students contribute pennies to an environmental issue. They save cans and paper for recycling. They clean up litter around the school grounds, and they do fund raisers for families when tragedy strikes. They respond to disasters around the world, like hurricanes and tsunamis, and they respond to the very personal and close-to-home heartbreak of the death of a student or teacher or principal. In the schools with the highest percentage of low-income students, children give what they have for those whose needs are great. Students learn that being part of a community means contributing to the needs of others.

It's opening night jitters all over again. The cast of "This Unsafe Star" has performed the play several times at Lincoln High, but tonight, the performance is at the Lied Center, the first ever stage performance at the Lied of a high school production. The playwright is Chris Maly, the drama teacher at Lincoln High, who tells the story of Emmett Till. Emmett is a 14-year-old African American child from the north who goes to Mississippi in 1955 to visit family. While there, he is abducted and killed; it's a racially motivated hate crime. His death, and the response to it by his mother and by the nation, is a precipitating event for the civil rights movement.

The large cast of Lincoln High students knows they are doing something wonderful, something big, this night on stage at the Lied.

They are telling a story that makes a difference, a story that matters. They are representing their school and their teacher; they are also representing a piece of history and a hope for the future.

Students in every high school have the opportunity to be on stage. One-act plays, dramas, musicals, all are performed every year. Hundreds of students find their niche, their place to belong, on stage or backstage, either as an actor or as part of the stage crew. The same is true, of course, for students who play in a band, sing in a choir, compete on an athletic team, or join a club. In addition to the opportunity to become proficient at something they love, the students also gain a place to belong, a group to call theirs, and a caring adult who helps them grow.

Sophie is a fourth grade student, a quiet, beautiful, grace-filled child. She's a good student, and she likes school. She has a younger sister in first grade, and little brother still at home. Sophie's mother has cancer, so Sophie is frequently the caretaker at home. Sophie's mother can't work, and Sophie's father is not a part of their lives. There is little food at home, and Sophie and her sister eat breakfast and lunch at school. On Fridays, before she leaves school at the end of the day, Sophie picks up a backpack, filled with food for the weekend, from a volunteer at school. The backpack, with staples like peanut butter and jelly, macaroni and cheese, cereal and juice, and a voucher for milk, will be food for the weekend for Sophie and her siblings. On Monday, Sophie will return the backpack to school, so it can be filled with food for the next weekend.

Nearly 40 percent of LPS elementary students come from families whose income is low enough that the students qualify for free or reduced-price breakfast and lunch. That's nearly 6000 students. Students of poverty are less likely to have good medical care, they are more likely to move and change schools during the school year, and they are less likely to start school with a typical five-year-old vocabulary than are students from non-low-income homes. And, they are likely to be hungry. These are the students who are glad for school to start again, whether it's on Monday after the weekend, the first day back after winter break, or the first day of the school year. For many low-income students, a school breakfast and a school lunch are their only meals. A partnership with the Lincoln Food Bank, including support from many groups and individuals in the community, provides backpacks of weekend food taken home by more than 500 children each Friday.

Katie looks a little scared, a little nervous, as she sits in her classroom right before lunch on the first day of school. She's in sixth grade, and she's starting middle school. The building is much bigger than her elementary school, and so far today she's figured out where her classrooms are and how to work the padlock on her locker. The next challenge will be the middle school lunch line, which has lots more choices than in elementary school! By the end of the day, she's relieved. By the end of the week, she's making new friends, and she declares that middle school is good. By the end of the year, she's confident, successful, and ready for seventh grade.

Time Warner Cable – a Company that Cares for Our Local Community!

Whether you find yourself at home, at work or out in the community, Time Warner Cable offers you the convenience of having all your communication services from one local company. Turn to Time Warner Cable for a wide range of communication and entertainment needs, including: **Basic and Digital Cable, HD, Digital Video Recorder, Road Runner High Speed Internet, Digital Home Phone and Pivot Wireless Service.** These services were created to simplify your life and to help you keep connected with your family and loved ones here in Lincoln and around the world.

nebOD **Nebraska On Demand** (channel 101), a unique channel available for free to digital cable subscribers, offers great programming under the following categories: *Around Nebraska, Sports, Arts & Entertainment, Huskers, Education, My TWC and Shop Nebraska.*

Lorie Safford from LPS Foundation receives grant check from Ann Shrewsbury with Time Warner Cable

Community service is woven into the fabric of who we are. The very nature of our business offers unique opportunities to our local employees to serve in the community and help Lincoln become a better place to live. Through the **Community Grant Program,** the Time Warner Cable Lincoln office has donated more than $300,000 in grants and half a million dollars in public service announcements to nonprofit organizations with focuses on education, athletics, the arts and technology. In addition, Time Warner Cable is a company that encourages volunteerism. Every year, more than 70 employees volunteer in the community, including at public schools events, Celebrate Lincoln Ethnic Festival, Lincoln Municipal Band concerts, City Impact, Nebraska State Fair, TeamMates Mentoring Program, Boy Scouts of America, among others. Since 2001, employees from the Lincoln office have also been helping raise thousands of dollars to purchase winter clothing for Clinton Elementary School students and People's City Mission, through the local Mittens & More Campaign.

Marcia Stewart, Spotlight Award Winner from Lefler Middle School

Education is our priority in all community service efforts. The Time Warner Cable Lincoln office annually invests thousands of dollars in cash and in-kind contributions into local schools through initiatives such as **Cable in the Classroom**. We also use our vast network to deliver the resources of cable programming and technology, including Digital Cable, at no cost to Lincoln schools' media centers, and also High Speed Internet to public libraries.

In addition, we reach out to educators, helping them to incorporate cable programming into their school curricula, through **Cable in the Classroom,** making a difference in the way the digital generation students learn. Every K-12 teacher within the Time Warner Cable Nebraska service area is eligible to take part in our teacher workshops and is encouraged to apply for our local annual **Spotlight Awards**, which recognize and reward educators who creatively integrate cable technology in the classroom. These educators are also eligible for the prestigious Time Warner Cable National Teacher Award, which offers cash prizes to winners and a trip to Washington D.C. .

The employees of Time Warner Cable are proud to be part of a company that cares for the communities we serve.

2007 National Teacher Award Winners from Nebraska with Sen. Chuck Hagel.

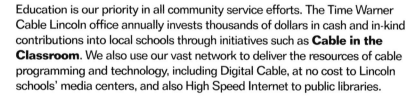
TIME WARNER CABLE
THE POWER OF YOU

Every year, more than 2300 students in LPS make the transition from elementary school to middle school. It's a big transition, for parents as well as students. The organization of middle schools has been planned so that sixth grade is much like fifth grade, and eighth grade is much like high school, and seventh grade is in the middle. Katie's sixth grade teachers, like sixth grade teachers in all middle schools, see it as part of their work to help students learn to "do" middle school. It works; there is no loss in academic performance from fifth grade to sixth grade. And, like Kelsey, sixth graders end the year confident and successful, and ready for seventh grade.

It's graduation day, and Anya and her parents are preparing the back yard for the party that will follow the graduation ceremony. Anya will graduate first in her class, having taken honors and Advanced Placement classes in English, history, math, and science. She has also excelled in speech and debate and in Future Business Leaders of America competitions. She's played in the band and been a member of student council. From many choices, she has decided to attend Duke University.

It's graduation day, and Shane and his parents are preparing the back yard for the part that will follow the graduation ceremony. Shane will graduate somewhere in the middle of his class. He didn't see a lot of relevance for many classes, especially math, until he took classes in Residential Construction. At that point, geometry became real, and so did reading, and Shane found his passion in life. He likes

building houses; he's a leader, and his teacher made him crew chief during his senior year. Shane talked about a house he and his classmates had built. "Every time I drive past that house, I see kids playing in the front yard, and I say to myself, 'We built that house, and a family lives there.' That makes me feel pretty good." Shane will enroll in the construction program at Southeast Community College; he also has a job with a local construction company.

LPS graduates have had many experiences in high school; there is probably no such thing as a "typical" student. All will have met graduation requirements, including demonstration of specified skill levels in math, reading, and writing. Some will have developed expertise in a content area like history or science while others will have found their hearts' calling in the arts. Still others will have discovered their talent to build, whether it is furniture, houses, or families. More than 75 percent of LPS graduates will be in some form of post-secondary education two years after graduation; most of them will also be employed on a part-time basis. Others will be working full-time, and some will have joined one of the branches of the armed services. LPS graduates give high marks to their education in math and English; they wish they had learned more about being a steward of the environment and working with people from different cultures.

It's summer, and far from the picture that most might have that school activity stops during the summer, the work continues. Students are in summer school, and teachers are working

with principals and district administrators to revise curriculum, prepare school improvement plans, and develop plans for individual students. Professional development classes are held all summer, with topics ranging from multicultural education to religious liberty to application of brain research to behavior systems. Science

Nebraska

JOEL SARTORE

teachers are spending days with scientists to update their content knowledge; kindergarten teachers are reviewing best practices for working with their young learners. The maintenance and custodial staff are preparing buildings for the next year, and newly hired teachers are wondering who their students will be and rehearsing what they will say when the bell rings on that first day. Principals and associate principals are putting the final touches on the schedule for the coming year, and the purchasing and accounting employees are trying to wrap up the current year and get ready for the next. All activities are pointed toward the first day of school, the day students get up early (with a groan, sometimes), put on their new school shoes, grab a backpack, and head out the door to start another year.

joelsartore.com

Any Joel Sartore image is available as a signed archival photographic print.

Starting at just $40, any image from *National Geographic* Photographer Joel Sartore's extensive collection is available as a signed archival print. The perfect gift for that hard-to-please person in your life.

Also available, *Nebraska: Under a Big Red Sky,* the heartland classic showcasing dozens of Joels's vibrant images. Soft cover only $19.95 plus tax and shipping.

To explore the thousands of possibilities, go to joelsartore.com or call 402/474-1006

Harvey Perlman

The Coins
of the Future

An individual's, an institution's, or a city's vision for the future is defined by its ambition. There are those who envision change with confidence that it can be managed with intelligence; there are those who find change frightening and can thus only envision the comfort and familiarity of the past.

But, of course, it is a false comfort because change is inevitable. The question is whether change will be driven by an ambitious vision, one that sees the potential for Lincoln and Nebraska to be competitive in the nation's and the world's economy, and in the process, to be positioned to build an improved quality of life for all its citizens.

The University of Nebraska-Lincoln has very high ambitions. We have created a campus culture that thrives on competition and success and we have demonstrated by our actions that our faculty and our students can compete against those from the very best Universities in the country and the world. The reality behind UNL's doubling of its research grants within a 6 year period is that its faculty went head to head in a competitive environment with faculty from other public and private research institutions and increasingly were recognized with the best proposals and with the talent to carry them out. We have high ambitions for our students and have always admired their ability to climb the ladders of corporate America, of the professions, of the arts, and of a variety of other endeavors. We

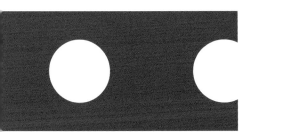

do not believe that our ambitions are unmatched by our talent or our potential.

These ambitions produce a vision for the University that is in keeping with the projected future course of the world. We intend to build a research capacity that works at the cutting edge of knowledge to produce new understandings about our world and innovative solutions to the problems that confront us. The fields of engineering and science will play the most visible role but we should not under-estimate the work in the social sciences that help understand and improve the interactions of people in our society and the work of the humanities and the arts that help understand and improve the human condition.

Research has two important purposes. First it is the outgrowth of man's interest in better understanding the world. For some, merely the understanding is sufficient; for others, that understanding is the tool with which one can address the

problems that confront us and improve the lives that we live. Albert Einstein said something like: 'if we knew what we were doing, we wouldn't call it research' and in many instances this is true. Discoveries often arise in surprising ways. Thus there are inherent but not always measurable advantages to creating a place where researchers can explore their own ideas, interact with others, and most importantly, engage students who will represent the researchers of tomorrow. The University of Nebraska-Lincoln is creating such a place.

The second important purpose of research is to generate economic growth. Innovation and talent are the coins of the future in economic competition. Nebraska faces stiff competition from other states for talent leading to innovation and the United States collectively faces that same competition from other countries. University innovation, if properly managed and supported, can generate products with commercial value and this, in turn, can generate companies with jobs to exploit that commercial value. It also attracts companies that see value in establishing relationships with research faculty and that

depend on highly trained students to complete their workforce. It is not accidental that areas of the country that have sustained real economic growth tend to cluster around research universities. Thus, there are inherent but not always measurable advantages to creating a place where university researchers and students can interact with private sector scientists and entrepreneurs on a daily basis. The University of Nebraska-Lincoln hopes to help create such a place.

This vision of the growth of a research university does not diminish, but rather enhances the importance of undergraduate and graduate education. The University places undergraduate education as its highest priority and we have developed, and envision continued development of, programs that permit each student, with his or her particular bundle of talents and interests, to become successful. Graduate students are the seed corn for future innovation as they prepare themselves for careers in research. We hope that both graduate and undergraduate students will become engaged in the research enterprise, learning the challenges and stimulation of finding new knowledge, but more importantly, of acquiring the habits of the innovative mind. The University not only produces innovations but also innovators and this combination can lead to expanded economic growth for Nebraska.

So, in summary, the vision we are pursuing at the University includes an academic program and a research enterprise of the highest quality, one that attracts young people not only from Nebraska but also from beyond, with the capacity to also generate the high quality jobs that will keep them here after graduation. We know this vision is possible and we have confidence it can be achieved. Yet, the vision is incomplete unless it engages both the State of Nebraska and the City of Lincoln in its pursuit.

The University of Nebraska-Lincoln is at the beginning of launching the Nebraska Innovation Center, a research corridor that will extend along Antelope Valley. The elimination of the flood plain by a massive and critically important public works project allows the University to pursue this vision. From Q Street through the recently acquired Textron plant, we envision University research facilities, providing the best environment for research and for engaging students in that process. Our efforts are now focused on Whittier School which we hope to revitalize as a building for research as well as for incubation space where we might nurture very early stage companies based on University research. A new physical science center will start to emerge on the corner of 16th and W and when completed will partner with the existing Engineering Center at 17th and Vine and the Beadle Center for Life

'if we knew what we were doing, we wouldn't call it research'

Illustration by Holly Pepper

Science Research at 19th and Vine as the core facilities in the research corridor. Additional facilities for nanotechnology, one of the most important new technologies that will generate new materials and new processes for many areas of our existence, and for expanding life science research are planned.

The full potential of the Nebraska Innovation Center will not be realized unless the City of Lincoln makes possible the location of private sector research companies in close proximity to the University. East downtown, once removed from the flood plain, provides such an opportunity. The University continues to explore the availability of a larger space to create an innovation campus, one that would attract a mixing of university and private-sector research and development companies, that would provide easy proximity for faculty, students, and private sector researchers to produce the synergies common to clustering innovative people from a variety of perspectives together in the pursuit of new ideas.

Lincoln has the potential to develop a very significant research and technology economic base. The existing advantages are numerous: a life style increasingly attractive to young professionals, relatively inexpensive electric power, a location within America's richest and increasingly important and diverse agricultural region and yet also astride the major information and physical highways of our country, and an expanding research university. The engagement of the business sector, through the newly formed 2015 Visioning Group, and the active support of the Lincoln Chamber of Commerce, provide a climate where real progress is possible.

Expanding beyond the City of Lincoln, Nebraska has a unique potential in the I-80 corridor and the opportunity it presents for economic development. Anchored on the West by the research potential of the University of Nebraska-Lincoln and on the East by the expanding research activity at the University of Nebraska Medical Center and the Peter Kiewit Institute, the corridor has a range of technologies, expertise, talent, and workforce skills, represented within a 50 mile radius. The potential is for each of these institutions to continue to generate companies through research, or to attract existing companies to this pool of talent. One can envision small start-up companies or outposts of larger companies locating adjacent or in close proximity to these research centers. As they grow and prosper, they can expand within the cities or along the I-80 corridor as they take advantage of the innovations generated by interacting with the Universities and with each other.

A properly planned I-80 corridor, one with the necessary infrastructure and the amenities to become attractive for high level technology companies, should be a part of every Nebraskan's vision. It is the future, and if it doesn't develop here producing benefits for Nebraska, it will develop elsewhere in competition with us.

With our focus on technology and research, we should not ignore the other investments that Nebraskans have traditionally made that have set us apart and which will continue to contribute to our success. Nebraska has historically made investments in arts and culture, from the Sheldon and Joselyn Art Galleries, the Lied and Holland Performing Arts Centers, and the enriching expanse of art and music that enliven our communities across Nebraska. Husker football and the other athletic programs of the University, give Nebraska an atmosphere that is unique. Any vision for the future must embrace all of our advantages and package them into a foundation for a future that is attractive to entrepreneurs and to young people generally.

Newt Gingrich reported that some 40 years ago the per capita income of South Korea and Ghana were the same. In that short period, South Korea has become an industrial and technological power house. It of course benefited from American investment but the point is that making the right investments, from whatever source, can allow one country or one state to succeed wildly beyond its current circumstance. I believe Nebraska is positioned so that it could achieve remarkable success in the next few decades. We have the work ethic, a manageable scale of population and the resources and infrastructure that are competitive, as well as a quality of life that is increasingly attractive to those who have grown tired of the intensity of living in more highly developed areas. An ambitious vision and the will to make the long-term investments are the essential requirements for future success.

Kent Seacrest

Launching: 2015

Lincoln faces serious challenges in the future. The city's isolated, geographic location in a predominately agricultural state, experiencing a stagnating population, raises major economic questions. National prosperity is shifting from the northern Rust Belt and coastal portions of the country and moving to the Sun Belt region of our country. Meanwhile, international competition has increased, placing additional economic tension on the Upper Midwest region. However, while most Upper Midwest region communities struggle, Lincoln is fortunate to have two important and unique attributes: (1) it is home to the State's Capitol and University; and (2) it is temporary residence to the best 8,000 young freshman minds each year who attend universities and colleges in Lincoln.

Vision

State's Capitol and University

There are seven cities that share the distinction of being both their state capitol as well as home to their state's major research university. They include Austin, Texas, Columbia, South Carolina, Columbus, Ohio, Lincoln, Nebraska, Madison, Wisconsin, Saint Paul, Minnesota, and Salt Lake City, Utah.

This is a distinct list of high quality communities. The seven cities have successfully leveraged the state capitol and state university combination to create unique balances of stable economies and dynamic growth, while free enterprise and the collective public good prosper together. The state capitol and state university combination is proving to be a winning formula. Over the last quarter century, Austin, Columbus, Madison, Saint Paul and Salt Lake have taken off and are praised as model cities for economic prosperity and social integrity. Over the last decade Columbia, South Carolina has launched many new economic initiatives and generated a higher quality of life. Is Lincoln next?

From 2000 to 2005, Columbia, South Carolina grew the fastest, followed by Madison, Wisconsin. Surprisingly, Lincoln's percentage growth rate over the five year period exceeded such great cities as Austin, Texas, Columbus, Ohio, Salt Lake City, Utah and Saint Paul, Minnesota. However, other economic and social indices suggest that Lincoln is not keeping up with these quality communities.

The State Capitol is very important in formulating sound State public policies. State government and its many wonderful state employees generate many attributes and benefits. Yet, the state governmental economy will not likely fuel Lincoln's launch. The greater potential lies with the State's flagship research University becoming the greater long term strategy for Lincoln's future. Already, the University of Nebraska—Lincoln (UNL) is Lincoln's largest generator of economic development and intellectual capital which improves Lincoln's quality of life. Lincoln's vision needs to include major initiatives to assist UNL in leveraging its research, technology, education, arts, community outreach and student social, political and athletic mission. Our community's future could launch with UNL.

Best 8,000 Young Minds

Each year 8,000 of the State's and the region's best 18 year old minds come to Lincoln to enroll as freshmen in our Capital City's fine universities and colleges. While attending school, they provide Lincoln needed vitality and creativity. Their presence creates many jobs for others in the community. Yet, upon completion of their formal education, we are not retaining enough of these fine young adults in Lincoln.

Many would like to stay and call Lincoln home. But they can not find quality jobs. Lincoln's job market is not dynamic enough to keep pace and provide a fitting job for these well trained minds. Meanwhile, building materials, energy costs and the community's infrastructure, financing and land use policies are increasing housing costs beyond their means. This younger generation wants to work hard, but they also want to play hard. For fun, this generation wants more than just the "O" Street bar scene. They seek more diverse and quality forms of entertainment and recreation, which Lincoln is not currently providing.

Lincoln's failure to keep pace with these 8,000 young minds every year with quality jobs, affordable housing or adequate entertainment and recreation leads to a serious brain drain. In turn, these are the issues preventing Lincoln from launching. These young minds have better choices or are forced to leave Lincoln for other communities to start their new careers and families. Consequently, many Lincoln moms and dads lose some of their quality of life by having to get on airplanes or in cars to see their young adult children and grandchildren in other far away communities.

The Angelou Report that was commissioned by the Lincoln Chamber of Commerce stated that 70% of our future community wealth will come from our own entrepreneurial citizens. When you think about it, the X generation (25-44 years of age) is the best bet to be Lincoln's next successful entrepreneurs. Lincoln's 50 and 60 year olds are starting to shift some of their entrepreneurial energies towards retirement. We can greatly influence Lincoln's future. It is our choice to be active or passive. We either start making the Capitol City more attractive for the X generation. Or else Lincoln

could start to trend like many smaller Nebraska communities by losing its young entrepreneurs. In turn, this results in a loss of community wealth and resources, leaving behind an "older and graying" population with many fixed costs. The results then lead to even "higher property taxes" or a "reduction of community services" and "quality of life".

Lincoln's 2015 Vision

Recently, a group of Lincoln business and community leaders decided to address these pressing issues. Formed at the end of 2006, 2015 Vision identifies ten pillars (projects) that need to be built for Lincoln to launch and reach its great potential. The pillars include the following (not in priority order):

1 West Haymarket Arena. As recommended by the Mayor's Arena Task Force, acquiring most of the Burlington Northern Santa Fe Railroad yard and constructing a new 15,000 seat Arena in the West Haymarket area behind Lincoln Station to replace the aging Pershing Auditorium;

2 New Convention Center and Headquarter Hotel. Encourage a redeveloper to construct a new convention, conference and exhibition center with a headquarter hotel next to the new West Haymarket Arena, utilizing the Lincoln Station as a major entry point;

3 Expand Haymarket Park to the south and north with new baseball, softball, soccer and football fields for city youth, adult, Lincoln Public School and higher education sporting and recreation events;

4 Create and market a new Nebraska Sports Triangle between Memorial Stadium, expanded Haymarket Park and the new West Haymarket Arena. This recreational and economic area would provide a special place for state and regional sports tournaments, while sharing parking and providing before and after game food, beverages, and shopping places;

5 Develop a University Arts and Humanities Center Block in the Haymarket to celebrate Nebraska's rich heritage in the pedestrian friendly Haymarket area. The Arts and Humanities Block would also include first floor retailing and upper story residential living units;

6 Implement Lincoln's "Town Square" at 13th and "P" Streets and develop the Tower project on top of the new City parking garage along "Q" Street between 13th and 14th Streets for downtown residential living, hotel and/or office uses;

7 Expand community and university related retail and entertainment along the town/gown "P" and "Q" Street zipper between the University and Downtown. Run a trolley along this corridor from the Haymarket to East Downtown Community Park and back. Other major University cities, such as Madison, Wisconsin, Lawrence, Kansas, Bloomington, Indiana, Iowa City, Iowa, etc., have successfully developed dynamic retail areas that cater to a multitude of generations who remain young of mind and heart;

8 Complete the Antelope Valley Waterway, Parkway, and Community Projects including constructing the high amenity East Downtown Community Park from "O" to "R" Streets and updating Trago Park from "R to "U" Streets. These improvements will revitalize the eastern edge of Downtown and UNL Campus, remove the designated 100-year flood plain from 800 dwellings, 200 businesses and over fifty acres of UNL Campus, as well as help reduce traffic congestion and remove arterial 16th and 17th Streets traffic through the University campus;

9 Develop a public and private sector research and development corridor along Antelope Valley improvements from "O" Street to State Fair Park. The R & D Corridor would include:

a. Redevelopment of Historic Whittier Junior High School into a premier University dry lab research facility;

b. Begin implementing the Board of Regent's UNL Master Plan that includes up to six new research and classroom facilities around the present Beadle Center and College of Engineering; and

c. Create locations for private research companies in the East Downtown area and other areas to be in close proximity to the University's public research facilities.

10 Finally, Expanded High Amenity Agricultural Exposition Center. Create an attractive, vibrant, year-round regional exhibition and events center at 84th and Havelock, one focused on agriculture, livestock and other compatible exhibitions. Co-locating the Nebraska State Fair and Lancaster County Fair would be the first step. Co-location could improve the viability of both fairs, reduce taxpayer assistance, and provide a state and local exposition center for year round activities. The State Fair campus could then be used by the University and City to provide additional lands in the Research and Development Corridor, as well as for recreation, parking and other community purposes.

The above ten pillars are not meant to be an exhaustive or an exclusive list of the community's imperatives. No doubt there are other important strategies that Lincoln needs to continue to address, such as K-12 education, infrastructure financing, community leadership, etc. The 2015 Vision leadership identified the above ten pillars as those that are most imperative to launch Lincoln's future. These ten ideas have already had extensive public process. The public sector has blessed and approved the concept of the ten pillars.

However, the public sector alone appears to lack the ability, resources and leadership to get these projects across the finish line. Lately, there is an increased distrust of government, both at the national level and local level. Taxes have become a four letter word. We give government a tax dollar and there is a perception (or reality) that we only get a few cents back on the dollar. Many Lincolnites are saying we have become too dependent upon our local government to lead, fund and guide Lincoln's entrepreneurial energies and spirits. For many years now, the private sector has been sleepy and not willing to work enough with government in a win, win way. Other citizens are quick to point out that the private sector has been nonexistent ever since the "O Street Gang" retired or died. Lincoln's public and private sectors are out of balance and not harmonious.

The 2015 Vision believes it is time to restore a better balance. It is time for the private sector to be more accountable and provide needed leadership and direction. The private sector needs to step it up and increase its investments in this dynamic community---through business investing, volunteering and philanthropic giving, so all the community ships rise together. It is time for the private sector to partner with government to complete these ten pillars and

really launch like the other six state government/university cities.

We need more public-private partnering to leverage both public dollars as well as private dollars in a time when resources are stretched thin. The construction and operation of Haymarket Park is a great example of a successful public-private partnership. Haymarket Park involves two governmental entities (City and University) joining with the private sector business (NEBCO, Inc.). The end result has been a facility much nicer than any one entity could begin to afford to build and operate on its own. Instead of cents on the dollar, one public dollar plus one private dollar can work together to produce three or four dollars of community benefits. The ten pillars are new, major, community investments that will require similar win, win, public-private partnering efforts to pool and leverage limited community dollars.

We talk a lot about the dollars, but at the end of the day a community needs to measure its success based upon the quality of life for all its citizens. The 2015 Vision seeks to implement pillars that will simultaneously improve the quality of the Capital City and the University of Nebraska Lincoln. The vision seeks to retain more of the 8,000 college minds every year to call Lincoln home. This is accomplished by these ten pillars providing these young minds with quality jobs, affordable housing and increased entertainment and recreation opportunities upon completion of their formal college education. If these strategies are implemented, all other segments of

the community will enjoy increased benefits and rewards as well.

In turn, this next young generation of entrepreneurs, along with the other generations, will dream of new community and business ideas. Together, we will take basic research and apply it to help our state and nation. We will expand primary jobs and attract new businesses. We will produce higher salaries and wages to allow more savings and investment. We will reinvest and rehabilitate the fine homes located in Lincoln's existing neighborhoods and build new quality and affordable homes in Lincoln's future neighborhoods. We will enjoy our time having fun in a variety of new recreational and entertainment venues. And we will produce investments and salaries that will lead to a net improvement in our tax base.

Change is inevitable. Lincoln can either elect to: (1) sit back, be late at reacting and be left behind the curve of change; or (2) implement a bold new vision that reenergizes the public and private sectors to build new community pillars that strengthen the Capitol City and University community and help retain Lincoln's young minds. The choice to launch is ours.

In many ways I look, think, and act like a Nebraskan. But it is more complex than that. Nebraska culture is not coherent and homogenous. We have many Native American tribes with powwows all through the year and we have strong African

American communities in Lincoln and Omaha. We have liberals and conservatives, sophisticates and provincials who have never left their country of birth. We have evangelicals and Sufis, hate groups and Nebraskans for Peace. Within Nebraska culture there are the

The Opportunit

Dr. Mary Pipher

Selected quotes from
The Middle of Everywhere
{Harcourt}

Even though people of color have a rich history in our state and, of course, the Native Americans were here first, our state's identity the last 150 years has been mainly European.

The real change occurred in the 1990s. Because Lincoln had almost no unemployment and a relatively low cost of living, we were selected by the U.S. Office of Refugee Resettlement as a preferred community for newly arrived refugees. Now we are one of the top-twenty cities in America for new arrivals from abroad. Our nonwhite population has grown 128 percent since 1990.

Suddenly, our supermarkets and schools are bursting with refugees from Russia, Serbia, Croatia, Bosnia, Hungary, and Ethiopia. Even as I write this, refugees from Afghanistan, Liberia, and Sierra Leone are coming into our community. ...We have children from fifty different nationalities who speak thirty-two different languages in our public schools.

Lincoln has often been described by disgruntled locals and insensitive outsiders as the middle of nowhere, but now it can truthfully be called the middle of everywhere.

o Get Things Right

Lincoln is our capital city. Its skyline is dominated by our capitol building with its golden dome crowned by The Sower scattering seed across the land. The year I wrote this book, the capitol was being repaired and refurbished for the new century, a nice metaphor for the changes in our state. The men who worked on the capitol scaffolding spoke thirty different languages, which prompted my friend Sarah to call our capitol "tower of Babel."

Globalization will change everything forever. Soon we will all be as mixed together as a bowl of salt and pepper. Refugees in our town offer us a heightened version of the experiences we'll all share as our world becomes one vast fusion culture. They are the harbingers of our future. The coping skills that refugees need—flexibility, the ability to make good decisions in the face of a dazzling number of choices, the ability to stay calm in a tough situation, and the ability to deal with people different than themselves—are the skills we will all need. All of us will require a global positioning system to tell us who and where we are.

"We think the world apart," said Parker Palmer. "What would it be like to think the world together?"

Teilhard de Chardin had a word—unfurling—to describe that "infinitely slow spasmodic movement towards the unity of a mankind." He saw education and love as the twin pillars of progress. At this amazing point in history, we have the opportunity to get things right.

Contributors

Krista Burlae is a published and acknowledged author of academic non-fiction, fiction and theatre. She has taught college writing as well as other disciplines. A former social worker, she identifies each author's unique, literary patterns and assists in enhancing and continuing those patterns within the writing process to create a piece of art. She holds a bachelor's in English, a Master's in Sociology and a Master's in Social Work. As a Writing Consultant, Krista has edited books, papers and stories in all different fields and genres and coached writers of equal diversity and skill levels. Her website address is www.writerswellspring.com.

Barbara Bartle has served as the Executive Director of the Foundation for Lincoln Public Schools for fifteen years, and is currently the organization's President. The Foundation was established in 1989 to provide the margin of excellence for the students and staff in the

Lincoln Public Schools in Lincoln, Nebraska. Prior to her affiliation with the Foundation, Ms. Bartle earned her B.S. in education from the University of Nebraska-Lincoln. She was a teacher at the elementary level and administrator at a performing arts center. While building the capacity of the Foundation, she has served as a consultant to other local education funds and school foundations across the country.

Wendy Birdsall is the President of the Lincoln Chamber of Commerce. As the president of the chamber, she also is President of the Lincoln Partnership for Economic Development, a coalition of the chamber, local government and private businesses financed with public and private money.

Wendy is a lifelong resident of Lincoln and a graduate of the University of Nebraska-Lincoln. She has served the chamber in a number of capacities for 16 years.

At press time, **Morgan L. Fry** is a s graduate candidate at St. Ambrose University, majoring in Marketing and Public Relations. A self-described "Mississippi River-rat," she has a deep understanding of the factors that make people call a place, "home." She also has a deep understanding of how to keep her family's pizza place customers happy. She is entertaining offers for post-graduate employment, something outside front-line food service.

Cindy Lange-Kubick has been a columnist and reporter at the Lincoln Journal Star since 1994, She writes about Life in Lincoln, its interesting places, people and quirks. Her essay for this book takes a look at the Lincoln she loves and the Lincoln she hopes her hometown grows up to be.

Lincoln Journal Star © 2005

When her three children were small she attended the University of Nebraska-Lincoln, majoring in journalism and sociology -- next spring she plans to graduate with her 22-year-old daughter.

Andrew L. McDonald is the senior pastor at Westminster Presbyterian Church and oversees a staff of twenty-two in the largest Presbyterian Church in Nebraska. As a relative newcomer to Lincoln, he brings a fresh sense of appreciation for what Lincoln has to offer. The Rev. Dr. McDonald earned a Bachelor of Social Work degree from the University of Illinois; a Masters of Divinity degree from Yale University; a Masters of Arts in religious ethics from Vanderbilt University; and a Doctor of Ministry degree from McCormick Theological Seminary. He has served congregations in Chicago, Illinois; Peoria, Illinois; and Nashville, Tennessee, among others. He and Parrish, as parents of Edison, Field and Trinity, have a

deep appreciation for all the people who make Lincoln a special place for children and young adults.

Award-winning art director **Larry McDonald** was born in Chicago and raised in rural Illinois. With degrees from Northern Illinois University, Mr. McDonald regularly advises clients as diverse as Alcoa, John Deere, the State of Illinois and local Quad Cities communities on communication and development matters.

"I'm all about architectural adaptive re-use. How can you make use of existing development, make it serve the current need and preserve the character for the future?"

He resides "in the house my grandfather built for my father to grow up," and maintains an active interest in the family farm near the intersection of Interstate 80 and the Mississippi River. His website address is www. thinktankworks.com.

Author **James L. McKee** brings broad expertise and a deep understanding of the history of Lincoln. Jim's biography appears on page 65.

Polly McMullen has served as President of the Downtown Lincoln Association (DLA) since 1997. She oversees the activities of a sixteen member staff and three Business Improvement Districts (BIDs) serving a sixty-six block downtown area.

Prior to joining DLA, McMullen served as an aide to former Lincoln Mayor, now U.S. Secretary of Agriculture, Mike Johanns. She

grew up in Omaha, has a masters degree from the University of Wisconsin and a bachelors degree from San Francisco College for Women. She currently serves on the boards of United Way, the United Way Foundation and Madonna Rehabilitation Hospital.

In 2005, DLA and the City of Lincoln completed a Downtown Master Plan, the first comprehensive plan for downtown Lincoln in over thirty years. The Master Plan process was led by Crandall Arambula, a nationally recognized urban design and planning firm from Portland, Oregon.

Polly was married for twenty-nine years to Lincoln physician Bruce McMullen, who passed away in 2000. She has two grown children.

Marilyn Moore is Associate Superintendent for Instruction in the Lincoln Public Schools. Her undergraduate, masters, and doctoral degrees are all from the University of Nebraska—Lincoln. She has been a middle school teacher and team leader, an administrator of a federal program, an adjunct faculty member of UNL, and an administrator in the Human Resources department at LPS. She brings these perspectives, plus those of a reader, musician, gardener, camp counselor, active church member, and softball player, to this essay. She is a storyteller and an advocate for children who looks for and marvels at the connectedness of our lives.

Edward J. Mueller is the past Publisher of *Chef* magazine, and currently is a consultant to the commercial food preparation industry. As an expert in "combat cuisine" (meals prepared while under extreme conditions such as at high-altitudes and on-board ships in stormy seas), he always serves up a sense of humor. Ed is a graduate of St. Ambrose University, and currently resides in Portage, Indiana.

Harvey Perlman was named the 19th Chancellor of the University of Nebraska-Lincoln on April 1, 2001. He had served as Interim Chancellor of the University of Nebraska-Lincoln since July 16, 2000.

A former dean of the University of Nebraska College of Law (1983-1998), Perlman has also served as interim senior vice chancellor for academic affairs at UNL (1995-96).

A Nebraska native, Perlman was raised in York, Neb., and earned a bachelor of arts in history and a juris doctorate from the University of Nebraska. He joined the NU law faculty in 1967 and taught until 1974 when he joined the faculty at the University of Virginia Law School. He returned to Nebraska in 1983 when he accepted the deanship of the Nebraska Law College, a post he held until 1998 when he returned to the professoriate. His area of legal expertise lies in torts and intellectual property.

He serves on the Council of the American Law Institute, a leading national law reform organization, as one of Nebraska's Commissioners of Uniform State Laws, and as Chair of the Board of Directors of the Big 12 Athletic Conference.

Perlman and his wife, Susan, an NU alumna, are the parents of two daughters. Anne, who earned degrees from UNL and the University of Nebraska Medical Center, practices medicine in Lincoln and is married to

UNL alumnus David Spinar; they are the parents of the Perlmans' three grandchildren, Will, Ava, and Marco, Husker fans all. Daughter Amie, who received BA and JD degrees from UNL, is a Nebraska Assistant Attorney-General and is married to UNL alumnus Ron Larson.

Dr. Mary Pipher received her BA in Cultural Anthropology at the University of California at Berkeley in 1969 and her Ph.D. in Clinical Psychology from the University of Nebraska in 1977. She received the American Psychological Association Presidential Citation in 1998. In 2001, she was a Rockefeller Foundation Scholar in Residence at Bellagio, Italy. Dr. Pipher's work combines her training in both the fields of psychology and anthropology. Her special area if interest is how American culture influences the mental health of its people. Dr. Pipher has appeared on the *Today Show, 20/20, The Charlie Rose Show*, the *NewsHour with Jim Lehrer*, and National Public Radio's *Fresh Air*. She has written articles for *Time* magazine, *Hope, Psychotherapy Networker, The Journal of Family Life*, and many other publications. Three of her books, *Reviving Ophelia, The Shelter of Each Other*, and *Another Country* were *New York Times* bestsellers. *Reviving Ophelia* was number one for twenty-seven weeks and on the *NYT* list for 154 weeks. Dr. Pipher travels all over the world sharing her ideas with community groups, schools, and health care professionals. Her articulate and passionate delivery creates enthusiasm in all types of audiences. Her down-to-earth stories of hope and resilience inspire people to work together to build a better community.

Photographer **Joel Sartore**'s biography is on page 33, to which he adds, "Whenever I'm on the road and mention that I live in Lincoln, people squint and ask, 'Why?' I don't go into much detail. I just say that my family lives nearby and leave it at that. I don't want to spoil the place.

I'm afraid that if I tell people what it's really like, they'll all want to move here, and I like things just as they are. Lincoln has all the amenities of a big city but the feel of a small town. There are no lines at the movies. Strangers say hi to each other on the street. Nobody honks their horn because they're too polite. I like that. A lot.

We get all four seasons, fabulous sunsets and a clean, wide-open sky to marvel at them. There are plenty of ponds and lakes to fish. Our airport has free luggage carts. They know me by name at the hardware store. My kids ride their bikes to the grocery store when we run out of eggs.

I could go on, but you get the point. Why would anyone not want to live here?"

Kent Seacrest is a shareholder in Seacrest & Kalkowski, PC, LLO in Lincoln, Nebraska. A graduate of the University of Iowa Law School and Urban and Regional Planning School, Kent practices almost exclusively in the real estate, land use, consensus building and planning areas. During his 27 years of practice, he has been involved in numerous multi-faceted real estate development transactions and projects in Lincoln and other Nebraska communities. In addition to major downtown Lincoln projects, such as the Cornhusker Square Project, Centerstone, Star Building, and University Square, Kent has also been involved in a number of residential and commercial projects and special projects, such as SouthPointe Pavilions, Wilderness Ridge, Regent Heights, Star Venture, Market Place, 84th and Highway 2 Shopping Center, Haymarket Baseball Park and Antelope Valley Major Investment Study. Kent has also been a member of Mayor Wesely's Public-Private Partnership Advisory Committee, Mayor's Infrastructure Finance Work Group, the Mayor's Acreage Resource Group, and the Mayor's Arena Task Force. Kent has taught planning law for the UNL Urban and Regional Planning program and most recently has become the spokesperson for the 2015 Vision Group.

Index

Smith, Anselmo B. 92

Smith, George Grant 170

Smith, J.D. 89

Smith, Prosper 132

Snell, Wm.H 113

South Platte 82

Sower, The 208, 209

Sprague 69, 76

St. Joseph 96

St. Mary's Catholic Church 193

St. Paul Methodist Church 157, 158

Starrels, Rabbi Solomon 104

State Board of Agriculture 89

State Penitentiary 76

Steam Wagon Road 86

Stevens Creek 70

Stewart, Lydia 148

Stine, Louis 105

Stout & Jamison 118

Stout, W.H.B. 111, 118, 190, 192

Stowager Automatic Phone 146

Strickland, Gen. S.A. 103

Stuart, Charles 189, 208

Stuart Building 209, 214

Stuart Investment Company 201, 209, 216

Stuart Theatre 224

Sunday, Billy 197

Swedish Lutheran Church 93

Sweet & Brock Bank 199

Sweet, James 97, 142

Swiss Bell Ringers 197

Syford, Dewitt 156

Syracuse 86

T

Talent Plus 9

Taft, Howard 197

Taylor, Rev. E.C. 79

Thayer, Gov. John M. 159

Thiehoff, W.F. 171

Thielsen, Hans 140

Thomas Price & Co. 164

Tiechnor House Hotel 115

TierOne Bank 28-29

Time Warner Cable 249

Touzalin, Albert E. 169

Towle, Max 217

Trinity Episcopal Church 185

Trinity Hall 172

Tucker, William 214

Tyler, James 153

U

U. S. Army Band 197

U. S. Courthouse 127

U. S. Land Office 96

U. S. Post Office 134

U. S. Secretary of Interior 103

Union Airport 221

Union Bank 115

Union Bus Terminal 196, 202

Union College 164, 165, 173, 180

United Synagogue of America 105

United Synagogue of Conservative Judaism 105

University Club 209

University Hall 112, 115, 129

University of Kansas 114

University of Nebraska 78, 93, 108, 109, 121, 156, 195, 196, 202

University of Nebraska Foundation 211

University of Nebraska Medical College 151

University Place 108, 156, 162, 169

V

Van Pelt, Robert 217

W

WRK, LLC 53

Walgreen Drug Store 220

Wallace, Mary 148

Wallingford, A.J. 77

Ward, Joseph 100

Warner, Dr. Amos G. 115

Warnes, E.W. 78

Washington, Booker T. 197

Watkins, Albert 101

Waverly 76

WCAJ 161

Weaver, Harry 203

Well, Morris 220

Wells & Frost 224

Western Union Independent Telephone Company 144, 146

Westfield Gateway 210

Westminster Presbyterian Church 42-43

Whiteman, Paul 214

Whittier Junior High 201

Wilcox, William H. 190

Wilderness Park 70, 76, 197

Willow Bend 88

Wilson, Homer 215

Wilson, Walter F. 209, 214

Winchell, John Keyes 103

Winkler, Gus 218

Winterset, Iowa 77

Woods, Alfred 160

Woods, Frank W. 144

Woods, George 144, 201, 214

Woods, Mark 144

Woods Brothers Company 148, 173, 175

Woods Brothers Silo & Manufacturing Company 173

Works Progress Administration 215

Worthington, Bishop 170

WPA 201

Y

Yankee Hill 70, 79, 86, 88, 97

Yankee Hill Brickyards 201

YMCA 197

York Seminary 157

Young's Steam Mill 100

Young, John M. 78

Young Ladies Library & Reading Room Association 132

Young Men's Library & Lecture Association 132

Z

Zehrung, Mayor and Mrs. Frank 148

Greetings from LINCOLN Nebraska

© C. T. & CO.

LOOKING EAST, LINCOLN, NEB.

7A-H3642

MEMB

LOCAL UNION NO. 22 O. P. I. A.

LINCOLN, NEBR.

LINCOLN WENT WET

PURTY GOOD HUH?

A. B. C. BEER

XXX RYE

J. M. EDMISTON STATE AGENT UNION CENTRAL LIFE Room 22, LINCOLN

Is Dry

Lincoln, Neb.

INDIVIDUAL SWEEP STAKE HONE ABSOLUTELY PUR NET WEIGHT 6 OZ PACKED BY VIEW APIA

GUARANTEE CLOTHING CO. ONE CENT UNITED STATES OF AMERICA

pe the